Mark Corner is a lecturer at the University of Leuven and an external speaker for the European Commission, providing introductory talks on the EU institutions. He is the author of *The Binding of Nations: From European Union to World Union*.

'At last: a completely common sense, no-nonsense, hands-on and eminently readable introduction to the European Union that does not lose itself in arcane abstractions but that clearly spells out what the Union is and what it is not, its achievements as well as its shortcomings – a must for every programme in European Studies, every course on post-WWII Europe, and an illuminating read for anyone interested in where Europe, and indeed the world, is heading.'

Theo D'haen, former Director of
European Studies, University of Leuven

THE EUROPEAN UNION

AN INTRODUCTION

UNION

MARK CORNER

I.B. TAURIS

LONDON · NEW YORK

Published in 2014 by I.B.Tauris & Co. Ltd
6 Salem Road, London W2 4BU
175 Fifth Avenue, New York NY 10010
www.ibtauris.com

Distributed in the United States and Canada Exclusively by Palgrave Macmillan
175 Fifth Avenue, New York NY 10010

ISBN (HB): 978 1 78076 684 3
ISBN (PB): 978 1 78076 685 0
eISBN: 978 0 85773 610 9

Library of European Studies 20

A full CIP record for this book is available from the British Library
A full CIP record is available from the Library of Congress

Library of Congress Catalog Card Number: available

Typeset by Data Standards Limited, Frome, Somerset, UK.

Printed and bound in Great Britain by T.J. International, Padstow, Cornwall

To Sacha and Jeremy, who will know whether the Quagga lives to be a hundred

Contents

Illustrations

Preface and acknowledgements

This book is a deliberate attempt to produce another work in an already crowded field. *The European Union: An Introduction* is being written not because there are no introductions to the European Union (EU) but because there are too many. They compete in updating each other's detailed inventories of how each institution is arranged and latch on to the latest abbreviation that has been added to the process of managing the Union. There is not a single bone of the animal that they fail to list and categorise. But they do not give any idea of how the EU lives and breathes. Though this book does not duck the requirements of analysing the Union's structure and institutions, it is an introduction that intends to focus upon the EU at work. It deliberately limits the 'academic' content (and references) in order to concentrate on what is being *done* (whether well or badly) at the European level.

It would not be difficult to write at great length about the paradoxes of belonging to the EU, where decisions are made at several levels and where 'multi-level governance' means that different centres of power are constantly nudging each other in different directions. But something more straightforward is needed at the moment. The second half of this decade is likely to be a momentous time for the EU. On the one hand, it has new Parliamentary elections, a new Commission (including a new president) and a Europe 2020 Strategy which it is determined to deliver on, though many of the inevitable 'targets' look unlikely to be met within five years. On the other hand, it is a body in crisis. Respected journals cover their front pages with headlines such as (to take one of dozens) 'The Sleepwalkers: a disaster waiting to happen' (*The Economist*, 25–31 May 2013), and the BBC's Europe correspondent Gavin Hewitt writes a book called *The Lost Continent* to tell us that this is Europe's 'darkest hour since the war'.[1] Two years ago the headlines were worse (the *Financial Times* moved from 'Eurozone woes' to 'Eurozone crisis' and finally 'Eurozone chaos' as the year progressed), but clearly there are many people who simply view the unhealthy state of the eurozone now as something fatal that briefly went into remission in 2012 and will soon be entering a more ominous stage in its inevitable decline.

A crisis about debt levels and managing markets becomes a crisis in people's lives if they find their savings threatened or their jobs going or the level of their pensions falling. The European Union began not out of theoretical considerations concerning sovereignty-sharing but out of practical considerations concerning how to secure peace and prosperity after a devastating war (see Chapter 2). In the same way, people are thinking of leaving the EU now (in the United Kingdom, but also elsewhere) not because of abstract ideas about where sovereignty should lie but because the prosperity that was supposed to be built around the formation of a single market and a single currency no longer seems to be there.

With popular concern about the EU being so obviously dominated by very down-to-earth considerations, anyone who writes about it has to be down-to-earth themselves. One of my jobs is to be an external speaker hired by the European Commission to give presentations to visitors about the nature of the European Union in general and the Commission in particular. Though the questions from these groups may be of the 'How can the high representative also be a vice-president of the European Commission?' type, they rarely are. If people are interested in the workings of the External Action Service at all, they will probably ask: 'What sort of things does the high representative do? What did she do last week? What does she consider her greatest successes and/or failures have been?' Above all, they will ask about unemployment, migration, poverty and (of course) the euro.

Preface and acknowledgements

This is not a book that explains how to 'solve' the eurozone crisis, but it recognises that offering yet another introduction to the EU means having to show that the institution can do something useful. 'Do something useful', of course, does not mean that it can wave a magic wand and cure all the present economic woes. But (to be parochial for a moment), like the dissenting voices who sat around John Cleese in Monty Python's *Life of Brian* and heard his rant 'What have the Romans ever done for us?', it helps to be able to point by way of reply to a few roads, aqueducts and baths.

I could not have done this without the assistance of several people. First, I would like to thank Joanna Godfrey of I.B.Tauris for being willing to risk the gamble of 'another EU Introduction'. Thus do angels rush in where fools refuse to tread. Second, I would like to thank a whole range of EU officials who have been more than willing to discuss their work at length with me and have been entirely open about the criticisms that might be levelled at what they are doing (which is not to say that my criticisms are theirs!). In particular, I would like to thank certain members of the European Commission: John McClintock of DG Agriculture and Rural Development, Michael Mann of the European External Action Service, Maria Fladl of DG Trade, Tom van Ierland of DG Climate Change and Richard Bates of DG Fisheries and Maritime Affairs. Michael McDadd of the UK Department of Work and Pensions, and three colleagues – Simon Pascoe, Liesje de Boeck and Johan Eyckmans – have also been very helpful. Finally, I would like to thank Professor Christopher Andrew, my history tutor at Cambridge a century ago (well, 40 years back) during the time of the (first?) referendum on the UK's membership of the (then) European Economic Community. His wit and insight were a great stimulus and some of his observations have found their way into these pages, as pertinent now as they were then.

Brussels, 2014

xiii

1

Introduction

Introducing the quagga

The key to understanding the European Union lies in recognising that it is not like anything else. Because it is always difficult to recognise and accept that something is different, the tendency is to see it instead as a disguised form of something familiar. Hence the quagga (a dangerous analogy, perhaps, seeing that this former inhabitant of South Africa, technically a subspecies of the plains zebra, is now extinct).The illustration in Figure 1 is a painting from the end of the eighteenth century of a quagga stallion in the menagerie of French King Louis XVI at Versailles. It is difficult to look at pictures of this creature and not to think that it should have made its mind up. Either it should have gone with the head and been a zebra, or it should have gone with the tail and been a horse. It is unsurprising that we think like this, because horses and zebras are all that we now know; the quagga looks odd because we never see one outside textbooks or computer screens.

Because of its uniqueness, the European Union is forever getting the quagga treatment and being told that it should 'sort itself out' as a horse or a zebra. It has become a candle burning at both ends, with one side trying to drag it back to being a collection of properly independent nation-states, and the other side trying to pull it forward in order to make it a single nation-state. The two positions are more alike than

Figure 1. Painting of a quagga: Watercolour on vellum parchment by Nicolas Marechal (1753–1802).

each would like to admit. At one end of the spectrum there might be a group of British or Hungarian nationalists; but at the other end of the spectrum is a group of European nationalists, waiting to wave their gold and blue flags with all the ardour of an American patriot waving the Star-Spangled Banner.

Both sides have the same problem – they cannot understand the nature of the European Union as a hybrid. They want to change it into what they are familiar with, and what they are both familiar with is the nation-state in its present form.

For one side, the 28 nations presently inside the EU are like 28 people stuck in a lift. They are all suffering from the foetid air, one has fainted, another claims to prefer to be dead and still the lift hovers between the third and fourth floors until the welcome sound of a firefighter (perhaps Mr Farage, the leader of the UK Independence Party) is heard cutting a way through to free them and give them back their 'space'. They will then go back to being autonomous nation-states living (and arguably quarrelling and fighting) together in the 'normal' manner.

From the other end of the spectrum comes the idea that a great nation-state in the making is being held up by extensive labour pains as it struggles to be born. A United States of Europe is to be created in the way that Italy and Germany were created in the nineteenth century. Those of this opinion would agree with the historian Benedetto Croce when he wrote:

> [J]ust as, seventy years ago, a Neapolitan of the old kingdom or a Piedmontese of the sub-Alpine kingdom became Italians, not by denying that which they had been, but by elevating it and incorporating it into that new existence, so will the French, Germans and Italians and all the others elevate themselves to become Europeans and their thoughts will turn to Europe, and their hearts will beat for it, as they have done for their smaller fatherlands, which they will not have forgotten, but love the more.[1]

Croce anticipated a 'greater Italy' in the way that Count Coudenhove-Kalergi later anticipated a greater Austria-Hungary in his influential *Paneuropa*, published in 1923, but in doing so they simply sought to reproduce the nation-state on a grander scale. As Michelle Cini puts it: 'If anything, the federalist rhetoric did little more than highlight the enduring qualities of the nation-state, in that it sought to replicate it on a European scale.'[2]

The word 'federalist' (one of the most elusive words where discussions of the EU are concerned) may not be the correct one, but Cini's point is a fair one. Both ends of the spectrum, whether 'eurosceptic' or 'federalist', are working with the same presupposition – that the present arrangement of nation-states is the only acceptable template. One side believes that the EU should become 28 autonomous nation-states; the other side believes that it should become one autonomous nation-state. Either way, they are both hooked on autonomous nation-states. But the EU is neither a knot that ought to unravel into a group of separate nation-states, nor a group of states in the process of turning themselves into the separate regions of a single nation-state. It is a body intended to deal with the limitations of the nation-state itself.

Dealing with theory

Political theories concerning the European Union can often seem abstruse. Is it a federation or is it a confederation (federation lite?). Is it heading in the direction of Germany or the USA ('federations') or more in the direction of the 13 American states with their Articles of Confederation after victory against the British in late eighteenth-century America (1771–88) or the German Confederation that followed the Congress of Vienna in 1815 and lasted till 1871 ('confederations')? Or will it be something 'in between' a federation and a confederation, like (on some views) Switzerland (which has in any case changed from being a 'confederation' to a 'federation' in the course of its history)? The permutations are endless, opening up infinite linguistic opportunities as the attempt is made to put a name to each one. Is it a sympolity or perhaps a compound polity? Is it a mixed commonwealth or an organised synarchy or a consociation?[3] Is it best seen as multidimensional with multilevel governance (and/or post-national governance)? On it goes, each new proposal generating a new discussion enabling academics to maintain their output and so stave off the lack of a productivity bonus.

But, ironically, this endless search for the right description of the EU comes partly from a failure to accept a point very simply put by Ben Rosamond: 'We need to break out of the "state fixation" that characterises so much of the routine academic and political discourse about the EU.'[4] For, when these descriptions of commonwealths, consocial mixes, synarchies and so on are unpacked (if they can be), it turns out that the intellectual problems are often created by an unwillingness to see the EU as it is and instead to fit it into existing models of international relations (IR) theory. As Rosamond says: 'rather than trying to fit the EU into IR theory, perhaps IR theorists need to look carefully at their established theoretical toolkits if they are to properly comprehend the EU.'[5]

In his book *Understanding the European Union: A Concise Introduction*, John McCormick quotes a saying that 'the EU works in practice but not in theory'.[6] Whatever such a remark is meant to mean, it surely provides us with some encouragement to get on with describing what the European Union does and not be too tied up with the complex theories about its nature. This book will try to allow the EU to speak for itself as the strange animal it undoubtedly is. Perhaps it lacks even the unity (despite its odd markings) of a quagga. It may be even stranger than that, and certainly not the sort of creature that easily heads the 'sponsor an animal' lists through which zoos help to maintain themselves. It is more of a duck-billed platypus, subject to frequent academic critiques of the 'surely it can't really be a mammal if it lays eggs' variety. But the important thing is to observe it in its habitat. That is why a substantial part of this book deals with practice.

Outline of the book

The European Union: An Introduction does not contain separate chapters going through each institution in turn. There is no need to repeat the familiar guided tours of Commission, Court of Justice, Parliament and so on that inform many other books. We are not going to go through the quagga stripe by stripe. There will be substantial chapters on the history (Chapter 2) and anatomy (Chapter 3) of the EU, but the emphasis of at least half the book will be upon examining EU activity in particular areas, providing specific examples. It is surprising how little attention is paid to this in introductions to the EU. As one of the best introductions to date, Anand Menon's *Europe: The State of the Union*, puts it:

> Actually, there is far too much discussion about how the EU works. Observers and practitioners alike spend inordinate amounts of time describing decision-making processes and institutional configurations, and far less examining what the Union actually does and how well it does it.[7]

It is this observation above all others that convinces me it is worth attempting another introduction to the EU, despite there being some very good introductions already (such as the McCormick book mentioned above). For even McCormick does very little to illustrate the EU at work, even though he concedes that 'polls find that most Europeans don't know how it [the European Union] works'.[8]

For instance, it is important to explain the complex (and still rather uncertain) place of the EU's new External Action Service, but does it not help in understanding it to describe some of the things it actually does, as this book tries to? That is why Chapter 7 on external relations looks at the situation in the Horn of Africa in some detail. Since the end of 2008, with a mandate to continue at least until the end of 2014, an EU naval force has been operating in and around the Gulf of Aden. Containing ships (mostly frigates) from various EU countries and reconnaissance aircraft from others, it has been mandated to deal with piracy and has a British rear admiral based in Northwood in the UK as its operation commander. Is that not relevant to the discussion? Does an EU introduction have to stop at a dry definition of what a particular policy area covers without examining some of the particular operations that take place within it? In each section of the chapters devoted to particular policy areas, this book will look carefully at specifics, giving examples in order to provide a clear illustration of how departments actually carry out their work and in order to give some concrete meaning to buzzwords and phrases such as 'multilevel governance'. If there are all these international, regional, national and sub-national 'actors' at work, we need to see some of the 'plays' they perform in order to understand what such expressions mean.

The chapters of this book lead naturally towards a conclusion concerning just what the EU is and what grandiose claims about 'the EU as a global leader' might mean. The argument here is that, once we recognise that the EU is neither a group of states crammed together in unfortunate circumstances and struggling to be free of one another, nor a single state struggling to be born, we can look at it as it is – 'Europe's experimental union', as the title of one book on the EU describes it.[9]

So is this a 'europhile' book? If it is a 'europhile' book, it is so only in the sense that it believes that, by letting the EU speak for itself, it will acquit itself well. But it is not a 'europhile' book in the sense of wanting to join all those who (confusingly) talk about 'ever more Europe', 'ever deepening integration', 'creating a single polity' and so on. It genuinely believes in the EU as a hybrid that works, but this is to set it against some of those 'europhiles' who think that a couple more treaties (and the relegation of the UK to some sort of ill-defined and self-inflicted 'associate membership') will allow the EU to sail on into the sunny waters of superstatedom.

As I have argued elsewhere,[10] the EU would have far more influence if it presented itself as a model of sovereignty-sharing between states that could be practised elsewhere (and even globally) than if it presented itself as a stage along the tortuous path from regionhood to statehood. If the latter were the case, all that would have been produced by 60 years of sovereignty-sharing would be another big state, a United States of Europe, which would simply become one of the 'big Six' players in a twenty-first-century rerun of the dangerous great power game that steadily tore Europe apart in the century after the Battle of Waterloo. Instead of being an example of how states could work together in a more peaceful and effective manner, the EU would just become another state rubbing up against, and risking conflict with, the rest. If the 28 (or however many it finally is) member states were to turn themselves into one big nation-state, then they would have ceased to demonstrate that their partial sovereignty-sharing system can enable states to coexist peaceably *while remaining themselves*. They would have forfeited what arguably entitled them to the Nobel Peace Prize awarded to the European Union in 2012, namely a system that has at the very least helped nation-states with a long history of conflict to live at peace with one another.

Therefore I would resist (if the choice were to be mine) the designation 'europhile' as much as that of 'eurosceptic'. I believe that the EU is a unique and precious institution (which is quite europhile enough for many people!), but precisely for that reason I have no desire to see it turned into a state. I have my suspicions of those for whom every crisis is an opportunity to move it up to another level of integration, because changing up a gear and becoming a state is as bad as changing down a gear and becoming several states. The EU is a system for keeping states but managing their relations with one another – and, given the carnage that states have caused through their *un*managed relations with each other in past centuries, this does not seem to be such a bad idea. To that extent at least, this is a book in favour of the quagga.

2

History

The nation-state at large: Europe 1648–1918

The European Union (EU) can only be understood on the basis of some understanding of history – not only the history of the organisation itself but also the history of Europe in the centuries that preceded its formation. If that is not done, then speaking about the unique nature of a partial sovereignty-sharing system between nation-states will not make sense. It will seem like an abstruse description of yet another international organisation.

The best place to begin is the middle of the seventeenth century. Though people may not be familiar with much in the history of political thought, they usually know a line from Thomas Hobbes' masterpiece *Leviathan*, written in exile in France at a time when, across the Channel, England was busy executing its king and abolishing the monarchy.[1] It comes in the passage where Hobbes tells us that in the 'natural state of mankind' (in effect a state lacking strong central government) we see 'the war of every man against every man'. The life of a human being under such a 'state of nature', he famously wrote, is 'solitary, poor, nasty, brutish and short'.

It was precisely in order to avoid such a 'nasty, brutish and short' existence, Hobbes argued, that people allow the state to emerge as a social construct, freely entered into by human beings who seek to overcome the endless conflict and vulnerability of living in a 'state of nature'. They agree to create a commonwealth, a 'Leviathan' (hence the title of Hobbes' book) or artificial man, whose soul (Hobbes tells us) is sovereignty, whose reason is law, whose strength is wealth, whose rewards and punishments are its nerves, and whose important officials are its joints.

Hobbes' description of recourse to a social contract in order to resolve conflicts between individuals in a 'state of nature' proved highly persuasive. But, by solving one problem, did Hobbes create another? What if the nations that resulted from the social contract he spoke about, receiving as they did (on Hobbes' own recommendation) the unswerving loyalty of their citizens, were *themselves* to become part of an outbreak of anarchic tribal warfare, not between individuals but between *states*? What if the states themselves acted as if they were in a 'state of nature'?

That was not an unreasonable question to ask in 1650. The Thirty Years' War had devastated much of Central Europe during the early part of the century. The war came to an end with the Treaty of Westphalia signed in 1648, just three years before the publication of *Leviathan*. The treaty brought an end to war in Europe by enshrining the principle of non-interference in the internal religious life of states, at least insofar as they chose from an acceptable list of Christian alternatives (it added Calvinism to the Catholic and Lutheran options permitted by the Peace of Augsburg a century earlier). The term 'Westphalian' later came to be used of any approach that rules out interference in the domestic affairs of another country, thereby extending what was originally applied to religious interference to all kinds of interference. Thus former diplomat Robert Cooper, for instance, talks of 'the old Westphalian concept of state sovereignty in which others do not interfere'[2] as a defining characteristic of the twenty-first century as much as of the seventeenth, and arguably just as much of a problem now as it was then. Life might be 'nasty, brutish and short' within a state that lacked suitable institutions such as a police force, but it was also likely to be 'nasty, brutish and short' if there was no control over states themselves, especially when technological development meant that the effects of wars increasingly spread across borders to affect civilian populations (this had even been true in the seventeenth century – the billeting of armies across Central

Europe and the impact of their destructive battles produced severe outbreaks of famine). The question of course was – and is – what sort of control over states is acceptable?

In his massive *Europe: A History*, Norman Davies declared that Westphalia 'set the ground plan of the international order in Central Europe for the next century and more',[3] presumably taking it as far as the time of Napoleon. No one told you what to do within your own borders, and when it came to other nations you did what you could to get the better of them in a constant diplomatic and, where necessary, military game. A number of sovereign nations then set about vying for power, making and breaking treaties and engaging in various wars in pursuit of their own interests, while subject to no higher authority.

Bearing in mind Davies's remark, did things change because of Napoleon? It is hard to see any significant change of approach at the beginning of the nineteenth century. There were some voices that spoke out against a dangerous vacuum in international relations. After the anticlerical triumph of the French Revolution, the end of the eighteenth century saw a notable revival of interest in 'Christendom', the mediaeval order that had regulated relations between peoples through the power of the Church and the papacy.[4] The romantic ideal of a *Europa Christiana* may have been an exercise in nostalgia, but it never quite died. Indeed some have argued that the idea of Christendom was an important impulse behind the Schuman Plan itself.[5]

However, the revival of Christendom was no more a practical prospect in the early nineteenth century than it would be today. Instead, the Napoleonic wars gave rise to the short-lived 'Congress' system of meetings between states in 1815, but barely a decade had gone by before British Foreign Secretary George Canning was falling out with the other powers over intervention to suppress the revolution in Spain and made his famous remark: 'things are getting back into a wholesome state. Every nation for itself, and God for us all.'[6] In effect, Britain scuppered the system. In Thomson's words, 'first among the important victorious Powers, she broke with the system and thereby made it crumble'.[7] However, despite what might be seen as an early example of euroscepticism on the part of Britain, the system would probably have collapsed in any case.

Whatever Canning meant by his curious reference to God being 'for us all', such pieties were never going to be translated into practical arrangements restoring the sort of ecclesiastical control that had been sanctioned during the Middle Ages. *Europa Christiana* had no chance against conservative realism and a firm belief in the balance of power. Many of those who mocked it also mocked Prince Metternich, foreign minister of the Austrian Empire from 1809 to 1848 and arguably chief architect of the system of international congresses for as long as they lasted, whom they dubbed the 'Baron de Balance'. But the critics had nothing to offer in its place. When the Congress system proved ineffective, the nineteenth century continued its attempts to manage an uneasy balance of power between states because this was the only system that they knew.

It is true that, compared with its successor, the nineteenth century was a time of relative peace in Europe (though not outside Europe, where imperial ambitions and rivalries led to a series of wars and occasional massacres). The only 'serious' conflict between states was the Crimean War of 1854–6, and that was restricted to a relatively small theatre of war in South-East Europe. However, the 'century of peace' can also be viewed as a century of preparation for war, culminating in a massive arms race and an explosion of colonial expansion.[8] Europe slid towards world war (few historians think that World War I was intended), while the only serious efforts at international negotiation were the Hague Peace Conferences of 1899 and 1907, with their many conventions and declarations (including the Geneva Convention of 1906, which sought to set out clearly the laws of war). But these conferences were essentially trying to mitigate the effects of a conflict they seemed unable to prevent. A third Hague Conference had been planned for 1915, but by that time the feared conflagration had already begun.

The war to end all wars?

The carnage of World War I might have been expected to concentrate the minds of European leaders after 1918. Hopes were pinned on the creation of the League of Nations, a body specifically intended to prevent anything like World War I from happening again. It was the first international authority, its supporters declared, that was not an empire. However, in two crucial respects it was hopelessly weak.

The first source of weakness lay in the fact that the two most powerful states in the world after 1918, the USA and the Soviet Union, were not members of the League. The US Senate voted not to join it in November 1919 and refused to ratify the Treaty of Versailles in March 1920. Meanwhile, the Soviet Union turned in on itself when the communist revolution failed to spread westwards, leaving the European powers and Japan to manage the League.

At the same time there were understandable reasons why Britain and France would be very reluctant enforcers of world peace. They had been severely weakened by four years of conflict fought on an unprecedented scale, leading to huge economic and military losses. The catastrophic World War I had crippled the European continent, and now it was the European powers that were being asked to ensure that no such catastrophe ever happened again. It had taken a disaster like the Great War to goad nations into supporting the League, but it had also weakened them too much to be able to manage it when it was created.

Unsurprisingly, therefore, the second source of weakness lay in the fact that there was no effective mechanism of enforcement. When a state was attacked, the Executive Council of the League could only advise members on how to fulfil their obligations to support it. It had no powers to impose any binding obligations on members. It could only make recommendations.

A further problem lay in the enduring tendency, even after such horrors as the World War I, to see in the conflict between states something 'natural' that could not be avoided, much as the social Darwinists of the late nineteenth century had seen the struggle of survival between nations as a 'natural' phenomenon. Oswald Spengler's *Untergang des Abendlandes* (Decline of the West) was immensely popular in this respect. Published in 1918, it painted a picture of cultures going through phases as if they had a life cycle like trees. The last phase was that of 'civilisation', but from this last phase a new cycle might be born, just as the 'barbarians' who destroyed the Roman Empire gave birth to a new culture in Europe. Though it would be simplistic to see in Spengler a joyous anticipation of Hitler as the leader of the new barbarian hordes, at once destructive and purging, it is not simplistic to view him as encouraging the sort of damaging fatalism that sees in the horrors of war something 'natural', rather than a tragic error to be avoided. One of the most important writings of the interwar era where ideas of a new European order were concerned, Coudenhove-Kalergi's *Paneuropa* (published in 1923), took Spengler to task on precisely this point:

> The cause of Europe's decline is political, not biological. Europe is not dying of old age, but because its inhabitants are killing and destroying one another with the instruments of modern science.[9]

Coudenhove-Kalergi co-founded the Pan-European Union, which held its first Congress in Vienna in 1926, and attracted luminaries from various walks of life, including Thomas Mann, Sigmund Freud and Albert Einstein. His *Paneuropa* had its limitations, however. It looked too much like the old Austria-Hungary writ large (understandably the idea never appealed to the first president of newly independent Czechoslovakia, Tomáš Masaryk). Without a clear idea of *how* the states were to cooperate, as opposed to disappear inside some kind of new Central European order, it was unlikely to progress very far.

The period that followed 'the war to end all wars' was unable to exploit the questioning of institutions that followed the mass slaughter of 1914–18. For those who did not subscribe to the view that conflict between nations was the natural (and therefore unavoidable) order of things, their alternative proposals were unable to make a dent in the basic canon of the 'Westphalian' system, the untouchability of the sovereign nation-state. One could try to create organisations in which those sovereign states would cooperate with one another – whether it was the League of Nations or the French Foreign Minister Aristide Briand's European Association. Or one could try to create a large European state out of the mass of states (including many new ones following the end of World War I) in Central Europe that would otherwise be unable to match the power and technological development of their bigger neighbours, as in Coudenhove-Kalergi's *Paneuropa*. One could pitch the nation-state at the European level (Coudenhove-Kalergi) or one could pitch the nation-state at its existing level (Briand), but one was still building one's ideas around the sacrosanct character of the sovereign nation-state. As mentioned in the previous chapter, this is still the problem with so much thinking about the EU today.

The rebuilding of Europe 1945-9

Within a generation, the so-called 'war to end all wars' had led to another world war. Once again the countries of Europe (not to mention much of the rest of the world) were desperate for peace, and once again there were new organisations to try to maintain that peace. The United Nations was formed as successor to the League of Nations, with the Security Council given powers of enforcement (unlike its predecessor, the Executive Council of the League of Nations). However, the condition of obtaining agreement on the exercise of those powers was a veto given to the five victorious powers of World War II. It was a restriction that, although arguably necessary at the time in order to bring the United Nations into being, was to limit its effectiveness considerably.

In Europe itself, pressure for new forms of European unity built up within the resistance movements and found expression in the *Manifesto of the European Resistance* published in Geneva in 1944 by members of the resistance from nine different countries. There was much talk of a new 'federal' Europe, and a Union of European Federalists was created in 1946. At one point during the war, the future prime minister of the postwar Labour government, Clement Attlee, declared that 'we must federate or perish'[10] and lent support to the Federal Union movement, but the aftermath of war and the practical problems of reconstruction brought a different perspective. Rather than paying too much attention to terms, it would be better to concentrate upon the situation that actually emerged after World War II.

The situation was close to what Coudenhove-Kalergi had originally predicted if Europe failed to overcome its divisions, namely a continent wedged between giants. The postwar order was to be dominated for two generations by the Soviet Union and the USA and the rivalry between them. Half a century earlier, Europe had been the location of colonial powers that then took their rivalries to the rest of the world. Now it was Europe itself that had become the battleground (in a Cold War sense) for rivalries between the new superpowers. Whatever was to develop in the way of a European Union would do so in the context of two other giant unions, one of Soviet Socialist republics and another of 50 states.

Two organisations emerged after World War II in the context of this superpower rivalry: the Organisation for European Economic Co-operation (OEEC) and the North Atlantic Treaty Organization (NATO). Both were important for the later development of the EU, but both were organised in a very different way.

The Organisation for European Economic Co-operation (OEEC) was established in order to manage the American economic aid programme that, in the form of the Marshall Plan, was provided to Western Europe on a massive scale after World War II. Whatever the philanthropic motives involved, there was also a clear economic incentive behind the Marshall Plan, perfectly expressed by CIA Director Allen Dulles: 'The Plan presupposes that we desire to help restore a Europe which can and will compete with us in the world markets and for that very reason will be able to buy substantial amounts of our products.'[11] However, such 'self-interest' was arguably a welcome advance upon the traditional attitude of the European nations themselves, whose colonies had been systematically deindustrialised in order to prevent them from competing with the manufacturing interests of their 'mother countries'.

There was also a political incentive. Marshall Plan aid was partly a reaction to the threat of communism. This threat was not just perceived as coming 'from the East': the communist parties of France and Italy were a particular worry, and it was seen as imperative to prevent them from coming to power by exploiting extreme economic hardship.

Though there was a marriage of self-interest and genuine humanitarian instinct in the Marshall Plan aid, it was clearly going to be conditional upon European cooperation. This is why, when George Marshall first announced the aid in 1947, he declared that 'the initiative must come from Europe'. The USA was not going to bankroll a return to the protectionist policies of the 1930s. Europe would cooperate as a condition of, as well as in the process of, receiving US aid. In other words, the requirement to manage Marshall Plan aid acclimatised European states to the sort of cooperation that was later to become essential to the formation of a common (and eventually a single) market.

When the Foreign Assistance Act of April 1948 enacted the Marshall Plan (which it called the European Recovery Program), it contained a passage in which (with perhaps a hint of justified condescension) it declared itself 'mindful of the advantages which the U.S. has enjoyed through the existence of a large domestic market with no internal trade barriers'. It was convinced that 'similar advantages can accrue to the countries of Europe' – if only, one can imagine them thinking, the occupants of those small countries bunched into the western peninsula of Asia could learn to get along with one another. It is not difficult to imagine these words part-inspiring and part-haunting European leaders as they struggled to develop economically during the next 50 years. It is no surprise that 1986, the year when, with Spanish and Portuguese accession, the European Economic Community (EEC) became the same size as the USA, was also the year when it signed the Single European Act in order to create the single market.

Then there was the question of developing an effective and united response to the growing power of the Soviet Union. This brings us to the other key organisation that emerged after World War II: NATO.

It is important to compare US policy towards Europe after World War II with what followed World War I. In the latter case, war was followed by a refusal to ratify the League of Nations, which the USA therefore failed to join, and a retreat into isolationism based on a degree of suspicion that the country had been lured against its better interest into an essentially 'European' conflict. Though the situation after World War II was very different, it was never taken for granted that the American reaction would be different too. American forces might return home as they had after World War I, leaving Western Europe exposed to a dangerous threat from the East.

In 1947, the United Kingdom (UK) and France had signed the Treaty of Dunkirk, in which the former agreed to maintain a permanent peacetime continental commitment. A year later, the UK, France and the Benelux countries (Belgium, the Netherlands and Luxembourg) signed the Treaty of Brussels, but, a month after it was signed, British Foreign Secretary Ernest Bevin was writing a joint letter with his French counterpart to President Truman, declaring that 'we shall require the assistance of the United States in order to organise the effective defence of Western Europe'.[12] Bevin himself described the Brussels Treaty as 'a sprat to catch a whale', the US military presence being the whale.

Between the letter to Truman and the formation of NATO a year later came the Berlin crisis, which lasted from the month that the Treaty of Brussels was signed in 1948 until May of 1949. The Soviet Union started to block Western access to the city of Berlin, eventually creating a total blockade of land access which led to the necessity of essential supplies being airlifted to the city. By the time the Berlin crisis was over, the North Atlantic Treaty had been signed – in Washington – by the USA, Canada and ten European states, thereby fulfilling Bevin's intentions. Judt quotes the words of the first secretary-general of NATO, Lord Ismay, that the purpose of NATO was 'to keep the Russians out, the Americans in and the Germans down'.[13] The first of these intentions was intensified by Soviet support for an invasion of South Korea in 1950; many in the West drew parallels between an invasion of South Korea from the North and an invasion of West Germany from the East. The second and third were realised by the presence of American forces in Germany. Certainly they were not strong enough to resist a Soviet invasion, but their presence meant that such an invasion would lead to American casualties and a full-scale world war, which even Stalin did not want. Moreover, those American troops, although not enough to repel a Soviet invasion, were enough to ensure that German rearmament would not make the country once again a threat to European peace.

By the end of the 1940s it looked as though two intergovernmental organisations, one (NATO) a military alliance to protect Western Europe from internal (Germany) and external (the Soviet Union) aggression, the other (OEEC) an organisation to mediate the delivery of aid to West European countries under the Marshall Plan, were in place to ensure a secure and prosperous future for the Western part of the continent. There was no need to add to them. Of course there would be grand speeches about a 'federal' future, but they need not be translated into any new organisations. Winston Churchill went to

Strasbourg in September 1946 and spoke of a 'United States of Europe', but such as 'to make the material strength of a single state less important', leaving open whether the projected United States of Europe would be a single state, and in any case talking of the UK as a 'friend and sponsor' of the new Europe rather than (presumably) a participant.[14] Two years later, in May 1948, 750 delegates met in The Hague for a Congress where Churchill as its honorary president welcomed the OEEC and the Brussels Treaty and added a reference to 'a parallel policy of political unity', once again vague enough to be consistent with any sort of agreement between states. Though full of grand speeches, the Hague Congress did not make clear exactly what that 'union' was to mean, or in what way it meant more than a period of cooperation between a set of previously warring nation-states. Plans for a 'European Assembly' emerged, but with no clear understanding of whether or how it was to be more than a consultative body.

The practical consequence of this Congress was the formation of the Council of Europe in May 1949, launched at a ceremony in London by ten states, including the UK (which successfully resisted a proposal from France and Italy that it should be called 'The European Union'). The meeting in London made it clear that the proposed 'European Assembly' agreed at the Hague Congress must have a merely consultative role, subject to a Committee of Ministers acting on the basis of unanimity. Thus the Council of Europe was going to be entirely in line with the intergovernmental principles outlined for the OEEC and about to be realised in the launch of NATO. Despite all the grand speeches at The Hague, there was apparently nothing new under the sun where the relation between states was concerned.

Yet there were some people for whom this was an unacceptable result of all the idealistic rhetoric that had been seen at the Hague Congress a year before. Several of them realised that the Council of Europe had limitations from the moment it was signed into being through the Statute of Westminster. Among their number was Robert Schuman, the French foreign minister, who signed the statute on behalf of France. Schuman came away from London determined to establish a new organisation, one that really would break new ground in the relations between nation-states.

How did it happen? In the context of the establishment of the OEEC and the imminent establishment of NATO, why should anyone think that the Council of Europe – which, for all its 'federalist' detractors, was precisely in line with the sort of organisation of nation-states that could be expected on the basis of past experience – was not the end of the story? Even as Europe struggled to recover from its worst conflict in history, why should anyone have expected to go further than these three organisations?

'In Cognac, they are good at waiting. It is the only way to make good brandy'

Just 11 days after he signed the Statute of Westminster in London, Schuman made an extraordinary speech in Strasbourg Festival Hall on 16 May 1949. Although it would be wrong to see the Strasbourg speech as a simple reaction to the events in London, they clearly provided essential background, as the following comment on the Council makes clear: 'the commencement [of the Council of Europe] is characterized by a timorousness which many people will find disappointing.'[15] Schuman's fear was that the Council would be another discussion forum, a talking shop – useful enough in the sense that it was always better, in Churchill's words, to have 'jaw, jaw' than 'war, war' – but falling short of what was needed for the rebuilding of Europe and the creation of a continent that was at last stable and peaceful as well as prosperous. For such a purpose it was necessary to envisage something entirely new, something that had not been attempted between nation-states before. He made the point clear in a speech at the Salon d'Horloge of the French Foreign Ministry a year later, on 20 June 1950:

> Never before has such a system that we advocate been tried out as a practical experiment. Never before have states delegated a fraction of their sovereignty jointly to an independent, supranational body. They have never even envisaged doing so.

The fact that states not only had never delegated a fraction of their sovereignty but had 'never even envisaged doing so' meant that it was only ever likely to happen in certain specific circumstances, of which the devastating effect on mainland Europe of World War II and the problem of rebuilding French–German relations afterwards were obviously crucial. This point is very well made by François Duchêne, in his classic biography of Jean Monnet (regarded by many as a chief architect of European unity): 'To recognise a relevant issue and opportunity demands a sense of timing. The right idea at the wrong moment cannot be concrete.'[16] He then quotes Monnet:

> Events that strike me and occupy my thoughts lead me to general conclusions about what has to be done. Then circumstances, which determine day-to-day events, suggest or supply the means of action. I can wait a long time for the right moment. In Cognac, they are good at waiting. It is the only way to make good brandy.

Duchêne concludes: 'Monnet had a version of the Schuman Plan in mind as early as 1941, but put it aside for nine years until France's German policy was about to collapse.'[17]

Why, then, just 11 days after Schuman had signed the Statute of Westminster, did he take this bold further step when it was increasingly clear that intergovernmental bodies were in place or in the process of being put in place in order to lift Europe out of economic devastation and protect it from military attack? American impatience with the way European states were cooperating under the OEEC may have played a part, but such impatience was hardly unexpected and was not going to lead to the switching off of aid. The key reason – which is perfectly in line with the sort of supposedly 'revisionist' theories of writers such as Alan Milward – is revealed in the title of one of Milward's most well-known books: *The European Rescue of the Nation*-State.[18] France and Germany (but not the UK) needed something more than the OEEC or NATO could offer if they were to re-emerge as nations after World War II.

Take Germany first. It was potentially the economic powerhouse of the continent. However, this was hardly the case in the immediate aftermath of World War II. Partly as a reaction to the myth that grew up between the wars that the armistice ending World War I represented an unnecessary 'betrayal' of the army by its leaders, the allies made sure that this time Germany was occupied. Many other factors intensified and prolonged this occupation. There was a huge refugee crisis to deal with as national boundaries were redrawn and ethnic Germans expelled by many of its neighbours. There was a push for the 're-education' of a nation whose war crimes (whether of its leaders or, through their complicity, of many others) were particularly horrendous, and considerable uncertainty about what to do in order to ensure that Germany did not become dangerous again. There was already a de facto division of the country into East and West, which prompted the French novelist François Mauriac to declare: 'J'aime tellement l'Allemagne que je suis heureux qu'il y en ait deux' (I love Germany so much I'm glad there are two of them). In the later stages of the war, moreover, there had been talk of dividing the country into several independent states on the grounds that this was the only way of rendering it harmless. Half a dozen 'Germanys' could have been created. If any country had an interest in a European project in order to save itself, it was Germany.

At the same time it was clear that, sooner or later, American pressure for a West European market and pressure for a European defence capability against the Soviet Union would make the advantages of a strong Germany irresistible. By the end of 1948, the Berlin airlift was in full swing, supplying beleaguered West Berlin from the air after all land routes had been cut off by the Soviet Union. Though the 'siege' of Berlin came to an end in the following year, the invasion of South Korea from the North in 1950 generated new fears of a similar invasion from East to West Germany. In such a climate of rising Cold War tensions, it appeared to be more dangerous to leave West Germany unarmed than to risk German rearmament. Rather than devising ways of keeping the country weak, the emphasis would be (at least so far as West Germany was concerned) upon how to make it strong. The same considerations applied in the economic field. Marshall Plan aid was trying to generate a West European recovery, in part in order to create a market for American exports, but the economic recovery of Germany was a condition of any progress at the European level. There could be no repeat of the reparations after World War I that had meant Germany was so overwhelmed by debt that it could no longer afford to be a market for other countries' exports. Europe (and the USA) needed a strong Germany both economically and militarily. Sooner or later that necessity was bound to make itself felt by those who for historical reasons were most reluctant to concede the point – the French.

This provided Monnet with his chance. He knew that it was France that had the most difficulty in coping with German recovery. It had refused, for instance, to merge its occupation zone (of Berlin) into the newly created Anglo-American zone when it was formed in May 1947. It felt that the British and American approach towards Germany was softening and wished to distance itself from that. Yet at the same time it had to recognise that the sort of factors outlined above were irresistible. Germany was not going to stay forever occupied, defenceless and poor.

What was necessary, Monnet realised, was not to fight against German postwar reovery but to find a way of locking it into the process of European recovery. The sharing of sovereignty would be acceptable to Germany while occupied Germany had barely any sovereignty to share and was struggling even to be able to form a government, hold elections and launch the Deutschmark. As Dinan puts it, shared sovereignty was better than limited sovereignty.[19] For this reason the Schuman declaration could reasonably be called 'grist to Adenauer's mill' (Adenauer was the first chancellor of West Germany). 'Das ist unser Durchbruch' (This is our breakthrough) was the Chancellor's response to the plan – a breakthough to respectability and to some sovereignty, even if shared.

But the idea of locking German strength into the process of European recovery was not only acceptable to Germany as a way back into the European family of nations. It was also highly desirable for France, if only France would realise it. This was what Monnet recognised. There was a window of opportunity for France while Germany was unsure whether it would be allowed to recover at all, and while there were still various controls upon its policies at home and abroad.

In particular, it was a window because of coal. France's need to have coking coal in order to produce steel had to be squared with the fact that Ruhr coke was under the control of an International Ruhr Authority, while the coal-rich Saarland was under French control but might not remain so (besides which, the coal of the Saar region was not very suitable for coking). This was not a new issue. An earlier

International Steel Pact, signed by Germany and France among others in 1926, reflected France's acceptance after World War I that its steel industry (now augmented by the return of Alsace-Lorraine) was dependent upon German coal and coke and needed to find some form of long-term arrangement that would guarantee supplies. In the aftermath of World War II, France was coming under growing pressure from its allies to 'find a solution' to the management of these regions. Would it not be better to find a 'European' solution through sovereignty-sharing, rather than to rely on what was bound to prove the temporary occupation of one area and being subject to the international control of another?

Germany needed sovereignty-sharing in order to survive as a nation, while France needed it in order to recover and in order to have the chance of continuing to be a 'great power'. The Schuman Plan was therefore acceptable to both – because it served the national interests of both. No one should doubt this, and it is no denial of the significance of supranationalism to assert it. France and Germany chose a supranational solution in order to benefit France and Germany. But, in doing so, they were doing something unique in the history of nations that would have a profound effect on their behaviour and that of the other nations that joined them during the years that followed.

A supranational structure takes hold

'Never before have States delegated a fraction of their sovereignty jointly to an independent, supranational body,' said Robert Schuman in the speech at the French Foreign Ministry in 1950 quoted above. In order to be clear about the implications of this action, we have to understand what 'delegated a fraction of their sovereignty' meant – and means. Chapter 3 attempts to do this in detail, but this chapter will remain focused on the history of the institutions rather than their structures. The key point is that six independent nation-states were collectively willing to be bound by the decisions of bodies that they created but that could not be controlled by any one of them acting alone. This was what Schuman recognised as a remarkable step forward. Nations were signing a new treaty – nothing new there. To that extent, the 1951 Treaty of Paris creating a European Coal and Steel Community (ECSC) was 'just another agreement between nation-states'. But these six went further than states had ever gone before when they created new supranational institutions that would ensure their adherence to the treaty they had themselves signed.

Unsurprisingly, an agreement to be bound by the decisions of a body that no one member state could control was unlikely to be acceptable in every area of government. Not long after the Coal and Steel Community came into being a crisis arose over a proposal initiated by René Pleven, the French defence minister, for a European Defence Community. But the plans for a European Defence Community were rejected by the French Senate (technically, it refused to put the matter to a vote), based on an unholy alliance of Gaullists and Communists. Since defence is probably the most sensitive area of all where a sense of national prerogative is concerned, the rejection of the proposal was hardly unexpected. Moreover, the specific circumstances that encouraged it in 1951 had changed by 1954. The Korean War was over, Stalin was dead and it was increasingly clear that the new North Atlantic Treaty Organization (and with it a continuing US military commitment to Western Europe) was not going to be undermined by any new outbreak of US isolationism. With increasing confidence in NATO and the US presence, the view that German rearmament could be permitted only under strict supranational control seemed less compelling.

The failure of the European Defence Community led to profound unease among supporters of sovereignty-sharing. The arrangement had been applied only in the area of coal and steel, and that had been difficult enough. Ratifying the Treaty of Paris had meant overcoming (or at least limiting) opposition from trade unions fearful of competition, politicians who saw national sovereignty as 'imperilled' and businesses who claimed there would be 'interference' in the market – arguments that were to become familiar during later treaty negotiations but that were there from the very start. The ECSC, with its headquarters in sleepy Luxembourg, might be as far as it went. Perhaps the whole sovereignty-sharing process would prove to be precisely what its opponents believed it to be, an 'unnatural' state of affairs that would disappear as circumstances changed. After all, the plan for a European Defence Community had brought in its wake another initiative which talked of a 'Political Community' that would encompass both defence and coal and steel (that is, the proposed European Defence Community and the already established ECSC). But the European 'Political' Community had died alongside the plans for a European Defence Community.

Monnet's technique was to proceed in a gradual manner, avoiding anything too ambitious (that, he felt, had been the mistake of the Defence Community and the Political Community). Like another shrewd operator after him, Jacques Delors, he preferred to keep close to what was politically feasible and tone down the rhetoric. If there was to be more sovereignty-sharing, it should be in an area close to that which already existed – coal and steel. His own preference was for an Atomic Energy Community. After all, atomic power was the energy resource of the future, whereas coal and steel were increasingly of the past. An Atomic Energy Community could therefore be presented both as technologically cutting edge and as a supplement designed to update the ECSC.

The leaders of the six member states of the ECSC agreed with Monnet's strategy, though with a different emphasis. When they met at Messina in Sicily in 1955 in order to try to rescue supranationalism from its defeat in the area of defence, they decided that it had been a mistake to try to introduce sovereignty-sharing in such a sensitive field. Returning to that area by seeking a new vote in the French Senate was recognised as unwise – after all, de Gaulle's popularity was growing and he was to hold the presidency of France for 11 years from 1958. It would be better to concentrate upon those areas where the pooling of sovereignty seemed to be acceptable, and these were likely to be in the economic sphere rather than defence and foreign relations. The leaders therefore determined to extend sovereignty-sharing in the economic realm and were attracted by Dutch proposals for a customs union and a series of steps towards further economic integration.

At their meeting in Messina, the foreign ministers listened favourably to the views of the Belgian foreign minister, Paul-Henri Spaak, when he supported both the Dutch proposals for a customs union and the proposals for an Atomic Energy Community. Spaak had been the first president of the Council of Europe, but resigned in 1951 because the Committee of Ministers was effectively blocking all the initiatives he supported. Now he could flourish. The Spaak report, published in 1956, proposed two separate organisations – which would later become the European Atomic Energy Community (EURATOM) and the EEC or the Common Market – and two separate treaties.

It worked. It may seem bizarre that, having succeeded in one area (coal and steel) and then failed in another (defence), the advocates of sovereignty-sharing should have attempted two more areas at the same time. In fact it was good politics. Presented with a choice of 'two or nothing', those who favoured only one proposal were persuaded to accept both for the sake of the one they wanted. France in 1956 became even more favourably inclined to an Atomic Energy Community, having been made aware by the Suez Crisis of the dangers that might arise from dependence upon imported oil. Meanwhile, the other five grew even more convinced of the economic benefits of a customs union, something that France was wary of because of the possible impact it might have upon its 'protected' industries and agriculture. In the end they, like France, were prepared to accept both for the sake of having one. The two treaties were signed at an elaborate ceremony in Rome in March 1957 (strictly speaking it is the Treaties rather than the Treaty of Rome), but as with subsequent treaties it was the process of ratification that mattered, and here Monnet's skills were crucial.

Monnet resigned as Chairman of the High Authority of the ECSC and lobbied on behalf of all the institutions, existing and planned, from outside them. He moved tirelessly among interest groups and governments to persuade them to accept the treaties. In the end, the Treaties of Rome were rightly seen as a great achievement, and are still the best known of all the treaties, the beginning of the road to European Union, even though sovereignty-sharing in fact began six years earlier with the ECSC.

There was arguably just one unfortunate aspect of Monnet's campaign. His lobbying group was called the 'Action Committee for the United States of Europe' (Le Comité d'Action pour Les Etats-Unis d'Europe), a name liable to suggest explosive 'federalist' ideas but that is accurately described by Bálint Szele as 'The European Lobby'[20] – a pressure group for more integration. Nevertheless, it was an ill-chosen title, one of many that were to give the misleading impression that what those who called for further integration really wanted was to create one single superstate.

By the end of the 1950s the essential character of a sovereignty-sharing community – whether a Coal and Steel Community or (later) a European Economic Community or (later still) a European Community or (later again) a European Union – had been established. On the one hand, there were going to be no-go areas so far as the sharing of sovereignty was concerned. On the other hand, there would be no going back on the decision to share sovereignty in some areas by creating supranational institutions. Many complications arose in the 60 years that followed these treaties, such as opt-outs and the debate over a 'two-speed Europe', or the recently developed open method of coordination (see Chapter 3). But, despite all these complications, what has not changed is the nature of the EU as a mixture of areas in which sovereignty is shared and areas in which it is not. Seven treaties have not changed that hybrid character but have embedded it. The Treaties of Rome did not begin the sharing of sovereignty, but they represented confirmation that it was to become a permanent feature of the European landscape. The quagga was to change a little as it grew, with a few new stripes here and there, but from now on no one could doubt the nature of the creature they were dealing with.

The paradox of de Gaulle – the European Economic Community in the 1960s

The first decade after the signing of the Treaties of Rome was dominated by the figure of Charles de Gaulle. The treaties came into force following ratification on 1 January 1958, and in the same year de Gaulle became president of France, remaining in the post until 1969. In terms of length, significance and policy impact, his period in power can be compared to the 11 years during which Margaret Thatcher was prime minister of the UK. Both were controversial and forthright, both gave their names to particular ideologies (Thatcherism/Gaullism), and both had a difficult relationship with the sovereignty-sharing approach of the Community. Despite this, both believed that there were benefits to be had from membership of the EEC and even that their national goals could be advanced through full participation within it.

It is important to remember that there were doubts about the future of the EEC when de Gaulle became president. People remembered his role in defeating the 'Pleven Plan', the proposal from French Minister of Defence René Pleven for a European Defence Community. Now he had become president of the Fifth Republic, under a new constitution that gave considerable powers to the president (especially in foreign policy) and that had been overwhelmingly supported in a referendum. Might he not seek to undo sovereignty-sharing altogether by withdrawing France from the EEC?

That he did not do so had a great deal to do with his recognition of the practical benefits of continuing to belong to the EEC. De Gaulle accepted that it was impossible to modernise France without it. That had essentially been the motivation for French involvement in the first place through the ECSC – without such an arrangement France could not develop economically and by doing so recover its standing in the world. In this opinion de Gaulle was at one with Schuman and Monnet.

In particular, he understood that such modernisation needed to be extended to the agricultural field through a Common Agricultural Policy. But how would that work? In a Europe that found itself 'at sixes and sevens' at the end of the 1960s – there were six members of the EEC and seven of the European Free Trade Area (EFTA) – it might have seemed possible to attract de Gaulle to EFTA. Surely as a 'nationalist' he would be in favour of free trade areas rather than the sovereignty-sharing approach of the EEC? But a free trade area would only remove customs duties – it would not guarantee a high price for French produce (by establishing a minimum floor price below which it is not possible for certain products to fall). Nor would it be able to keep out cheaper produce from abroad through a common external tariff or provide any subsidies for exports (see Chapters 4 and 5). If de Gaulle wanted to support his farmers, the price for doing so was a form of regulation in the agricultural sphere that meant supranational institutions. In exactly the same way, such institutions were essential to Margaret Thatcher's pursuit of the single market a generation later.

De Gaulle's passionate belief in France was combined with a realisation that France could not act alone to restore its national greatness. That had been clear in the dark days of 1940 when he founded the Free French and made sure that, whatever happened to a country that had been made to suffer occupation, there would always be a France that was part of the international campaign against Nazism. Now the need was economic recovery, but that too could not be managed alone.

In one sense de Gaulle had a distrust of supranational institutions as strong as that of successive UK governments, including those headed by Margaret Thatcher. He suspected that what the Commission in particular was seeking to do was to create a single state. He described the ambitions of the first president of the European Commission, Walter Hallstein, in the following terms: 'He does not even hide his plan, which is to transpose to the European level the institutional structure of federal Germany.'[21]

De Gaulle effectively stamped on any notion of the EEC as a greater Germany in the making, but he was not perhaps quite so averse to the idea of a greater France in the making. Where he differed from British concerns about the threat to national sovereignty was in his determination to form a common European front on a number of issues, not least that of defence. The problem was that a common European front meant either submitting to supranational institutions or making France's own wishes prevail over those of everyone else. De Gaulle was unwilling to accept the former, but the other five states were unwilling to accept the latter.

The issue came to a head over the Fouchet Plan (see Chapter 7). De Gaulle disliked NATO, withdrew France from the military wing of it and sought to develop a common foreign and defence policy for the six member states of the EEC through a plan drawn up by his ambassador to Denmark, Christian Fouchet. The plan called for a 'Union of European Peoples' without supranational institutions and gives a fascinating insight into what an unravelling in the 1960s of the sovereignty-sharing arrangements entered into during the previous decade might have meant. The Commission would have been turned into a secretariat of the Council, with similarities to a civil service. The Parliament (at that time an Assembly made up of delegates from the national parliaments) would offer recommendations or questions to the Council but would never develop decision-making powers, while real decision-making power would lie with the Council, which would act on the basis of unanimity with no clear understanding of how its decisions would be enforced (since there would be no Court of Justice enforcing European Law). Money for the 'Union' would come from annual contributions made by member states (thus ending progress towards 'own resources'). In effect, de Gaulle's Union of the European Peoples was an old-style intergovernmental body with a lot of window-dressing about shared values and civilisation. It was an object lesson in the dangers of becoming too attached to words and phrases. 'Union of European Peoples' sounds much like 'European Union', and yet it was completely different in reality.

The Fouchet Plan got nowhere, because de Gaulle was in an impossible position. The Benelux countries, the three smaller members of the Six, remained supportive of supranational institutions, particularly the Commission, seeing them as ways of preventing too much power being exercised by the larger countries of the Community, particularly France. They were not going to be forced into a common foreign and defence policy when that was a matter of accepting the foreign and defence policy of the French. For one thing, they did not share de Gaulle's hostility towards NATO. They had been part of the campaign to keep (and strengthen) US forces in Europe and they were not about to change their view of that. They were as happy as Bevin had been to have caught the whale, and they were not in any mood to be told that they might be swallowed by it. When de Gaulle decided to salvage a specifically Franco-German agreement from the wreckage of the Fouchet Plan, he found his Treaty of Friendship and Reconciliation, signed at the Elysée Palace in January 1963, crucially modified by the German parliament. It added a codicil asserting that Germany's commitment to fulfilling its NATO obligations took priority over anything else. De Gaulle had to accept that the other five had a different view of NATO from that of France.

Where the UK's delusion in the 1950s had been that it could manage its affairs without the Six, France's delusion in the 1960s was that it could manage the Six in its own interests. This goes some way towards explaining the fact that France twice vetoed the UK's application to join. De Gaulle's EEC had to be big enough to dominate Europe but small enough to be dominated by France. Though the other five were desperate for France to stay inside the Community, and were prepared to support French interests as far as they could, there were limits to the degree to which they were prepared to succumb to French wishes. NATO was one example of such limits.

Difficulties came to a head with the famous Empty Chair Crisis of 1965 and ended with the Luxembourg 'Compromise' of the following year. It is easy to see why the Commission thought that it was not going to encounter too many problems in 1965 when it proposed to bring forward a system of 'own resources' (essentially giving the Community a budget of its own rather than making it dependent upon regular national contributions from member states). After all, a considerable part of these 'own resources' were going to fund the proposed Common Agricultural Policy, of which de Gaulle was a fervent supporter. But the proposal for 'own resources' was being made without consulting de Gaulle in advance. The schedule established by the Treaty of Rome envisaged a considerable extension of voting by Qualified Majority Voting (QMV) in the following year, and de Gaulle took the view that the 'own resources' issue was a way of acclimatising France to the idea that it might be outvoted on crucial issues, something he was not prepared to accept under any circumstances. He promptly created 'empty chairs' by withdrawing French participation in all but run-of-the-mill business by the Council of Ministers.

De Gaulle won his battle. The Luxembourg Compromise stated that, where a vital national interest of any one member state was concerned, the Council would find a consensus (effectively a unanimous) solution. The Council agreed to the extension of majority voting as planned in the following year, but it did so partly because it knew that a member state could always exercise a de facto veto by declaring that its 'national interest' was at stake. However, what made the Community acceptable to France was also what made the rest of it (even without the UK) unwilling to conform to French wishes. The extraordinary approach made by de Gaulle to the UK in February 1969, suggesting that the EEC be recast as an intergovernmental free trade area with the UK inside it (which the Foreign Office happily reported to the other members of the Six),[22] may have reflected an awareness by de Gaulle, weakened in any case by the events of May 1968, of the impossible dilemma that he faced. He had remained part of the Six because it suited France's interests to do so, but he could never make it a sheer extension of those interests. Even when the UK was kept out, there were enough protests against such a policy from within. Though de Gaulle understood far earlier than did the British the advantages to his country of membership of the Community, he had a similar distaste for the 'community method'. In the end he was even prepared to make their joint distaste for such a method the grounds for an Anglo-French rapprochement around the principles of EFTA. Since this would have been totally unacceptable to the other five and would in any case have destroyed all the obvious advantages to France of its membership of the system it had helped to create, it can be seen as the last desperate gambit of a man about to lose power. But the same contradictions were to re-emerge 20 years later when it was the UK's turn to shake the Community to its foundations.

The paradox of Margaret Thatcher: the Community in the 1970s and 1980s

The 1960s might have been a time when de Gaulle rocked the European Economic Community to its core, but the decade had also been a time of prosperity for Western Europe, with growth rates in the Six at around 4 or 5 per cent and unemployment rates at less than 2 per cent. Such economic conditions helped the Community to weather the Gaullist storm. It also helped the installation of the three key features of the Common Market – a customs union, a common trade policy and a common agricultural policy.

In December 1969, shortly after de Gaulle's resignation as president of France, the leaders of the Six had their first meeting in two years at The Hague, and the new French president, Georges Pompidou, expressed his willingness to accept enlargement 'in principle'. After two vetoes from de Gaulle, UK entry was at last on the cards, and the leaders left the summit referring in positive terms to 'the spirit of The Hague'. There was talk from Pompidou of foreign policy cooperation, though it was received with some caution by the other five, who remembered the problems of the Fouchet Plan. There was also talk of further economic and monetary cooperation. The Luxembourg prime minister, Pierre Werner, was asked to draft a report on Economic and Monetary Union. And the Community finally got its budget ('own resources'), not least as a means of being able to fund the Common Agricultural Policy (CAP) in advance of British entry. All in all there was some reason for confidence that the Community not only was about to enlarge but was moving forward the process of integration.

In fact the 1970s proved a very difficult time, partly because the boom years of the 1960s were over. Indeed, it was one of the misfortunes of the UK's twice-vetoed application to join the EEC that it was finally accepted in 1973, just as the good times were coming to an end. This naturally fed a *post hoc ergo propter hoc* supposition that joining the 'Common Market' had inhibited rather than encouraged British economic success. British entry was in any case dogged by disputes. It was the only country not to have a referendum over joining (Ireland and Denmark had one and voted to enter, Norway had one and voted to stay out, and France had one and voted to allow the enlargement to proceed). In the end, the British had their referendum two years later, in 1975, when a new Labour government under Harold Wilson agreed to one, essentially in order to avoid splitting his party. But why have a referendum two years after entry (except, of course, as a ruse to overcome the fissiparous tendencies of the Labour Party)? To justify a referendum two years after entry, Wilson had to say that the terms had been 'renegotiated', and lost no time in exaggerating or even inventing the changes he had made (single-handedly fending off plans for a 'euro-loaf' and 'euro-beer', for instance). Though some changes were introduced in the course of the 'negotiation', concerning matters such as New Zealand lamb and the UK's budget rebate (an issue that was to blow up later under Margaret Thatcher's leadership), nothing was achieved in the 'renegotiation' that could not have been achieved anyway in the course of routine discussions between European leaders. The result, wrote Roy Denman, was 'the minimum of gain for the maximum of irritation'.[23]

There is no doubt that many of the factors involved in ending the economic boom, such as the quadrupling of oil prices in 1973 and a further doubling in 1979, were nothing to do with the creation of the

EEC. However, the whole sovereignty-sharing enterprise had been based upon ensuring a successful economic outcome; this was the area in which it had begun and the area in which, after the debacle of the planned European Defence Community, the willingness to share sovereignty had been reaffirmed and extended in the Treaties of Rome. It was therefore built into the expectations of those engaged in the sovereignty-sharing enterprise that they would reap some economic reward from it. The 1960s had been good years for the six founder members of the EEC – good for other countries too, such as the UK, but not nearly as good as they had been for Germany, France and Italy. At the same time, high growth rates and low rates of unemployment made high levels of welfare affordable and ensured a reasonable level of industrial harmony. Though the focus of the Common Market was upon wealth creation, it was always recognised that economic success was the precondition of successful social policies, which were also vitally important. Now it seemed as though the whole social and economic fabric was endangered. In this respect it was a feeling not unlike that which the present economic crisis sometimes engenders.

The question by the end of the 1970s, then, was one of how to recover the economic strength that had been in decline since the beginning of the decade. Regular meetings of European leaders of the (now) Nine had been established through the launch of the European Council in 1975. Could they steer the Community in the direction of economic renewal through some of the policies concerning Economic and Monetary Union outlined in the Werner Report at the beginning of the decade? Currency volatility was an obvious inhibitor to trade – might not something be done in this area? The German Chancellor (Helmut Schmidt) was becoming increasingly concerned that German economic recovery was being inhibited by deliberate depreciation of the dollar. Surely there must be some way of preventing currency manipulation and bringing back the sort of stability that had once been there under the Bretton Woods system.

The result, the European Monetary System (EMS) of 1979, was the first step on the way to the creation of a single currency. Currencies would not be able to fluctuate by more than a certain amount from an agreed level (weaker economies such as that of Italy were allowed more wiggle room than stronger economies such as that of Germany), with central banks agreeing to intervene by buying or selling a currency that looked as though it was going to go above or below the band. The system actually managed to work reasonably well during the 1980s, though the UK stayed away from it until 1991 (only to be forced out ignominiously a year later on 'Black Wednesday', the day that ruined the Major government's reputation for economic competence forever). Its eventual collapse, however, set the scene for the transition to a single currency a decade later, the consequences of which are still very much a feature of the European Union today.

The attempt to ensure some currency stability through the EMS went hand in hand with an effort to reinvigorate the Common Market. After all, the customs union had been achieved by the end of the 1960s. Goods should have been circulating freely between member states. But they were not – or not as much as they should have been. The Community had been enlarging – to 9 in 1973, and then to 10 (with Greece) in 1981 and to 12 (with Spain and Portugal) in 1986. By the mid-1980s membership of the EEC had doubled, and its population had increased by more than one-third. It was now an Economic Community of over 300 million people – in terms of numbers bigger than the USA and the Soviet Union – yet it was losing market share to the USA and to another much-envied economic giant of the time, Japan. It became increasingly frustrating to see that what was supposed to be an 'Economic Community' apparently lacked economic coherence.

Once the EEC had a market as big as America's but a less vibrant economy, it was inevitable that people would compare the relative ease with which a Nebraskan without a job moved to find work in California with the unwillingness of a jobless Italian to seek work in Germany. As they did so, further drivers of integration were bound to come into play as a necessary means of ensuring the economic strength that had always been at the heart of the 'European project'. What sense did it make to have a single market if it was not made easy for citizens of any of the 12 member states to live, to be employed, to open a bank account, to have their children educated, to have access to medical care and to receive a pension anywhere in the EEC? These things did not happen all at once, but they were now part of the logic of the single market. Some of them were strictly speaking outside the economic arena, but they were part of making the economic arrangements workable (see Chapter 4).

The desire to progress further with the single market was also the reason for the signing of the Single European Act (SEA) in 1986. And this is where another towering European leader of the second half of the twentieth century, Margaret Thatcher, becomes important (she was UK prime minister from 1979 to 1990), and where a similar contradiction emerges to that which faced de Gaulle.

Though they shared a fierce commitment to national sovereignty, the key difference between de Gaulle and Thatcher is this. De Gaulle wanted France to run the Community, and was frustrated when it proved impossible (even when the UK was kept out) to do so. Thatcher wanted not to be run *by* the Community, and was frustrated when time and time again she had to accept that membership of the EEC was unavoidable. De Gaulle wanted the Community to exist for the greater glory of France. Thatcher wanted the greater glory of the UK to exist outside the Community. Neither could have their way, and in practice both made compromises.

In the first half of the 1980s, it seemed as though the problems of the British Budget Question (BBQ also meant 'Bloody British Question' when the UK delegations were out of hearing) would go on forever. For Thatcher it was a question of 'getting my money back', as if the Community was a foreign body to whom money had been lent and was now taking its time about returning it. Like many prime ministers before and since, she easily turned the EEC into a 'they' who had nothing to do with 'us'. Even though the budget question was finally resolved at the Fontainebleau Summit in 1984, there was no reason to believe that it would be any easier to deal with Thatcher in the second half of the decade.

Except for one thing – she was a committed believer in the single market. The role of Jacques Delors, president of the Commission 1985–94, in ensuring that she was always encouraged in this approach should not be underestimated. Delors recognised that every European leader, whether it was the 'eurosceptic' Margaret Thatcher or the 'euro-enthusiast' Helmut Kohl, extolled the virtues of the single market. Delors therefore put the emphasis in the preparation of what was to become the SEA upon market integration. He was also aware that the single market was bound to appeal to industry and that it would be helpful to his cause to have vocal support from the private sector. He encouraged the commissioner for industry and the single market, Etienne Davignon, to call for an initiative from industry. Davignon repeated Henry Kissinger's famous question concerning whom he should call when he wanted to speak to Europe by asking: 'whom do I call when I want to speak to European Industry?' The Round Table, launched by a group of 17 business leaders in Paris on 6–7 April 1983, was crucial in providing an answer. It continues (now as a group of 50 or so CEOs of multinationals with European parentage) to emphasise the advantages, in terms of competitiveness and economies of scale, of building a single market, though the issues have changed. Delors helped to make sure that no leader – even a prime minister such as Margaret Thatcher who was often accused of neglecting industry's needs in favour of finance – could ignore the views of business leaders.

Delors emphasised the purely financial benefits of further economic integration. The Commission commissioned a study of what it called 'the cost of non-Europe', more specifically the estimated cost of failing to complete the single market. The result of this was the Cecchini Report (Paolo Cecchini was a former Commission official), which used data from the four largest member states and comparisons with the USA in order to to put a price on failure to achieve a single market. To some extent Cecchini was quantifying the unquantifiable, but his 16-volume report (eventually published in 1988; a condensed version is available in English)[24] examined the financial costs to firms of all the administrative hurdles erected to make it difficult to do business in another member state and estimated the costs in terms of lost trade at 200 billion European currency units (ECUs).[25]

Delors was therefore able to present the SEA as something that would make everyone inside the EEC richer and that had considerable support from the business community. This helps to explain why Margaret Thatcher was enthusiastic about it and proved manipulable (a word not used lightly of her) when it came to certain key policy developments. It was, after all, the first major agreement in 30 years (the last had been the Treaties of Rome signed in 1957). Its modest title (it was not even called a treaty) belied its import, just as some 20 years later the grandiose title 'Constitutional Treaty' was to exaggerate the significance of another – and in the end prove its undoing. The SEA did not transform the EEC overnight, and many of its measures were not fully implemented. But it was arguably the most important of the five treaties (in effect it was a treaty) that followed the Treaties of Rome. Nearly 300 pieces of legislation were agreed (they were drafted by UK Commissioner Lord Cockfield, who had previously been a minister in Thatcher's government) to remove what were divided into 'physical', 'fiscal' and 'technical' barriers to integration. The treaty recalled the intention of the Treaties of Rome to create 'an area without physical frontiers in which the free movement of goods, persons, services and capital is assured' and set about trying to do so.

There is a certain paradox about the attempt to create a free market – it actually needs a lot of legislation! Deregulation cannot work without regulations. The point of the paradox (see Chapter 4) is that, without a large number of rules, enforceable through the European Court, ensuring that the market is not being distorted through subsidies or bureaucratic walls erected by member states against each other, the natural tendency towards protectionism (particularly in difficult economic times) will prevail. In her memoirs, Thatcher refers to the single European market in positive terms as 'intended to give real substance to the Treaty of Rome and to revive its liberal, free trade, deregulatory purpose'.[26] But a deregulated, free trade and liberal economic environment involving a number of different nation-states could not happen automatically. It needed to be made legally binding upon them and constantly monitored by authorities with the power to intervene in order to make sure that such an environment was maintained. If you take the view that it is not appropriate for nation-states to share sovereignty, then you cannot form a single market – as those who have attempted to form one in other parts of the world under the auspices of the Association of Southeast Asian Nations or the African Union have found out.

In practice Margaret Thatcher recognised this. In signing up to the SEA, she signed up to a treaty that effectively unlocked the possibility of QMV, which had been in quarantine since the Luxembourg Compromise of 1966. Doubtless she had in mind forms of French and German protectionism being overcome as a majority of states voted for the single market. But there was always the possibility that the UK could be outvoted too.

After the signing of the SEA in 1986, Thatcher continued to be willing to compromise. Unlike Cameron when similar negotiations over the EU's budgetary framework took place in 2013, she was willing to allow the EEC budget to increase in 1988. Her 'surprising tractability'[27] is not difficult to explain – it was to maintain the momentum towards realising the single market. To do that she would even accept a higher budget in order to provide increased regional spending to poorer members of the EEC (who made their support of the single market conditional upon their receiving such 'compensation').

This aspect of Margaret Thatcher's premiership needs to be remembered despite the attitude to the Community expressed in the very same year (1988) in her speech to the College of Europe in Bruges. 'We have not successfully rolled back the frontiers of the state in Britain, only to see them reimposed at a European level, with a European superstate exercising a new dominance from Brussels', she famously declared. As the reference to a 'European superstate' shows, she was like de Gaulle in suspecting plans to turn the EEC into a single European state. But she herself voted through the SEA, which had extended QMV and had given additional authority to the European Parliament, directly elected since 1979. Without some imposition at European level, the single market that she wanted to see further embedded in the Community would be unenforceable. She could not at one and the same time condemn Europe for 'interfering' and require it to facilitate a single market of 12 different nation-states. She might resent the Community, but in the making of the single market she could not do without it. If she tried to, as her colleagues began to realise at the end of the decade, there would be a considerable economic price to pay.

There was, of course, one key step in the formation of a single market to which she, most of her colleagues and all of her successors as prime minister have remained adamantly opposed – the single currency. As already stated, there was nothing new about this idea. There had been various efforts to avoid currency fluctuations following the end of the Bretton Woods system, and that this should eventually lead to a proposal for a single currency as the most effective way of supporting a single market was hardly a surprise. But a single currency means giving up control of interest rates and exchange rates at the national level (not that in practical economic terms that 'control' at national level is always very assured), and this in turn means that the members of what was to become the eurozone had to be working within a common macroeconomic framework so that a cut in interest rates, for instance, would not benefit one state while harming another. The implications of this are still being worked out in the second decade of the twenty-first century with the persistent crisis in the eurozone.

From Maastricht to Nice

Following the SEA, treaties started to come at roughly the same intervals as parliamentary elections. Maastricht was ratified in 1993, Amsterdam in 1999 and Nice in 2003. The fact that the dates of these treaties in the textbooks differ reflects the controversy surrounding each of them – and the fact that their passage requires the unanimous agreement of all member states. If the time at which the heads of government signed these treaties is taken as the moment of their being passed, then the correct dates would be 1992, 1997 and 2001. But that was only the beginning of the story. Parliaments in all the member states had to pass legislation approving the treaties, and in some cases referendums had to be held (member states can choose their system of ratification). This takes time. Moreover, a popular vote may lead to a 'No', in which case the country is invited to explain the reasons for its opposition, the proposed treaty is then amended and a further referendum produces (it is hoped) a 'Yes'. Thus Denmark voted 'No' in 1992 and was granted four exemptions ('opt-outs') as a consequence, the most important of which was from the single currency planned for later in the decade (like the UK, Denmark does not use the single currency, though unlike the UK it pegs the Danish crown to the euro). A second referendum then produced a narrowly won 'Yes' vote, though the speed of it was bitterly resented and led to riots in Copenhagen and even gunshots from a cornered group of police, injuring several protesters. Denmark's reluctant 'Yes' was matched by a similarly reluctant 'Yes' from France (its so-called *petit oui*), which also held a referendum on Maastricht.

The long-drawn-out process of treaty ratification led to a lot of talk about Maastricht as 'a treaty too far' (more were to come), but, though the controversy was real (in terms of divided electorates and bitter arguments between member states over issues such as the size of their representation in Parliament or the Council), the reality was that these treaties remained solidly within the framework established by Paris, Rome and the SEA. Like the Constitutional Treaty to come, Maastricht's grand title of 'Treaty on European Union' and the decision to make the EEC part of a new entity called 'The European Union', encouraged the idea that a new creature was being born rather than an old one being trimmed and groomed. As was made clear at the time by Prime Minister John Major's reaction to the 'f-word' (federalism), it was foolish to give in to the temptation to claim too much for a treaty. By suggesting that a tidying-up exercise was a transformation, some of Europe's leaders nearly wrecked the Maastricht Treaty (as they were later to wreck the Constitutional Treaty).

The Maastricht Treaty is well known for having established the European Union on the basis of three 'pillars'. Whatever the pros and cons of this arrangement, it clearly represented continuity with everything that had gone before, namely a system of *partial sovereignty-sharing*. Two pillars, those concerned with the Common Foreign and Security Policy on the one hand, and with justice and home affairs on the other, were intergovernmental, whereas in the third pillar – which covered everything to do with the former EEC and the agreements on Coal and Steel and EURATOM – sovereignty was shared. Although it was possible to argue that significant changes had taken place through greater use of QMV in the Council and the power of 'co-decision' between Council and Parliament, which gave the latter a veto in some areas of policy, Maastricht's pillar system effectively provided a rationalisation of existing practice.

Maastricht is also famous for laying down a procedure and timetable for moving towards a single currency. The decision showed that, even after a doubling in size, the 'Franco-German engine' was essential to what was now renamed the European Union. It recalled the same principle that had originally drawn Schuman to propose the Coal and Steel Community and Adenauer to embrace the idea as a 'breakthough', namely that there was a window of opportunity in which Germany would be willing to be the economic engine of European recovery in return for acceptance within the family of European nations. That was an obvious point in the late 1940s; 40 years later it had resonance again because the Soviet Union's reformist leader Mikhail Gorbachev had unexpectedly agreed to a reunited Germany within NATO. The Western powers were suddenly confronted with the prospect of German reunification and a Germany whose 80 million inhabitants would be significantly more than the 60 million that had made West Germany roughly the same size as Italy, France and the UK. Would there be difficulties accepting Germany's new position as the 'bull moose', the 20 million inhabitants of the former Deutsche Demokratische Republik (DDR or East Germany) appearing overnight as members of the Union? The creation of the eurozone made it possible for the giving up of the Deutschmark to be a continuation of the principle that, in return for acceptance, Germany should affirm its commitment to the whole of the EU. It could grow (and in doing so help everyone else to grow) only by being European. A single currency was the price of a single Germany.

The treaties of Amsterdam and Nice were more focused on dealing with enlargement than on changing the nature of the European Union. By 1995 there were 15 members, but all eyes were on the arrival of a dozen new member states, mostly from the former satellite countries of (and even some former parts of) the Soviet Union. Amsterdam and Nice were therefore mostly taken up with some not very flattering (to the EU) arguments over the how institutions were to be streamlined in the light of enlargement: would the Commission get too big, should there be more use of QMV, who should have how many votes in Council or how many members of the European Parliament should there be in a larger (but how large could it get?) Parliament? Nice extended once again the range of decisions covered by QMV, but it also introduced the possibility of blocking a decision in Council if those opposed represented a certain percentage of the EU's population. Since all the candidate countries (bar Poland) had populations only one-quarter or one-third those of member states such as France, the

UK, Italy and Germany, it is reasonable to suppose that this was a form of 'streamlining' the Union that in effect meant curbing the powers of the new member states. QMV was extended in order to make sure that any 'eccentricities' on the part of some of the new members could be outvoted, while the blocking provision ensured that any eccentricities on the part of some of the old ones could not be outvoted. If anything ought to have shown the 'eurosceptics' that this was not a case of 15 nation-states trying to turn themselves into the different regions of a European 'superstate', it was the unsightly scrambling for national voting rights or seats at both Amsterdam and Nice.

False starts and genuine progress: the European Union after Nice

The suspicion that a new nation-state was in the making undoubtedly contributed to the failure of the Treaty Establishing a Constitution for Europe. Moves towards such a treaty were initially expressed in much more measured tones. The European Council meeting that issued the Laeken Declaration on the Future of the European Union in December 2001 simply talked about a Union that needed to be 'more democratic, more transparent and more efficient'. This was eminently sensible given the imminent growth of the European Union from 15 to 25 members, a 60 per cent increase in the Union's membership. As the previous section mentioned, the issues raised by enlargement had hardly been dealt with adequately by the Amsterdam and Nice treaties. The largest enlargements so far at any one time had been of three new members (in 1973 and 1995). Now there was to be an increase of ten. Though it was less significant in terms of population (an additional 80 million – something like a 20 per cent increase in the population of the Union), the impact in terms of a need for some reorganisation was clear. After all, there would never be an enlargement like this again. Even if all of Europe were eventually to become part of the European Union (and assuming that an acceptable definition of Europe could be found), new members would come in twos and threes as they usually had in the past.

Had that point been recognised in terms of the requirements it imposed upon existing members for some practical moves towards streamlining institutions, what followed would probably have been relatively uncontroversial. Instead, the Laeken Declaration decided that such changes would be overseen by a so-called Convention on the Future of Europe, as if adding a few new members was akin to redefining a continent. The Council went on to talk about 'the adoption of a constitutional text in the Union'. Once the 'c-word' was out, it was latched onto as clear evidence of the state-building designs of the Council (despite the fact that it was the least likely institution to have such designs).

The British foreign secretary at the time, Jack Straw, pointed out that constitutions were relatively harmless things, enjoyed by golf clubs and the Conservative Party as much as (potentially) the EU, and that a document that clearly set out a voter-friendly 'who does what' guide to the EU could only be beneficial.[28] Unfortunately, such a straightforward and much-needed guide to the workings of the Union was not what the Constitution turned out to be: 400 articles, 36 protocols, 2 annexes and 50 deliberations hardly made up a concise introduction to the life of the quagga – one might as well have made a list of all the bones in its body. Effectively it was a bringing together of what had been agreeed in treaties so far and what was proposed for the new treaty. It would have been perfectly happy as the Treaty of Laeken or wherever the Council happened to be meeting when it was signed. But no, it had to be the 'Constitutional' Treaty. There had to be a 'constitution'. And once there was a mention of 'constitutions', the new treaty was bound to be seen as more than it was – and therefore as more threatening than it was. The way was open for the UK Conservative opposition at the time (in the form of Michael Ancram, shadow foreign secretary) to describe the proposal as caving in to 'the people who want to see political union'. Like 'constitution', 'political union' is another deeply confusing expression and is one that is being resurrected by those who are anxious for another treaty to follow the Lisbon Treaty. Like 'constitution', it is something that might be seen as suggesting the creation of a single nation-state, the greater Italy of Benedetto Croce or the greater Austria-Hungary of Coudenhove-Kalergi.

The perception that the Constitutional Treaty was a blueprint for a superstate on the other side of the Atlantic, a United States of Europe to match the USA, was a misreading but also a a warning to be careful about language (naturally the fact that everything is published in many languages – there are currently 24 official ones – complicates this point). President of the Convention and former French President Valéry Giscard d'Estaing was keen to strengthen the European Council and in many ways reflected traditional concerns of the French right for protecting national sovereignty. But the reality was lost in the rhetoric. As a 'Constitutional' Treaty this could not be a treaty like any other – even though this was precisely what it was. The many annexes, declarations and so on could not be seen as the useful codification of treaty provisions and instead became a horribly flatulent equivalent of 'We the people'. Nemesis came in an unexpected manner (though it should not be forgotten that the French nearly rejected the Treaty of Maastricht in a referendum) when French voters rejected the proposed treaty, closely followed by the Dutch.

It was all a storm in a teacup. A few years later the Treaty of Lisbon, containing the vast majority of the proposals contained in the Constitutional Treaty, was agreed and ratified. In fact it had simply been a consolidating treaty all along, one in which the balance between the 'intergovernmental' and the 'supranational' elements remained roughly as they were. However, the unfortunate consequence of the disaster over the Constitutional Treaty was to make the Lisbon Treaty itself seem more radical than it was. After all, if most of the measures being introduced at Lisbon had been in its aborted predecessor, was not this an example of introducing massive changes by stealth? Governments were saying that the Treaty of Lisbon (unlike the Constitutional Treaty) did not require a referendum because it was just an amendment to existing treaties. But, if that was the case, why were so many of its provisions carbon copies of those that had been made in the Constitutional Treaty? Precisely because the Constitutional Treaty had been paraded as more than it was, the Treaty of Lisbon was suspected of being more than it claimed to be. The verbose trumpetings of the former produced concerns about the apparently false modesty of the latter.

In reality, what the Lisbon Treaty dropped from the Constitutional Treaty were the trappings of statehood – the word 'constitution', the official adoption of a flag and anthem, the title 'foreign minister' for the high representative (whose powers, in contrast to her title, were almost exactly as envisaged in the Constitutional Treaty). In reality, neither treaty sought to change the hybrid character of the EU. But the ability of language (and over-ambitious politicians carried away by their own rhetoric) to make something more than it is shows just how misleading a wrong choice of words can be. Had European leaders learned their lesson with the ratification of the Treaty of Lisbon?

Looking forward: the Treaty on Political Union?

In September 2012 the president of the Commission, José Manuel Barroso, delivered his annual 'State of the Union' address to a plenary session of the European Parliament in Strasbourg. Clearly he was concerned about the euro crisis, declaring that 'securing the stability of the Euro area is our most urgent challenge'. Moves towards completing 'economic and monetary union', 'banking union' and 'fiscal union' were all part of solving this crisis and preventing another. However, he then went on to talk of 'political union' and declared: 'Let's not be afraid of the words: we will need to move towards a federation of nation states.' Barroso then went on to explain what this meant, or, more specifically, what it did not mean: 'I call for a federation of nation states. Not a superstate.' He then explained: 'Creating this federation of nation states will ultimately require a new treaty. I do not say this lightly. We are all aware how difficult treaty change has become.' Nevertheless, he proposed to 'present explicit proposals for the necessary treaty changes ahead of the next European Parliamentary election in 2014. This is our project. A project which is step by step but with a big ambition for the future with a Federation as our horizon for Europe.'

Barroso thereby set the scene for what can be guaranteed to be another storm in another teacup. Of course, like any leader conscious that his time is coming to a close (he cannot remain president of the Commission beyond 2014), his thoughts have turned to legacy. But what invariably happens is that leaders in such a state of mind talk up the grand projects they have ('a big ambition for the future'), latch on to a grandiose title ('a Federation of nation states . . . a Federation as our horizon for Europe') and then set all the hares running just in time for the European elections in June 2014.

Inevitably it will be asked why it is so important for a European 'Union' (which was previously a European 'Community') to become a European 'Federation'? What is this 'horizon' towards which we are all supposed to be moving? Why change the name? Why have a new treaty? The answer would appear to be that nothing else will do for a legacy-hunting president of the Commission. 'Let's not be afraid of the words' – but words matter (George Orwell should be compulsory reading for every president of the Commission), because they are so easily open to misinterpretation (not least when they come in 24 different official languages).

Conclusion

A study of the historical context shows that there is nothing radically new in what Barroso was proposing. 'I call for a federation of nation states. Not a superstate.' These words of his are absolutely consistent with what this chapter has tried to show to be the enduring principle throughout. All the partial sovereignty-sharing arrangements that have characterised the relations between an increasing number of European states since 1951 have had something in common. Whether it is a Coal and Steel Community or a European Economic Community or a European Community or a European Union or (conceivably in the future) a Political Union or a Federation of Nation-States, this whole process has never been one of bringing a superstate into being. The story of the EU is not the story of a nation-state in the making. It is the story of a unique arrangement between nation-states, one that has helped to secure peace in a continent whose history has so often been characterised by devastating war.

Of course there have been changes along the way as a group of 6 has become a group of 28. Such expansion is bound to affect the institutional structure in one way or another. It is also true that the attempt to establish a common and later a single market has had spin-off outside the purely economic domain, as it inevitably will. But this spin-off has never threatened to make foreign policy, for instance, a 'Community competence' – such a thing would be as unthinkable in

2014 as it was when the French Senate refused to put the Pleven Plan to the vote 60 years earlier. The underlying character of the partial sovereignty-sharing arrangement has become more embedded in the structures of the EU, not less, in the course of seven treaties (see Chapter 3 for more details).

The EU has a budgetary framework now until 2021 and a lot of important practical policies to implement during that budgetary period (see Chapter 6). It is putting in place a new Commission under a new president after a new five-year Parliament elected in June 2014. It will almost certainly be enlarging, though the formal right of withdrawal confirmed by the Treaty of Lisbon means that one or two states might leave. These will be interesting times. But a study of the historical background provides convincing evidence that it will lead neither to a return to the sort of loose arrangements between nation-states that characterised treaties before the Treaty of Paris was signed, nor to the creation of a single state.

The most formidable leaders of the two most powerful states in the European Community/Union (militarily if not economically) during the last 50 years, de Gaulle and Thatcher, both had their fears about the creation of a superstate, but both ended up working with a body that (to some extent) they both despised. De Gaulle never sought to withdraw France from the EEC, despite his hostility to Hallstein and despite the Empty Chair Crisis. That the Community was still there in 1969 when he resigned was something of a surprise to those who had reacted with concern to his election as president of France 11 years earlier. Thatcher's hostility took longer to materialise. She supported a 'Yes' vote in the referendum on UK membership in 1975 and, despite the long and bruising campagn over the 'British rebate', she signed up to the first revision of the Treaties of Rome in 30 years (the SEA) and supported increases in the EU budget to smooth the path of enlargement when Spain and Portugal entered. Though her Bruges speech and the circumstances of her downfall (ironically, preferring to be at a meeting of European leaders in Paris than ensuring that she got a few more votes in the leadership election back home) have been used to highlight her 'euroscepticism', she certainly accepted that Britain's economic interests were best served by membership of the EEC and even by a process of strengthening its institutions and legal powers.

Sovereignty-sharing will always grate most with the 'big beasts', and yet the history of the EU has shown that even big beasts can be tamed.

This chapter began with the Treaty of Westphalia signed over 300 years ago and arguably ushering in the era of the 'nation-state'. Nation-states have to find a way of living together that neither fails to restrain their bellicose tendencies nor undermines their identity. The story of Europe since 1648 has been one of wars and bloodshed on a sometimes grand scale. Whether or not the European Union is seen to have deserved the Nobel Peace Prize awarded to it in 2012, there is no doubt that it has contributed to making Europe a more peaceful continent (despite five wars in South-East Europe in the 1990s that should not be overlooked). The nations that emerged from the traumatising experience of World War II did not simply ramp up the rhetoric about peace while doing nothing to provide for it in reality (though there was some of that). They built institutional structures that would help to make war as impractical and unthinkable as it could possibly be made to be. Those who developed these novel institutional structures deserve some credit. When the windy rhetoric has passed away it is the practical arrangements that have been made to give it substance which must remain, if anything at all is to remain (apart from the warm glow that soon disappears) when the speeches are over.

3

Anatomy

Introduction

Though a tour of institutions can be found in most introductions to the European Union (EU), they do not always make clear how the different institutions relate to each other or how they can be seen as forming a coherent whole together. This chapter will try to remedy that defect. It does not deny that there are problems and inconsistencies in the way the institutions relate to one another (there are), but there is still an underlying logic to the whole process that needs to be brought out. The EU may be a quagga or a duck-billed platypus, but it is still an animal that moves.

This book has already tried to make clear that the central nervous system of the European Union is the sharing of sovereignty. That is what enables us to talk of the European Coal and Steel Community (ECSC), the European Economic Community (EEC), the European Community (EC) and the European Union (EU) as one evolving arrangement that has undergone many changes (not least of name). Take the sovereignty-sharing away and there is nothing unique about the EU. It becomes part of the herd, another grouping of nations like all the others in the alphabet soup of regional, subregional and international organisations.

The sharing of sovereignty is what began the process of creating the key institutions that exist today – in particular the Council of Ministers, the European Parliament (originally the Assembly), the Commission (originally the High Authority), the Court of Justice and the Consultative Committees (now the Economic and Social Committee and the Committee of the Regions). However, this creates some obvious difficulties. For one thing, there are clearly a lot of institutions and the relations between them constantly change as they jockey for power. It therefore becomes all too easy to write a list-based account of them saying 'this treaty gave more power to the Council,' 'that treaty gave more power to the Parliament', when what the reader needs above all is to know how all these institutions fit together, if they do at all.

A second difficulty lies in the fact that the uniqueness of the EU is reflected in the uniqueness of its institutions. This means that the attempt to see the institutions in terms of their 'national equivalents' will be misleading. As suggested in the introductory chapter, there is a tendency to mistake the EU either as a gathering of nation-states like all the others or as a single state in the making – a new Austria-Hungary struggling to be born. I suggested that both these apparently opposite positions take the nation-state as the fundamental unit of government to which everything else must be reduced. In the same way, national institutions are often taken as the template according to which their EU equivalents are judged. The EU Parliament is 'not quite right' because it appears to be a parliament without a government. The Commission is stuck between being a mere civil service (which it is more than, because it has the right of initiative to propose new laws) and being a legislature (which it is less than, because it cannot pass the laws it proposes). The Court of Justice is not quite a supreme court. And so on. Each institution is measured against its national equivalents.

A great deal of the criticism of EU institutions is based on this sort of approach. A 'federalist' member of the European Parliament (MEP) who sees the development of the EU as that of a single state in the making will say that the Parliament 'ought' to have the right of initiative at present held exclusively (in most areas) by the Commission. The need for the European Parliament to have a government with a clear policy agenda will be stressed. In reality the 'federalist' is impatient to see the European Parliament acquire the powers of a national parliament and begin to look like what (s)he considers a 'real' parliament. The 'eurosceptic', on the other hand, will look at the Commission and say that it 'ought' to be no more than a civil service, carrying out only what the Council decides, in the way that a civil service at national level implements the decisions of ministers. Then it will be a 'real' civil service.

These arguments soon become enmeshed in a horrific mass of detail, but it helps to see that both critics are really basing their views on the same principle: EU institutions must be like their counterparts at the level of the nation-state, and only when they are identical to these counterparts will they be coherent. This book will take precisely the opposite approach. Starting out from the premise that a sovereignty-sharing union of states is something unique, it will expect the institutions of that Union to be unique too. It will not expect them to be like – or to be struggling to become like – their national equivalents.

A different kind of treaty

Understanding the institutional origins of the EU can be made easier by comparing it with the institutional origins of the Council of Europe, founded in 1949. French Foreign Minister Robert Schuman (see Chapter 2) deliberately set out to create something different from the Council of Europe when he pushed for a Coal and Steel Community. Of course there were institutional similarities. The Council of Europe had a Committee of Ministers (the foreign ministers of each member state), just as the Coal and Steel Community (and now the EU) had a Council of Ministers. The Council of Europe had a consultative assembly made up of MPs from each member state – and the Coal and Steel Community had an assembly made up initially of MPs from each member state. The Council of Europe used some grandiose language, language that spoke about striving to 'achieve a closer union between its members', language that might suggest the 'ever-closer union' spoken of in the Treaties of Rome.

But the institutional structure of the ECSC was different. The Treaty of London, which established the Council of Europe in 1949, required a secretariat whose job was to ensure the functioning of the Council's decision-making body, the Committee of Ministers. However, the Treaty of Paris of 1951, which established the ECSC, created a High

Authority that was far more than a secretariat (it had executive powers) and a Court of Justice. What was different in 1951, in other words, was that the nations who signed the Treaty of Paris created institutions *empowered to implement the treaty that they had agreed*.

This is the crucial step taken with the Treaty of Paris. After all, there was nothing new about signing a treaty. Nations had been making (and breaking) treaties for centuries. The flowery language in which Robert Schuman hailed this new treaty as something wholly new (see Chapter 2) had to have some point to it. The difference from the Treaty of Paris was that the signatories agreed to a new mechanism to ensure that this particular treaty was not yet another that was made and then unmade. They voluntarily delegated, to independent institutions that they would create but not control, the task of implementing their own treaty; in other words, if they had regrets about what they had agreed the morning after, they could not go back on the treaty because it was no longer exclusively in their hands.

The High Authority (later the Commission) and the Court of Justice were the two bodies that the member states that signed the Treaty of Paris agreed to create. These bodies were empowered (under conditions that will be considered later) to implement what had been agreed. It is important to stress that the two institutions had (and today in the form of the Commission and the Court of Justice have) this power only because the member states granted and grant them. The states chose to confer 'supranational competence', and they could choose to do so no longer. The ECSC was created to last 50 years, and in 2002 the member states decided to wrap it up rather than extend its remit. They could do exactly the same with the European Union as a whole. An eighth treaty could be signed, for instance, revoking the process by which member states voluntarily confer upon the Commission the right to implement the treaties. The show goes on because the member states choose to let it do so. They could bring it to an end.

A balance – not a fight to the finish

This should make clear that the European Union is not an interim stage in the creation of a single large nation-state covering much of Europe, or what I have called the creation of a 'greater Italy' or a 'greater Austria-Hungary'. The nation-states remain in charge of the process. The institution in which the ministers of the individual member states meet in various 'configurations', depending upon which policy area is under discussion, is the Council of Ministers. It is here that proposed legislation is discussed, amended and adopted or rejected. There is nothing temporary about this institution. It is not preparing to hand over power to a new central government, after which it will be demoted to some kind of assembly of the regions. The Council is a permanent institution, which has if anything been strengthened over the decades. Moreover, in 1975 the European Council was launched, bringing together the EU's top leaders (presidents and prime ministers) in regular quarterly summits (more meetings are possible if needed) to provide the EU with general political direction and priorities (summed up in the 'conclusions' issued at the end of each meeting). If anything it has become more clear with time, not less, that the whole institutional edifice of the EU rests upon the collective willingness of the member states to sustain it.

Hence the EU is – and was from the beginning – a balancing act. It created powerful supranational institutions (the Commission and the Court of Justice), which would not be needed if the EU was little more than a discussion forum between states. But it also has powerful intergovernmental institutions (the Council of Ministers and the European Council), which would not be needed if the EU was a single state in the making. Being what it is, the EU has both types of institution, which exist in a certain creative tension with one another, jockey for power and influence and argue about what their exact status should be; but through all the changes that have taken place over more than 60 years the overall design has not altered in any fundamental way.

This introduction will not examine this 'creative tension' in detail but will give just one example. Desmond Dinan, in his *Ever Closer Union*, explains that 'ardent eurofederalists often lament the European Council's ascendancy'. However, he goes on:

> Yet the emergence of the European Council in the 1970s contributed to a gradual strengthening, rather than weakening, of supranationalism. Aware of the intergovernmentalism inherent in regular summitry,

national leaders agreed when they launched the European Council in 1975 to organise direct elections to the European Parliament in order to shore up supranationalism.[1]

Hundreds of such nuances attend the histories and institutional analyses of the EU. More power for the Council, so more power for the Parliament. Move A strengthens intergovernmentalism, so Move B is brought in to strengthen supranationalism. And so on. It is useful to know the developments in detail (and Dinan's book is a wonderful cornucopia of detail), but they all take place within the context of a single overall framework, which demands that each side recognise that the other will never go away. Moreover, they reflect an acceptance that a move to strengthen the institutions on one 'side' may need to be offset by strengthening those on the other 'side'. Only for those who believe that the end of sovereignty-sharing is the only viable political arrangement are all these adjustments part of a 'fight to the finish'. For others they are simply an attempt to maintain a balance. Indeed, it is arguable that every treaty has moved further in the direction of embedding *both* sides within the institutional framework, so that the most unlikely development at the institutional level now would be for one side to triumph over the other.

The developing framework

The last section stressed the importance of a decision by six independent nation-states not only to sign a treaty but to create a High Authority, a 'supranational' institution in the sense that it was staffed by members of each of the six member states, and to delegate to that body the power to implement their treaty. This system has not changed fundamentally during the last 60 years. Nowadays the European Commission, staffed by people from the 28 current member states of the EU, has the task of implementing what are now seven treaties, which have been agreed unanimously by the member states.

Three points have to made clear about this system. The first is that it applies to some, but not all, of the activities of member states. The European Union is, and always has been, a *partial* sovereignty-sharing system. The six states that signed the Treaty of Paris, and created the High Authority with the authority to implement it, were very clear that such authority must be confined to the terms of the treaty (at that time limited to the coal and steel industries). Three years later they rejected a proposal to create a European Defence Community (see Chapter 2). Meeting at Messina in Sicily a year after the European Defence Community was rejected, the Six essentially went back to the economic areas in which sovereignty-sharing had proved acceptable. The Treaties of Rome effectively reaffirmed the sovereignty-sharing process after earlier setbacks. They could do so only because by the end of the 1950s it was already accepted that member states would not let the system they had agreed on to extend to every policy area.

The second important point to understand about this system is that it required two institutions, not one. It was not only the High Authority that was created by the Treaty of Paris, but also the Court of Justice. It was not enough to create a High Authority and give it the task of implementing the treaty; another institution had to be created in order to ensure that this implementation was legally binding. There were bound to be conflicts, with the High Authority being seen as telling proud and independent states what to do, even though these states had themselves agreed to create it, and even though it had been created only in order to hold those member states to nothing more than the details of a treaty they had unanimously agreed upon. Such a process was bound to be fraught with difficulties once the precise details of what they had already agreed upon came to be worked out. There needed to be a way of ensuring that the provisions of the Treaty of Paris were *enforceable – legally* enforceable – and that each member state was therefore legally obliged to respect them. The Court of Justice was and is a vital part of the implementation process. A separate section later in the chapter will look at this institution in more detail.

The third important point about the system is that the empowerment of the High Authority, and later the Commission, to implement the treaties did not mean that it was given carte blanche to decide exactly what that implementation was. What it received and has kept ever since is the 'right of initiative' – that is, the right to propose new laws. How else, after all, could it possibly implement any treaty?

Since the Commission is there to implement treaties but not to go beyond them, the first thing it must do when proposing a new law is to go round like someone with a coat in search of a peg, in order to show on what article of the treaties its proposal is based. If it cannot succeed in doing so, the proposal has to be dropped. Hence the laws it proposes are technically 'secondary legislation', whereas the articles of the treaties are 'primary legislation'.

Moreover, its right of initiative is a right only to *propose* new laws. It is entirely unsurprising that the member states, even after they had agreed to create the High Authority (later the Commission) and the Court of Justice in order to implement the Treaty of Paris, should have wished to remain part of the overall institutional framework. They insisted upon the creation of two other institutions: the Council of Ministers and a Common Assembly made up of delegates from national parliaments (the forerunner of the European Parliament, the name taken in 1979 when it ceased to be made up of national delegates and instead was directly elected).

A (necessarily simplified) diagram of the EU's decision-making process is shown in Figure 2. The diagram makes clear that new laws are proposed by the Commission, the body empowered to implement

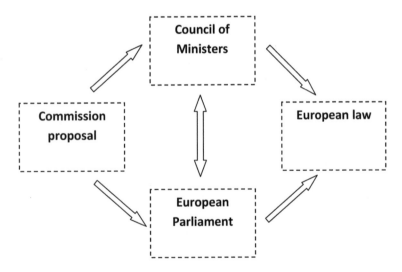

Figure 2. Diagram of the EU's decision-making process.

the treaties. The Council and the Assembly (now the Parliament) then consider, amend and pass or reject those proposed laws. Once passed, they may become part of the body of European Law, which is binding upon member states.

Whereas in the case of the Council of Europe the Committee of Ministers *controls* the process of decision making, in the case of the EU the Council of Ministers (and later the European Council, essentially the Council of 'top ministers') is a *part* of the process. But it is an essential part, and the 'licence' of the Commission should not be exaggerated. The Commission is empowered to implement these unanimously agreed treaties but is forbidden to go beyond them. And it can do so only to the extent that the Council and Parliament agree to the terms of the proposed implementation. The Commission has a right of inititative that exceeds the powers of a civil service, but it cannot pass the laws it proposes, which means that its power is less than that of a legislature.

How a new law gets made

Before going through the institutions one by one, it is useful to look at the process outlined in the diagram above in a little more detail.

As the diagram makes clear, new legislation begins with a proposal from the Commission. This may come from a number of different departments (known as Directorates-General or DGs) working together (for example, Environment, Climate Change and Energy working on a proposal concerning renewable energy sources), though there will always be a 'lead' department. The proposal from the Commission will be the product of a lot of prior consultation with experts, interest groups, lobbyists and other institutions. The Treaty of Lisbon also introduced a 'Cititzens' Initiative', enabling the Commission to propose a new law as a response to public demand expressed in the form of 1 million signatures representing at least one-quarter of the member states (seven). The initiative must be for something within the Commission's remit, that is to say an area within which it is entitled to propose new legislation.

Once a new proposal is framed, opinions are sought from national parliaments. This is intended to give national parliaments the opportunity to say that the proposal would be better dealt with at national or regional level than at European level (in line with the principle of subsidiarity) or that it is taking a sledgehammer to crack a nut (the principle of proportionality). If enough national parliaments dislike the proposal on this basis (one-third or more), it has to be reconsidered by the Commission, and, if the Commission persists with it, the Council (by a majority of 55 per cent) or the Parliament (by a simple majority) can throw it out.

The proposal also travels (in most areas) to the two consultative committees, the Economic and Social Committee and the Committee of the Regions. The former has existed since the 1950s and brings together civil society groups, which are divided into three groups: employers, workers' organisations and 'other interests'. Its members are nominated by national governments and then appointed by the Council. The Committee of the Regions is more recent, dating from the 1990s (see Chapter 6), and is made up of elected regional or local politicians nominated by their national governments and appointed by the Council. Though these committees are merely consultative bodies, the requirement to consult them gives them an opportunity to advise, influence and delay (one could say they had 'House of Lords' powers).

The range of consultations does highlight a genuine attempt to be as participatory as possible and bring in as many 'actors' as one can. The people may band together to propose a law. The Commission proposes nothing without input from experts, interest groups and lobbying organisations. The proposal travels horizontally between units at the same level within various departments of the Commission before travelling upwards to their Directorates and finally for consideration and approval to the College of Commissioners – that is, all 28 commissioners meeting together and, if necessary, taking a vote. And then the process of consultation goes on, with national parliaments and with the consultative committees representing particular groups in society – cumbersome, bureaucratic, often slow, but some would say that this is the price of democracy, especially when it has to exist at many levels.

When the process of consultation is complete, the institutions that decide whether the proposal is or is not to be passed (the Council and the Parliament) come into play, though the Parliament will make a first reading of proposals at the same time as the consultative committees. This can be a quick process or it can involve a degree of ping pong between all three. Even when the final stage is reached and 'the act is adopted', there is still room for negotiation and complicated manoeuvring as it is implemented. The implementation process has spawned the word 'comitology' and, though the process is technically the responsibility of the Commission, the Council and the Parliament oversee it, making comitology what Dinan calls 'one of the most arcane activities in the EU'.[2] National officials collaborate with officials from the Commission in formal committees that oversee the implementation process.

There is a constant process of interaction (or, if things go badly, of haggling, stalling and prevaricating) between these three institutions as everything possible is done to reach agreement (in the case of comitology, extending even to a complicated process of agreeing what they have agreed). But recognising the complexity of this process is more important (at least for those who do not work inside the labyrinth) than knowing the detail: as many bodies as possible are consulted; proposals go back and forth between the major 'players'; the Commission puts the ball into play but retrieves it at a later stage of the game before once again letting it go. Everything that can be done is done to prevent the ball from being kicked out of the stadium. This means that, in controversial areas, adjustments and amendments are to be expected, and probably no one will be entirely happy with the result.

EU legislation may come in binding or non-binding forms, and the binding forms come as 'decisions', 'directives' or 'regulations'. Decisions are specific to member states or even particular businesses, perhaps allowing a company an exemption from a particular measure (thus a small car firm might be allowed an exemption from rules governing vehicle emissions – see Chapter 8). Regulations require no national implementing measures – they are normally so specific that there is no need for them (for example, a specific adjustment to the floor price for a particular agricultural product). Directives are by far the most important form of ruling. They are binding as to the result to be achieved but allow member states to determine how they will achieve that result, although they are given a deadline and are obliged to report on their progress towards meeting it (see, for instance, the discussion of renewable energy in Chapter 6).

The important fact that what is often arrived at, after the Commission has made its proposals and the Court of Justice and the Parliament have passed them, is *binding* legislation, requiring the compliance of member states or other bodies such as companies, points to the vital role of the Court of Justice. It therefore seems appropriate to begin a closer examination of the particular institutions with this body.

The Court of Justice: establishing the principles of direct effect and supremacy

Tucked away in Luxembourg alongside the High Authority, the Court of Justice was hardly in the limelight in the 1950s. However, it had huge potential significance. If the member states had created a High Authority and had delegated to it the task of implementing what those member states had agreed to in their treaty, then the Court of Justice must be at its side in order to make that process of implementation legally binding upon them. Otherwise the High Authority would seek to implement the treaty and the member states would merely ignore it.

It was the 1960s before the Court flexed its muscles. The test came in 1962, after the signing of the Treaties of Rome establishing the European Economic Community. Article 12 of the treaty establishing the EEC had stipulated that, in the process of moving towards a customs union, member states should refrain from introducing new customs duties or increasing those that already applied. Eventually they were going to abolish customs duties altogether. But that was to be achieved by the end of the 1960s. In the meantime they agreed to avoid any new duties while they phased the existing ones out.

The Van Gend en Loos Company claimed in 1962 that the Dutch customs authorities had raised the duties for some chemical fertiliser (ureaformaldehyde) that the company had imported into the Netherlands from West Germany. This was contrary to Article 12. When the *Van Gend en Loos* case became an issue, the Dutch government did not try to defend itself by claiming that its customs officials had acted correctly; it claimed that the Court of Justice had a strictly limited part to play in the process. There may have been a breach of Community law by a member state, but if there *had* been such a breach the right procedure for dealing with it was at member state level through 'infringement proceedings'. The role of the Court was to report an offence to the member states and leave them to deal with it.

The problem was that this was arguably too narrow a view of the role of the Court. It had been created in 1951 (with seven members for six member states in order to ensure a tie-breaker, the seventh member rotating between the three largest states) with the task of 'ensuring that in the interpretation and application of the law the Treaty [establishing the Coal and Steel Community] was observed'.[3] If the Court was seeing that the treaty was observed not just in the 'application' of the law but also, as stated above, in its 'interpretation', then it was certainly more than a police officer handing over miscreants to the authorities. It was part of the authorities itself.

Van Gend en Loos therefore became the occasion of the Court asserting its powers. It was no longer a debate about the rights and wrongs of the level of duty on fertilisers entering the Netherlands. It was about the competence of the Court of Justice. Article 12 had been absolutely clear in its prohibition of any increase in customs duties, the Court pointed out. There was no ambiguity here. So why were member states trying to take the case away from the Court and somehow insert themselves into the process? They had created a Court to be a Court and they had agreed to the creation of a body of law that gave binding form to the treaties they had agreed. This must take effect without the member states trying to interpose themselves between the law and its application. The law must have 'direct effect'. No intermediate body was needed in order to confirm or deny its application – not national courts; not national governments trying to horse-trade a compromise. 'The Community', the Court declared, 'constitutes a new legal order' and the subjects of that new legal order are not only member states but 'their nationals', individual persons or legal persons such as the Van Gend en Loos Company.

Once that principle had been established and accepted by the member states, the Court of Justice had made itself a powerful institution. The only possible way of deflecting its authority was to accept that European Law was in the hands of the Court but to make it of secondary importance. However, the Court of Justice was ready for that too. In *Costa* v. ENEL (1964) it gave a ruling establishing the principle of supremacy, insisting that Community law could not be overridden by domestic legal provision – not without the legal basis of the Community itself being called into question. The *Simmenthal* case some time later (*Simmenthal* v. *Commission*, 1978) produced an absolutely clear formulation of the principle. It declared that 'every national court must [...] apply Community law in its entirety [...] and must accordingly set aside any provision of national law which may conflict with it'.[4]

Arguably the development of the powers of the Court of Justice through the principles of supremacy and direct effect was half-unexpected by the member states themselves when they created the ECSC and later the EEC. They knew there would be a Court, yes; they knew it would keep an eye on whether they observed the treaty, yes. But the idea that it would not report infringements to the member states and leave them to decide the outcome but would rather rule on these matters itself, and that any national laws found to be inconsistent with these rulings must be set aside, and furthermore that an (eventual) army of natural and legal persons could bring cases claiming (among other things) unfair trade practices to the Court – even if these were implications of what the member states had originally agreed in the Treaty of Paris, they were ones they had not fully understood themselves at the time.

The Court of Justice: engine of economic integration

The Court deliberately used the judicial powers it laid claim to in order to encourage economic integration. After the *Van Gend en Loos* case, other firms recognised that they could make use of European Law and the Court of Justice in order to protect their interests. The way was open for companies or individuals to go to their own national courts and claim that a particular measure contravened European Law. A company could, for instance, use the Community legal system in order to challenge restrictions on its ability to operate across national borders. It could go to the Court and ask it whether particular

Figure 3. The Court of Justice today.
Note: The twin towers nearby are for translators and interpreters (the EU has 24 official languages, which means over 500 possible language combinations).

restrictions were legitimate under the treaty. Hence all those famous cases such as *Cassis de Dijon* in which the attempt of one member state to keep the products of another one out are overcome by the application of European Law through the decisions of the Court of Justice (see Chapter 4). Without such binding decisions, the single market would have been drowned out by the cries of states trying to protect their 'national champions' at all costs.

At the same time, individuals – for instance a group of employees – could seek compensation for losses suffered as a result of member states failing to comply with Community law. One example of this was the *Francovich* case of 1991, in which applicants successfully sued the Italian government for compensation when it failed to implement a directive concerning employees' rights to protection against their employer's insolvency. The fact that the government of a member state could successfully be sued established the principle of state liability. Member states had envisaged that, when the Court of Justice ordered that financial compensation be given, this would concern illegal acts on the part of Community institutions. That was indeed what the relevant part of the treaty establishing the European Economic

Community in 1957 had stated. But the Court argued that 'inherent in the system of the Treaty' was a remedy against *states* breaching Community law.[5] As suggested above, the states had perhaps started with the expectation that the Court of Justice would have a policing role, handing over miscreants who would then be dealt with by the member states themselves, acting as both judge and jury. Now they were finding themselves not as judge and jury but as defendants!

The Court of Justice continues to exercise its power in accordance with the principles of 'direct effect' and 'supremacy' established in the 1960s, and continues to do battle in the long and grinding (and still unfinished) process of creating a single market (nowadays most of the battles are in the area of services rather than goods) out of 28 member states that are naturally protective of their own interests. It is now made up of one judge from each of the 28 member states and is divided into two bodies. One deals with requests for rulings from national courts. The very fact that national courts ask the Court of Justice for a binding 'preliminary ruling' shows that they recognise its authority and is a practical demonstration of the principle of supremacy. The other body, the General Court, rules on actions for annulment brought by individuals and companies (and sometimes member states). Because of the landmark rulings concerning 'direct effect' mentioned above, individuals and businesses have become used to taking cases directly to the Court.

Like the Commission (originally the High Authority), the Court of Justice originated with the decision of a group of member states not only to sign yet another treaty but also to create new institutions by whose decisions they agreed to be bound. To some extent (as the discussion of the Court of Justice has tried to show), they may have ended up delegating more powers than they intended, or at least they did not fully appreciate what their own act of delegation really meant. But the EU would hardly be the first body to develop in ways that were beyond what its founders intended.

The Commission: its structure

As suggested at the beginning of this chapter, it is not unlikely that people will look at the Commission and feel that it is, or ought to be, a

Figure 4. The Berlaymont building, headquarters of the European
Commission.
*Note: This shows a message from happier times – the banner is welcoming
Slovenia to the euro in 2007.*

civil service. They will think 'eurocrats, bureaucrats' and wonder what
its 'right of initiative' is. A civil service does not propose new
legislation, they will feel; ministers do that. But this is the whole point
of the creation of supranational institutions with executive powers.
The Commission is not allowed to go outside the terms of the treaties
('primary legislation') agreed by the heads of state, but it is entrusted
with formulating secondary legislation that specifies what those
treaties mean. In practice, this means a right to propose a great deal of
new legislation, even in new policy areas, so long as its proposals are in
line with what has been agreed in the treaties.

The composition of the Commission reflects its unique role. It has a permanent civil service working in various departments (Directorates-General) divided up into directorates and units. These are civil servants who have passed what are essentially the aptitude tests through which people enter a national civil service. But that is not the whole picture. There are also 28 commissioners (one per member state), very often with a political background (President José Manuel Barroso, for instance, was formerly the prime minister of Portugal), who have 'cabinets' (essentially teams of advisers) attached to them and a political agenda that, whatever their nationality, has to be framed from an EU-wide perspective (the Treaty of Lisbon encourages this wider perspective by requiring that the members of their cabinets come from at least three different countries). This political agenda they will then seek to advance. That, after all, is the way in which they will have been used to working in their previous (and in some cases future) careers. When Roy Jenkins, or Neil Kinnock, or Chris Patten or Peter Mandelson (for instance) became UK commissioners (Jenkins was president of the Commission before he returned to UK politics in order to build up the Social Democratic Party in the 1980s), they did not become civil servants. They continued the political activity that was bred into their bones. But they had to do so in a new way, framing policy within an institution that was more than a civil service but lacked the legislative powers that they were used to.

For, though it drafts the laws, we have seen that the Commission cannot pass them. This 'more than a civil service, less than a legislature' may seem strange (which in national terms it is), but it is entirely appropriate to the European Union's overall framework as a balance between supranational and intergovernmental elements. If the Commission could not propose laws, it would lose the right it has always had to possess a 'conferred competence', a right to develop legislation in accordance with the treaties. But if it could not only propose but pass laws, then what check would there be upon its activities? How could the Council or the Parliament judge whether or not the Commission was going beyond the terms of the treaties?

The Treaty of Lisbon says that the president of the Commission is 'elected' by the Parliament, the name being proposed by the member states. One might think that this was more confirmation than election, and there is pressure for the Parliament to be able at least to choose from a shortlist of names. In his State of the Union address to the Parliament in September 2012, the president of the Commission, José Manuel Barroso, proposed that European parties should present their nominee for the president of the Commission during the Parliamentary elections of 2014, so that voters would recognise that they were indirectly voting for a particular nominee as Commission president. This not only would add to the democratic legitimacy of the Commission, but would give a genuine 'European' flavour to European elections. The president of the Parliament, Martin Schulz, took up this idea enthusiastically in the spring of 2013 and the Parliament has since voted in support of it. As so often, however, it is the heads of state who may turn out to be the most reluctant to accept new forms of democracy at the European level. They are unlikely to concede the right to nominate the new president of the Commission to the European voters.

When the president of the Commission has been decided, the other commissioners are then chosen by the member states and the president-designate acting together. There is always one commissioner per member state. It is noteworthy that the two 'supranational' institutions (the Court and the Commission) have equal representation for each member state, whatever its size (as in the US Senate), whereas the Parliament and the Council have a more complicated (and much haggled over) system of 'degressive proportionality', with a degree of weighting in favour of smaller states (in the case of the Council, a manifestly unfair one).

When all the new commissioners have been nominated for particular portfolios, the Parliament interviews each one for the equivalent of Senate hearings in the USA. It may not approve of them. Thus the Parliament rejected two commissioners proposed for the 2009 College of Commissioners (their renewable term of office is five years) and two proposed for the 2004 College. Replacements had to be nominated by the member states concerned. Indeed the Parliament has the power to dismiss the whole College, and in effect used this power in 1999 when all the commissioners resigned, falling on their swords before they could be run through.

Member states certainly feel that, through the power to have 'their' commissioner, they are able to exercise important influence at EU level, and it is a right they guard jealously. A proposal to reduce the number of commissioners to fewer than the number of member states had to be withdrawn before Ireland voted 'Yes' to the Lisbon Treaty in a second referendum. This is not to deny the point that commissioners must act in the interests of the EU as a whole, but it is still true that they carry a particular national perspective into the heart of the Commission. That Ray MacSharry was the first commissioner to tackle the problems of the Common Agricultural Policy (CAP; see Chapter 5) was not unrelated to the national perspective of a country that experienced one of the worst famines in history and the personal perspective of a man born in Sligo in the west of Ireland and who worked as a livestock dealer in Sligo and Mayo, getting to know at first hand the problems of small farmers there. The result was a combination of absolute commitment to the principles of the CAP and an absolute determination to reform it in practice. It was also fair to describe it as an 'Irish perspective' on the CAP, even though MacSharry worked very hard to support the interests of the EU as a whole.

The president of the Commission can attend meetings of the European Council. Though they cannot vote, they can influence decisions, particularly when national leaders cannot agree and a compromise position can only come from outside. The Commission president also attends sessions of Parliament, ostensibly to account for Commission policy but also with an opportunity to influence Parliamentary thinking. This foot in the door of other 'camps' gives a good president of the Commission (such as Jacques Delors in the 1980s) a chance to act proactively and exploit to the full the 'right of initiative'. Less effective presidents tend to perceive this role negatively as a way of finding out in advance what they cannot hope to achieve. This is a reminder that institutional structures are only as effective as the individuals who embody them.

The Commission: activity

The practical effectiveness of the Commission is hugely dependent upon the *binding* forms of EU legislation. Created in order to hold member states to treaties they had agreed, it could hardly carry out this remit without the ability to do more than simply remind them of the decisions they had made. It had to be able (in certain areas at least) to enforce adherence. This has already been made clear in the discussion above of the evolution of the Court of Justice, and it can be seen from numerous examples in the chapters examining specific policy areas in the rest of this book. How, then, does the Commission carry out the role that it somewhat grandly describes in terms of being 'Guardian of the Treaties'?

First, there is the use of infringement proceedings. These are usually cases initiated by the Commission when it believes that a member state is failing to fulfil its obligations under EU Law. The Maastricht Treaty added to the power of both the Court and the Commission by giving the latter the right to ask for, and the former the right to impose, financial penalties upon states that failed to comply. It always needs to be borne in mind that such penalties are very rarely applied. Member states are used to transposing and complying with EU Law, and know that it benefits them when other states are made to do so as well.

But sometimes it happens, and the amounts are not a mere slap on the wrist. Nugent gives the example of France being fined 20 million euros in July 2005 for catching and selling fish that were too small, plus a further 60 million every six months until it complied.[6] In the absence of such sanctions, EU policy in this (controversial) area would be even harder to enforce. Fish are in demand, the edible species are often in short supply, binding rules are arrived at only after a great deal of discussion (between the Commission and scientific experts/interest groups) and compromise (when Commission proposals are amended before finally being passed by the Council and Parliament). However, once they are finally agreed (including the limits for Total Allowable Catches), the rules have to be enforced. Doubtless UK fishers bobbing up and down on the North Sea may complain that they are being told how many fish they can catch by 'people in Brussels'. The reply is that, without binding EU-wide agreements, those edible species (and the fishing industries with them) will be even further threatened. Moreover, the sharing of sovereignty means that those UK (for instance) fishers or their representatives, although they do not exclusively determine what will be caught in UK waters, do have a say in what will be caught off the coasts of Ireland or France or Spain.

Because of binding legislation (particularly directives) backed up by the threat of financial sanctions, there is much more likelihood that member states will meet targets in the environmental field, for instance, than in areas where no binding directives can be applied. An example of the latter would be the target of 3 per cent of gross domestic product (GDP) being spent on research and development by 2020, as agreed by the Europe 2020 Strategy. Though it would be wrong to label these targets 'pious hopes', and though it is true that member states are obliged to report on their progress towards meeting them (under the 'open method of coordination'), the targets are not binding. Arguably a great deal of jargon has sprung up in order to muddy the distinction between what is binding and what is not. Officials talk of 'soft governance tools', of 'benchmarking', of 'best practice guidelines', of 'peer evaluation', which is linked to 'naming and shaming' (that is, publicising lists of who has managed to get close to achieving a certain target), of guidelines, of timetables and (of course) of lots of 'actors' (to ensure 'partnership' and 'multilevel participation') being brought into the discussions (or 'social dialogue') taking place at endless meetings – and so on. The result may well be that the targets are not reached. The main reason for this is that a member state that does not reach 3 per cent by 2020 will not find the Commission going to the Court and requesting that it be fined a substantial amount of money, something that could happen in the case of a member state failing to implement a directive.

However, it would be wrong to conclude that, in policy areas where directives do not or seldom apply, the Commission can do nothing important. Chapter 7 will argue that effective coodination of nearly 30 member states in the peacekeeping sphere may lead to very significant actions, even though such coordination can be based only upon the consent of all. Indeed, there is a case for saying that coordination in the defence sphere matters even more than levels of spending.

To give another example. In a sphere such as education, although all matters of curriculum content, school policy and the structure of primary, secondary and tertiary education are national competences, the huge strides made in terms of getting both young people and adults to take courses in other countries would have been impossible without the work of DG Education and Culture and its various programmes at secondary, tertiary (academic and vocational) and adult level – Comenius, Erasmus, Leonardo da Vinci and Gruntvig. This was not work intended to impose standardised education programmes upon member states; it was intended to enable each country to share information with others about whatever education system it chose to adopt. The EU played a part, alongside institutions such as UNESCO and the Council of Europe, in the creation, through the so-called Bologna Process, of a European Higher Educational Area in 2010. If students and teachers at tertiary level are to be able to move around the EU (and European countries that are currently outside it) there needs to be a clear and transparent system for understanding and accrediting courses in all those countries. The abbreviations that flow from this – EQF (European Qualifications Framework), ECTS (European Credit Transfer System), and so on – are vital constituents of the free flow of traffic at tertiary level – the academic exchanges that should in turn bolster employment prospects and economic growth. None of this involves more than enabling different national systems to work with one another. As in the defence sphere, it is interoperability rather than harmonisation (in the sense of standardisation) that is sought. It remains, however, essential work.

Undoubtedly it is the protection and encouragement of the single market that represent the most important aspect of the Commission's work. With current debates about completing a single market in services, not to mention the thorny issue of whether or not a single market requires a single currency and, if so, what the implications are in terms of moving towards 'fiscal union', it is easy to forget just how much progress has already been made (see Chapter 4). It is also important to see that maintaining and policing the single market involve not only watching out for the activities of member states but also keeping an eye on what particular businesses are doing.

Competition policy is another Commission activity (listed by the Treaty of Lisbon as one of the six areas of exclusive EU competence). This may involve dealing with states – for instance by preventing public subsidies to firms, or by promoting liberalisation where certain companies have been blessed as 'national champions' and incur special favours, particular in the energy and communications sector. But it may also mean preventing cartels or monopolies on the part of private businesses. It is in this area that the really big fines tend to be imposed (such as the fine of half a billion euros imposed on Microsoft in 2004 for anticompetitive behaviour). Because the EU market is so large, firms that do not want to lose lucrative market share have to comply with these rulings.

A great deal has been achieved in order to benefit consumers by action in this area. Without it, for instance, there would be no cheap air travel in Europe or reduced roaming charges for using mobile phones (see Chapter 4). Moreover, without it the nations of the EU-28 would be far less wealthy than they are, whatever the current malaise over the eurozone.

This may be seen as 'soft' rather than 'hard' power, but it is power nevertheless, allowing the EU to have considerable influence globally (see Chapter 7), whether in terms of relations with other states or in terms of a more general influence. It is possible, for instance, not only to force international companies to be competitive but to force them to take environmental concerns into account (see Chapters 5 and 8). In all the actions that the Commission takes in these various areas, whether controlling vehicle emissions or fining Microsoft or protecting wild bird habitats, the Commission is doing no more than implementing laws passed by the Council and Parliament and shown to have been in line with treaties agreed unanimously by the member states. But because those laws are legally binding upon the member states, the Commission has been able to hold them to what they have agreed, and thereby to check (especially in difficult economic times) the natural protectionist tendencies that would otherwise have prevented a huge and influential trading bloc from emerging, one that could set rules on economic activity both for itself and, to some extent, globally.

The Council of Ministers and the European Council

As the earlier part of this chapter made clear, when the member states agreed a unique system of delegating the authority to implement their treaties, they did not walk away from the process but remained part of it, overseeing the very institutions to which they granted delegated powers. Hence the existence of the Council of Ministers from the very beginning. This body consists of ministers of member states (one minister from each national government), who meet in various 'configurations' depending on the subject under discussion. If the subject concerns the environment, for instance, then all the environment ministers of member states go, and are said to be attending the 'Environment' Council. The presidency of the Council rotates between member states, each of which gets 'six months in the sun' setting the agenda and chairing meetings (with the exception of the Foreign Affairs Council). The UK will hold the Council presidency in the second half of 2017, which is probably why this is the year chosen for a possible referendum on the country's membership of the EU.

The most important issue that has arisen in the course of the Council's history (apart from endless wranglings over relative voting strengths) is that of Qualified Majority Voting (QMV). This is crucial because, if there are to be areas in which unanimity is not required, then that amounts to the loss of a national veto. Even when unanimity is given up, the complex formula for QMV agreed by the Treaty of Lisbon and to be applied from 2014 (a double majority of 55 per cent of the votes representing 65 per cent of the EU's population) reflects the serious haggling that went into agreeing it. Countries clearly hoped that even without a veto they could find enough like-minded other states to block anything they did not like.

The introduction of QMV in the Council of Ministers was anticipated by the Treaties of Rome but delayed by what is generally considered the greatest crisis in the history of the sovereignty-sharing institutions, the so-called Empty Chair Crisis of 1965–6 (see Chapter 2). The result of that, the Luxembourg 'Compromise', in effect maintained the veto, allowing a member state to reject anything it considered to be vital to its national interest. In reality, the Council of Ministers spent 20 years after the Luxembourg Compromise knowing that that they had to achieve a consensus in order to get anything passed.

The breakthrough for QMV came with the passing of the Single European Act in 1986. It was the urgent need to develop the single market that finally persuaded European leaders (including Margaret

Thatcher) that they had to introduce such a system. Without sovereignty-sharing, a single market will always fall prey to the protectionist tendencies of member states, as Thatcher realised (see Chapters 2 and 4).

There is no doubt that QMV has allowed some controversial measures to be passed that might otherwise have been impossible, such as the MacSharry reforms to the CAP (see Chapter 5). On the other hand, one should not underestimate the extent to which the principle of the Luxembourg Compromise still lingers on. The Treaty of Amsterdam in 1997 spoke of the right of member states to prevent a vote being taken on closer cooperation between member states if 'important and stated reasons of national policy' were at stake. The Treaty of Lisbon introduced the idea of 'emergency brakes' that governments could apply in certain policy areas if their 'national interests' were endangered. These provisions are simply the Luxembourg Compromise by another name. There is no doubt that the Council still prefers to decide everything by consensus, though this does not mean that the provision for QMV is insignificant. Dinan suggests that QMV is important not so much because many items *are* put to the vote but because they *can* be – what he calls 'the shadow of the vote'.[7]

In most areas the Council's work is focused upon passing legislation jointly with the Parliament on the basis of proposals from the Commission, the 'ordinary legislative procedure' already described. However, there are some areas in which the Council of Ministers (together with the European Council) has exclusive competence, such as the implementation of the Common Foreign and Security Policy.

The words 'together with the European Council' introduce an inevitable complication. Unsurprisingly, a system of ministers meeting under various formations depending on the topic under discussion (Environment Council, Competitiveness Council, etc.) has to make room for the desire of 'top ministers' (that is, presidents and prime ministers) to meet. Moreover, meetings between heads of state are obviously crucial. The whole sovereignty-sharing exercise began with a meeting of heads of state, it is heads of state who agree (unanimously) the treaties (which then have to be ratified by their national parliaments and in some cases through national referendums) and it is heads of state who meet when there is a crisis (for instance in 2008, when Russian intervention in Georgia provoked an Extraordinary Meeting of the European Council). Yet it took a lot of time for meetings of heads of state to become part of the EU 'system'. Only in 1974 did summits of heads of state become known as European Council meetings (thereby guaranteeing confusion, since the similarly named Council of Europe is an altogether separate body). Only in 1993 (when the Maastricht Treaty was ratified) was its composition and number of meetings codified (it meets on a quarterly basis with provision for additional emergency meetings) and a broad description of its tasks given (amounting to the setting of general guidelines for the EU). Only in 2009, when the Treaty of Lisbon was ratified, did the European Council become recognised as a formal institution, its role still being couched in broad terms as one of defining 'the general political directions and priorities' of the EU.

Of course, such broad considerations depend on circumstances. Sometimes they can focus on what genuinely are 'general political directions and priorities', such as the development of the Europe 2020 Strategy. But sometimes they find themselves wrestling with something much more specific – such as the levels of Greek debt.

The reason for such apparent coyness on the part of heads of state is not difficult to ascertain. They preferred (and perhaps still prefer) to play the role of *deus* (or *dei*) *ex machina*, setting up and maintaining the machinery without themselves being part of it. In a sense this a perfectly understandable, and goes back to a point that cannot be made too often – the EU is not a single state in the making. It is therefore constantly in the hands of the heads of state, it continues in existence only because of their blessing and any one of them can take their country out of the EU altogether (the Treaty of Lisbon formalised the right of withdrawal, which Greenland had already exercised de facto by withdrawing from the EEC). This is currently being considered as a possibility for the UK in 2017. Compare the situation in the USA, where there is also a great deal of autonomy at state level, but where (as the outcome of the American Civil War made clear) there is no right of secession. The EU exists – and continues – because of an ongoing agreement between nation-states. This remains the key to understanding it even though it is also true that these member states agreed a unique system of supranational authorities to implement and enforce their treaties. The nation-states remain the final arbiters – they are not about to hand over that role to another body. This may help to explain their rather strange position of trying to remain for so long in the institutional world but not of it.

The Parliament

The European Parliament is difficult to define. It began as an Assembly made up of delegates from the individual nation-states. In that role it could be seen as part of the intergovernmental control mechanism monitoring the way in which the Commission and the Court of Justice implemented the first treaties. At the same time, however, its emergence since 1979 as a directly elected body has led to its being seen in increasingly supranational terms, not least by the more 'federalist' of its members. In fact, it is quite hard to define it in terms of either camp.

Like the Commission, the Parliament is often judged in terms of whether it conforms to the structure of national parliaments. It does not, but, as I have argued in the case of the Commission, this is not automatically 'a bad thing' – it is the form appropriate to a union of 28 nation-states. The Parliament has had direct elections since 1979, held in June of every year ending with a four or a nine, by various systems of proportional representation over a long weekend of voting. Its parties are required to be in European 'family groups', the fear being that otherwise the states might form into a number of different 'national' parties. British MEPs might form into a British party, French MEPs into a French party, and suddenly there would be a re-enactment of the Napoleonic Wars on the floor of the chamber. According to the rules of procedure for the European Parliament (Rule 30), 'a political group shall comprise Members elected in at least one quarter of the Member states. The minimum number of Members required to form a political group shall be twenty-five.'

This was the requirement that put a great strain on David Cameron when he sought to carry out a pledge first made during the Conservative Party leadership campaign in the UK in 2005, namely that the Conservative MEPs leave the main centre-right grouping,

Figure 5. The two European Parliament buildings: the headquarters of the European Parliament in Strasbourg and the Parliament building in Brussels. *Note: If the Members of the European Parliament could decide for themselves where to meet, they would vote for it to be in one place.*

which in fact was the largest party in the Parliament, and instead form a new party outside it. There were already enough British Conservative MEPs to cross the 25 barrier, but he needed people from at least six other countries in order to make it an acceptable political grouping. There followed a much-publicised trawl of MEPs, apparently of increasing degrees of eccentricity, from other countries in the Union, eventually drawing in members from parties such as 'Poland Comes First' (from Poland) and 'For Fatherland and Freedom' (from Latvia) in order to make up the requisite quota. The result was the European Conservatives and Reformists Group, which had 53 MEPs from ten countries in the 2009–14 Parliament (one fewer than the Greens), though 25 were from the UK and seven countries had only one member.

It might be asked why the Conservative MEPs were willing to move from a party (the European People's Party) with considerable influence in the Parliament, within which many of them were personally happy to work and which gave them great influence. One of them, Edward McMillan-Scott, was four times elected vice-president of the European Parliament. Now they were leaving for what Nick Clegg, the Liberal Democrat leader and now coalition partner of David Cameron in the UK Parliament of 2010, described during the 2010 UK election campaign as 'a bunch of nutters, homophobes, anti-Semites and climate-change deniers'.[8] The reason was that parties campaign for elections to the European Parliament on the basis of national lists drawn up by their national party establishments. Had they not gone along with Cameron's wish that they join the new party, the Conservative MEPs would have been unable to stand as Conservative candidates in the subsequent European election. They had to either change party (as McMillan-Scott did in 2010 by joining the Liberal Democrats) or do what the leader at home wanted.

What the complex tale of the European Conservatives and Reformists reveals is the extent to which the European Parliament – often described and often seeking to describe itself as a 'supranational' institution, the only parliament in the world elected by several different nation-states – remains in reality closely tied to the interests of its member states. In his State of the Union address to the Parliament in September 2012, the president of the Commision, José Manuel

Barroso, reminded MEPs that 'even in the European elections we do not see the name of the European political parties on the ballot box, we see a national debate between national political parties'. The European political parties in effect remain coalitions of national parties rather than having their own clear European identity. There has been talk of changing this in future, but it remains to be seen whether anything will be done. In 2012 the Parliament rejected Liberal MEP Andrew Duff's proposal for 25 members (a very small proportion of the total and no more than a top-up to the national lists) who would be nationals of at least nine different member states chosen by the European political parties and would be elected for a single pan-European constituency. Duff's report in the *EUobserver* on the Parliament's rejection of his proposal, even though it had been passed by its own Constitutional Committee, raised the question of whether the Parliament had acquired more powers without acquiring more legitimacy.[9]

An EU citizen can vote in European elections for the candidate in the country in which he or she is living, whether or not they are a citizen of that country. But whereas voters can think of themselves as 'EU citizens' voting for an 'EU Parliament', the people they are voting for tend to be chosen by national party establishments and to be citizens of the country in which they are standing.

That does not have to be the case. A person may stand in the country in which he or she is residing, despite being a citizen of another member state. This has happened already in several instances, usually when there is no or little language problem (thus Irish citizens have been elected for constituencies in the UK and Dutch citizens have been elected in Belgium and Germany), but not always. For instance, in 2009 an Argentine with Spanish nationality, Marta Andreasen, was elected in the UK, somewhat ironically winning the election as a candidate for the United Kingdom Independence Party (UKIP). But such things are unusual, showing how far people still think in national rather than European terms. People in the UK can (relatively) easily accept a Londoner standing for a constituency in Bradford because he or she is British; they do not accept quite so easily that a Romanian should stand for North-East England because he or she is European.

The European Parliament therefore remains a compromise between the national attachments that people feel most strongly and the

European attachments that certainly need to play a role in their national life. It is not quite the 'supranational' body that it tends to make itself out to be. The European Parliament for 2009–14 has been a Parliament of the Nations rather than a national parliament in the making, and there is little sign yet that the 2014–19 Parliament will be any different. Sometimes it is MEPs themselves who are least able to see this.

The other key point about the European Parliament is that it is a 'parliament without a government'. It does not have the power to be a government. As explained earlier, in most areas the Commission proposes a new law, which is then passed by the Council and Parliament jointly under a 'co-decision' procedure. The Parliament cannot draft a law (it can and does invite the Commission to do so, of course) and it cannot (on its own) pass a law. Its authority over the budget is also shared with the Council. It has supervisory powers over EU institutions – as already pointed out, it can approve or reject the nomination of the commissioners – but these alone do not add up to the role of a government.

It is true that the Parliament enjoys important powers, which have been steadily increasing over the years (from a requirement that it be consulted by the Council to a right to make joint decisions with it in an ever-growing number of areas). This steady increase in powers has not yet been noted very clearly at national level, but it is significant. The Treaty of Lisbon, for instance, gave the Parliament the power to decide whether to accept the seven-year budgetary framework hammered out and eventually agreed between national leaders in Brussels in January 2013. National leaders only woke up to this power when the Parliament proposed changes to the budget in March 2013, just in time for the leaders to 'reconsider' them in the March meeting of the European Council.

The Parliament has been able to justify its increasing powers by pointing to the fact that it is directly elected (although, as pointed out, with an inescapably 'national' flavour to its candidates). And, although levels of turn-out have been bad (and are falling), they are still not far from those who turn out to elect the (arguably) most powerful person in the world, a US president. It is also true that, where the question of a 'parliament without a government' is concerned, there can always be an argument about definition: after all, there are plenty of governments at least some of whose laws are considered by more than one chamber (Senate and Congress in the USA, Bundestag and Bundesrat in Germany, House of Commons and House of Lords in the UK). However, in the case of the European Parliament it not only has to share in the passing of laws but has no direct 'right of initiative' – it cannot propose new laws.

A government requires at the very least the capacity to be able to adopt a programme, translating (in UK terms) the manifesto it has explained to the voters before the general election into the equivalent of a 'Queen's Speech' outlining what legislation it proposes for the next session of Parliament. The European Parliament can do this only indirectly, by outlining its priorities and inviting the Commission to formulate legislation in accordance with them. Unsurprisingly, this right of inititative is something that many in the Parliament would like to see coming their way, either exclusively or in a joint arrangement with the Commission. However, this book has already explained why the right of initiative is seen as lying appropriately with the Commission, since this is the body given the task of implementing the treaties.

Being (on some definitions) without a government means a tendency to lack overall policy direction for the five-year Parliament. Thus, in the 2009–14 Parliament, the leader of the party with the most seats (the European People's Party), a right-wing Pole named Jerzy Buzek, was nominated president of the Parliament for the first half of the Parliamentary term. Then in January 2010 a left-wing German, Martin Schulz, took over as president, because he was leader of the second-biggest party (the Progressive Alliance of Socialists and Democrats). It would be the equivalent of David Cameron in 2010 agreeing to be prime minister for the first half of the Parliament and then handing over to Ed Miliband for the second half – after all, they were the biggest two parties and neither had an overall majority in 2010, precisely the situation in the European Parliament. But in a UK context such an arrangement would be unthinkable without a formal coalition and an agreed 'red–blue' programme. In the European Parliament it can happen more easily because there is less pressure for an overall policy programme. This is perhaps partly why turn-out has fallen in European elections even though its powers have grown; voters are unclear what the overall programmes are between which they are being invited to choose. This in turn further encourages the unfortunate tendency to think in merely national terms: not seeing any clear European agenda, voters decide to vote on national issues instead.

This lack of a clear policy programme may be considered a disadvantage. Even so, it would be wrong to say that the Parliament is not a 'real' parliament or that its lack of a government (at least on some definitions) is nothing but a disadvantage. The members of national parliaments are subject to strict controls, instructed how to vote by party whips and required to be 'on message'. MEPs are not on a leash in this sense. This gives them a certain freedom, though as we have seen they can still be pressured by national leaders back home, and this makes for some indirect 'whipping'. It was noteworthy that, as they prepared to vote on the highly controversial 2014–20 budgetary framework in 2013, many MEPs, worried about being left off 'party lists' for the forthcoming European elections, were concerned about their national leaders finding out how they had voted. While this remains an overriding concern for MEPs, it is doubtful whether they can rightly be called members of a 'supranational' institution. The truth is that there are elements of both supranationalism and intergovernmentalism within the European Parliament.

Other institutions and 'important players'

This chapter has concentrated on five institutions (if the European Council and the Council of Ministers are taken as separate institutions, as they are considered to be under the Treaty of Lisbon) and two important consultative committees. However, there are other institutions and bodies that must be taken into consideration in order to complete an 'anatomical survey'. They will not be described in detail, but they should not go unmentioned.

The European Central Bank (ECB) was set up in 1998 when the euro was introduced, and it manages monetary policy in the euro area. It is unsurprising that this should be the one major EU institution to be located in Germany (its headquarters are in Frankfurt). As discussed in Chapter 2, the creation of the eurozone was a continuation of the

Figure 6. The headquarters of the European Central Bank in Frankfurt.
Note: The European Central Bank is the first major EU institution to be located in Germany.

principle that, in return for acceptance, Germany should affirm its commitment to the whole of the EU. In this case 'acceptance' applied to the former Deutsche Demokratische Republik (the DDR or East Germany), which made the newly united Germany (effectively overnight, in 1990) the largest member of the EU. The implicit condition for this painless process of enlargement was acceptance of the single currency.

The ECB sets interest rates within the eurozone and concentrates above all on maintaining price stability (keeping inflation below but close to 2 per cent). It is independent, taking no instructions from governments, though some see the emphasis on price stability (above economic growth) as a reflection of 'German' economic thinking.

Though it has a Governing Council that manages the eurosystem, it also has a General Council of the European System of Central Banks, which includes the governors of all central banks, whether inside or outside the eurosystem. This is a reminder of the fact that it is technically an institution of Economic and Monetary Union to which all 28 member states belong. It is also a reminder of the fact that, though not all member states are part of the eurozone, they cannot isolate their economies from the decisions of the ECB.

The seventh institution (upgraded to institutional status by the Treaty of Maastricht in 1993, though it has existed since 1975) is the Court of Auditors. Like the Commission and the Court of Justice, it has one member per member state and is appointed by the Council (after consultation with the Parliament) on the basis of nominations from member states. The Court has no judicial authority. Instead, its role is to examine the EU's financial affairs. Hence the Maastricht update reflected two things: in the first place, the fact that the Union had more money to spend, and, in the second place, a certain reputation for not spending it properly.

Each year the Court of Auditors produces a 'statement of assurance' concerning EU expenditure, for which the Commission has responsibility, and each year the assurance (based on a sample of the transactions in which the EU engages) fails to be unqualified. It is possible to argue that, with so many transactions, unqualified assurance is not to be expected, though Dinan points out that the budget commissioner under Barroso's first presidency (2004–9) promised that he would obtain one by the time his five-year term ended in 2009.[10]

He did not. A more sensible approach would have been to point out that management of EU spending is decentralised to a considerable extent. It is national governments that are responsible for the daily administration of most EU expenditure. As so often where the EU is concerned, the national (especially) and subnational players like to pretend that they were not on the pitch when some foul is called. Just as they are adept at claiming the credit for successes at the EU level, so they are adept at avoiding the blame for any failure lower down.

Apart from the seven 'institutions', there are other bodies of importance. The European Investment Bank (EIB) was established by the Treaties of Rome in 1958 to promote economic development by lending to both public and private sectors and at the same time providing guarantees for loans from other institutions (hence it can act as a catalyst, leveraging money from other sources). It does not use money from the EU budget but finances itself by issuing bonds on world financial markets. Being AAA-rated, it does not find this difficult, and in fact the EIB borrows more than any other international financial institution, including the World Bank. Its shareholders are the member states, whose subscription depends on their economic weight. Most (but not all) of its money goes to investment projects within the EU, with a focus on energy and transport networks and schemes that support innovation and environmental sustainability. Its Board of Governors is made up of ministers (normally finance ministers) from the member states.

Generally speaking, the EIB puts up 50 per cent of project costs. Examples of projects it has supported are France's TGV (high-speed train) lines and the Athens metro (in the transport sphere) or wind farms in the UK and flood protection in Venice (in the energy and environmental fields; see Chapter 6).

The sums involved are considerable. In 2011, for instance, the EIB lent 61 billion euros, over 50 billion of which was directed towards schemes within the EU. Needless to say, programmes such as the Lisbon Strategy (for the first decade of the twenty-first century) and its successor the Europe 2020 Strategy (for the second decade) have called for more EIB investment, and the global financial crisis of 2008–9 provoked the same reaction. In January 2013, heads of state unanimously agreed to boost the capital of the EIB by 10 billion euros as part of a European Growth Pact agreed the previous summer.

There are other bodies to which a proper Cook's tour would pay more attention, such as the Ombudsman, who investigates complaints of maladministration by EU institutions, or the 40-odd agencies that undertake a series of technical tasks assisting the Commission (which keeps overall control of policy implementation). But they are not essential to an introduction.

The one other thing that should not be forgotten by anyone engaging in the usual run-through of institutions is the importance of bodies that are in no way, directly or indirectly, part of the EU institutional framework, namely the various interest groups (or lobbyists) that are present (in Brussels in particular) in their thousands. They may be business groups or political/social interest groups or non-governmental organisations (NGOs) – or business groups that call themselves NGOs in order to give an aura of selflessness to the pressure they exert. Some take these groups as evidence of EU institutions that are open and transparent and welcoming to civil society participation. Others lament them as an example of the susceptibility of those same institutions to powerful groups that are well financed and can make sure that their voices are the ones to be heard. Whichever view is taken, their existence shows that for many businesses and other organisations there is now a 'European dimension' to their lobbying. A business no longer thinks that the 'European level' is something that can be left to others or to national government departments.[11] If there is one thing that all sides can agree on, it is that the presence of the lobbyists circling around these institutions, whether or not they are bees round a honeypot, shows that for all their failings and cumbersome arrangements these are institutions that matter.

Conclusion

The sort of institutional complexity that anyone considering the EU today is likely to observe has a long pedigree. The collection of one Court of Justice, one Assembly, a High Authority, two Commissions and three Councils by the end of the 1950s was already a very cumbersome arrangement! But it must always be borne in mind that what was being done was unique and involved a very careful determination of powers by six nation-states. Make the intergovernmental elements too strong, and treaties cease to be effective. Make them too weak, and they cease to be acceptable to powerful and independent nation-states. That tension is there now, and it was there then.

As the institutions slowly began to take shape, Jean Monnet made a pitch for a European equivalent of the 'District of Columbia', the DC in Washington DC which makes it clear that the federal institutions of the USA are not in one particular state (thereby perhaps being seen as favouring it) but are located outside any of the 50 states. However, the national governments decided otherwise and the High Authority, with Monnet as its first president, began its work in Luxembourg.

As the Treaties of Rome approached, Monnet once again pushed for containing all the institutions in a single 'European District'. Luxembourg was already coping with the organisation of officials for the Coal and Steel Community and did not want more. In the end Brussels was chosen for the new institutions, partly because a lot of the meetings that led to the Treaties of Rome had been held there, and partly perhaps because it was largely French-speaking (acceptable therefore to France) but not itself in France (acceptable therefore to the other five). Major institutions were not established among the losers of World War II until the level of German reluctance to accept the creation of the common currency was (very slightly) reduced by the siting of the European Central Bank in Frankfurt.

Arguably it was unfortunate that Monnet did not succeed. The bickering among countries over 'who will have which institution' is hardly an attractive accompaniment to expressions of commitment to 'ever-closer union'. Such bickering does not look like going away. Arguments continue, for instance, over whether the European Parliament should continue to meet for one week each month in Strasbourg and three weeks in Brussels (not to mention having its administrative support staff in Luxembourg). Bringing them together in one place, simple if there were a 'European District', becomes instead the possibility of 'France losing an institution'. A framework that should reflect the coherence of the EU is thereby reduced to a bitter battle for the institutional spoils between nation-states. It also gives a distorting national flavour ('Brussels decides') to what are essentially Community decisions.

Does this anatomical survey allow a coherent picture of the EU and its institutions to emerge? I hope it gives at least some overall picture. The key point is the willingness to share sovereignty, but that required institutional mechanisms, and those who set these mechanisms up made themselves part of the institutional scheme of things too in order to ensure that the supranational institutions did not get out of hand. The result is a combination of institutions implementing the treaties (the Commission with the aid of the Court of Justice), institutions monitoring that process of implementation and thereby inevitably a part of it (the Council of Ministers and European Council) and an institution (the Parliament) that initially began as part of the monitoring process (when it was an Assembly of national delegates) but has since acquired some (but by no means all) of the characteristics of a supranational institution. Inevitably such a system produced not only a large number of institutions but, at times, a lack of policy coherence.

The existence of so many institutional 'players' also produces a lack of efficiency at times, particularly when responsibility is at several levels – the European, the national, the subnational. This is illustrated by the failure of the Court of Auditors, in its annual reports, to give the Commission a clean bill of health for its overseeing of the budget. The Commission argues that it cannot easily oversee what has to be largely managed at national or subnational level.

Out of all this complex institutional cross-referencing and (at times) haggling and bickering comes the key question raised by so many who write about the EU: what about the democratic deficit? There is certainly a lot of sensitivity about this, and measures such as the Citizens' Initiative (a million signatures from citizens which invite the Commission to propose new legislation) are undoubtedly part of an attempt to respond to it.

However, there is a certain irony where the democratic deficit is concerned. It is above all the heads of state (and to a lesser extent the Council of Ministers) who are most resistant to democracy at the European level. Treaty after treaty negotiation has produced the most ungainly horse-trading on votes in the Council, and it has ended up with a totally skewed form of 'weighted voting' that gives the Germans no more votes than the French, the British or the Italians (it is in order to compensate to some extent for this discrimination that Lisbon requires a double majority, taking into account the size of a country's population). It is the Council of Ministers that has been most resistant to having its proceedings open to scrutiny. It is the Council that refuses to use its common sense and allow the Parliament to meet in one place (MEPs themselves would vote overwhelmingly to meet in one place), the Council that may refuse the Parliament the right to propose as well as consent to the name of the president of the Commission.

What always needs to be made clear (and this was plainly stated in President Barroso's State of the Union speech in the autumn of 2012) is that the EU contains 28 member states, that there may one day be more or (conceivably) fewer or a revolving door whereby some come in and some go out, but, in whatever combination they are, nothing will seek to supplant them or make them regions of a single 'superstate'. Once that is clearly stated, the problem of the democratic deficit can be addressed at all levels (for it is a problem at *all* levels, not just the European). The point of the democratic deficit is that representative government must work at the regional, the national and the European levels, and that, through the principle of subsidiarity, they should complement rather than rival one another.

Though a lot is said about failures at the EU level, in the end it may be at the national level that this lesson has to be learned most effectively. The example of the UK is a good one. Like the proverbial pushmi-pullyu of Hugh Lofting's Doctor Dolittle stories, it feels itself pulled in two directions at once by two different 'heads'. One minute Westminster worries about losing powers to Brussels. The next minute it worries about losing powers to Edinburgh. One minute it talks about a referendum on whether the UK stays in the EU. The next minute it agrees to a referendum on whether Scotland should stay in the UK. Caught between the two centres of power it sometimes seems to be paralysed. When the Scots claim that they can stay in the EU after leaving the UK, the Prime Minister is the first to warn them that this may not be so. But when they hear his stern lectures to the EU and about a possible 'Brexit' (British exit) after 2017, they may well feel that leaving the UK is actually the only way of ensuring that they *stay* in the EU. Paradoxically, the more UKIP calls for the UK to leave the EU, the more Scots may feel that their safest bet is to leave the UK (though all the evidence is that most of them would prefer not to), leaving UKIP presumably to campaign in 2017 as the Former United Kingdom Independence Party, a situation that at the very least will give the party an unfortunate acronym.

However it turns out, the British situation shows how the different layers of government – subnational, national and European, – need to move towards mutual acceptance and co-working rather than see themselves as rivals in a 'winner takes all' fight to the death. The democratic deficit will not be solved by each level claiming it is the only one at which representative government can be true to the people's wishes.

Such cooperation is also the only way of dealing effectively with the challenges Europe faces in a globalised environment, in which major problems can rarely be solved at one level alone. This raises a question that anyone who has ploughed through the standard textbooks on the European Union so often finds themselves asking: why do these worthy tomes not do more to show what the complex creature they are so determined to describe down to the last bone in its ankle actually does? Why not throw away your microscope and watch it feeding or raising its young or building dams or dealing with predators? Each of the next five chapters will introduce a policy area and then attempt to move outside the laboratory in order to observe the animal in its habitat.

4

The single market

There are those who think that the single market is a rather lacklustre example of a 'union' between nation-states. They see it as a fallback onto the safe and 'easy' territory of economic integration dating back to the meeting at Messina in Sicily of the six founder members of the European Coal and Steel Community. After the failure of their plans for a European Defence Community in 1954, they hurriedly moved towards the creation of a European Economic Community (EEC).

Francis Fukuyama wrote an immediately famous (and, like much that is immediately famous, later highly contentious) article in 1989 entitled 'The End of History?' Penned in the year the Berlin Wall collapsed and peaceful revolutions broke the stranglehold of Soviet power on Central and East European states, while the Soviet Union itself was in the process of collapse, Fukuyama wrote about a world apparently so completely delivered over to a single economic system dominated by the only 'hyperpower' that historians would no longer have anything interesting to write about. In the process, he managed to take a swipe at 'those flabby, prosperous, self-satisfied, inward-looking weak-willed states whose grandest project was nothing more heroic than the Common Market'.[1] A single market was for those without ambition. 'Real' nations (presumably) fought battles, won wars and brought their opponents low through the superiority of their 'Star Wars' technology.[2]

Fukuyama's characterisation of the EU in this manner (followed up by a range of other clichéd analyses of the 'Americans are from Mars, Europeans are from Venus' variety) not only fails to recognise the important ways in which the EU is developing in more 'Martian' areas (see Chapter 7) but fails to see just how much is involved even on the strictly Venusian side of things. The single market may be an economic issue, but creating one is a highly politically charged activity. After all, the 'economic' issues are those that in almost all cases (in European but also, it may be said, in US elections) matter most to voters. That national leaders, responsive and accountable to their national electorates, have nevertheless gone a long way towards creating a single market in Europe is a remarkable development, with nothing wimpish about it.

And there is nothing finished about it either. The single market is obviously central to understanding the European Union, but it remains work in progress. The current debate about the single currency and how to save it or make it prosper, for instance, can be seen only in the context of more than half a century spent trying to create a single market. The euro is part of a wider process of economic integration that set out to make it as easy to do business in another member state as to do business in another region of the same member state.

The Treaty of Lisbon uses the term 'internal' market rather than 'single market' to convey the idea that the EU market should correspond as closely as possible to the market within a single state. Essential to that process were the so-called four freedoms: the free movement of persons and of capital (essentially the inputs to production), and the free movement of goods and services (essentially the outputs of production). Both areas threw up and continue to throw up difficulties. Does the free movement of persons mean that an insupportable number of Romanians and Bulgarians, for instance, are making their way to the United Kingdom (see the latter half of this chapter)? Does the free movement of goods mean that the market in Germany, to give another example, can be overwhelmed with 'unpleasant' foreign beers that breach its centuries-old purity laws, laws that reflect a proud national tradition of ensuring that beer is always free of chemical additives? The process of making this market was bound to lead to strong feelings in particular countries about 'invaders' from outside, whether animate or inanimate.

The record of the Six in implementing the treaty creating the European Economic Community was patchy. It had talked of developing common agricultural, trade and transport policies. By the end of the 1960s the common transport policy was nowhere to be seen. The Common Agricultural Policy was up and running by 1962 but provoked a political crisis over the way it was funded. So far as trade was concerned, movement towards a customs union progressed steadily and was completed ahead of schedule before the end of the decade. There was also talk of removing restrictions upon the internal movement of people, money and services between member states, but a decade later this had hardly moved beyond a declaration of intent.

However, one very important thing had happened – something that is often underemphasised in treatments that like to focus on particular 'areas' when in fact all the areas are interrelated. The European Court of Justice (ECJ) began to flex its muscles. As has been made clear in Chapter 3, this was a vital development. An economic agreement between member states, even if is clearly a way of enabling everyone to prosper (and the economies of the Six *did* all prosper in the decade after the treaties were signed), is bound to provoke a clash between perceived national interests and Community interests. The successful completion of the project to abolish internal customs duties required some instrument to ensure that, when domestic businesses that relied on such duties started to put pressure on their own governments, those governments would not give in to such pressure. The ECJ was that instrument.

Without the moves of the ECJ to assert its authority through the principles of supremacy and direct effect (see Chapter 3), the single market would never have been able to develop. In fact, the Court deliberately used the judicial powers it laid claim to in order to encourage economic integration. Firms grew used to the idea that they could use the Community legal system in order to challenge restrictions on their ability to operate across national borders.

The case of Belgian margarine

And the Community legal system was going to be needed. By the 1970s the Common Market had been established so far as the removal of internal customs duties was concerned, but there were many other barriers that could be used by member states in order to make it hard to trade across national borders. Quotas could be set upon imports of particular products, though it was relatively easy to declare this illegal. A more difficult issue was the many regulations concerning the testing and certification of products coming from other member states, which, while not making it impossible to trade in another country, made it more bureaucratic and costly. Many of these restrictions seem almost comic, but they have serious implications. Here is an example involving Belgium. The text I am quoting from is a judgment of the ECJ made in 1982 and available on the EUR-Lex website, which gives access to European Law.[3]

The issue was as follows (there is some legalese here, but it is still worth quoting):

> [A] question as to the interpretation of Article 30 of the EEC Treaty in order to enable it [the Court] to decide whether a requirement laid down by Belgian legislation as to the shape of packaging of margarine sold by retail (royal decree of 2 October 1980, Moniteur Belge of 14 October 1980, p. 11845) is compatible with Community law.

Belgian law specified that margarine had to be sold in containers that were cube-shaped. A German seller wanted to sell margarine in tubs shaped like a 'truncated cone'. When the Belgian recipient refused to accept the margarine in the different shape, the case went before the ECJ. The Belgian position was that its legislation prescribing the shape of margarine was essential in order to enable shoppers to distinguish it from butter!

> [T]he Belgian government contends that the requirement of the cubic form is necessary for the protection of the consumer in order to prevent confusion between butter and margarine. It states that the cubic form used for the sale of margarine is 'rooted ' in the habits of Belgian consumers and is therefore an effective safeguard in that respect.

The ECJ ruled against Belgium, noting that:

> consumers may in fact be protected just as effectively by other measures, for example by rules on labelling, which hinder the free movement of goods less.

And it observed that Belgian rules had made it very difficult for other countries to sell their margarine in Belgium:

> [T]he protective effect of the Belgian rules is moreover demonstrated by the fact, affirmed by the Commission and not disputed by the Belgian government, that despite prices appreciably higher than those in some other member states there is practically no margarine of foreign origin to be found on the Belgian market.

It may be a relatively small issue, but it illustrates the effect of having binding Community or European Law that member states have to comply with. A state wanted to protect its own manufacturers of a particular good. It could no longer do so by means of customs duties at the border or by imposing quotas, but it *was* able to do so through measures that had 'equivalent effect', in this case by requiring other member states to provide that good (margarine) only in the particular form in which it was sold in Belgium. By so doing it kept out foreign suppliers (and at the same time kept the prices for its own consumers high, there being no foreign competition). The ECJ ruled that this practice was illegal under European Law. It pointed out that it would hardly be difficult to find alternative ways of alerting Belgian shoppers to the fact that they were buying margarine even if it was not in the sort of container they were used to – after all, manufacturers could surely devise some garish warning label! The result was almost certainly to help Belgian consumers by increasing competition and thereby bringing down the price of margarine.

National authorities were bound to do as much as possible to safeguard their own national interests (and those of the national electorates who elected them). Though everyone would benefit from a single market (even the producers of expensive Belgian margarine would benefit as consumers), it would not be possible to create such a market without supranational authorities that could face down national governments (or provide them with suitable cover for their preparedness to comply with Community law). The obligation of the ECJ to play the role of single market enforcer is absolutely crucial, because without it the forces of protectionism would have simply been too strong.

The free movement of goods

As the last section made clear, progress towards a single market was crucially dependent upon landmark rulings of the ECJ. Two key ones from the 1970s involved alcohol. One, the *Dassonville* case in 1974, concerned a Belgian importer of whisky from France. The whisky was coming to Belgium not directly from the producers but indirectly via a third country (France), and the Belgian authorities claimed that this could not be permitted without the correct documentation. The plaintiffs argued that if the whisky had entered the French market legally it must be allowed to circulate among other member states, and the ECJ confirmed this in a ruling that declared that 'all trading rules that hinder trade, whether directly or indirectly, actually or potentially, are inadmissible'.

The most important case, however, was *Cassis de Dijon* in 1979. This 'Ribena with punch' is a blackcurrant liqueur made in France. Germany sought to ban its sale in their country, essentially because, at 19 per cent proof, its alcohol content was not sufficient for them to accept it as a liqueur. Behind what, as in the case of Belgian margarine, seems to be an almost farcical aspect to the case – Germany claimed that the low alcohol content was a health risk, presumably because its citizens might be tempted to treat it as lemonade and consume it in excessively high quantities – a serious principle lay struggling to get out. By ruling that 'there was no valid reason why products produced and marketed in one member state could not be introduced into another member state', the ECJ opened up the possibility of easing trade between member states without the process of wholesale harmonisation that some had seen as a precondition of liberalisation.

To elaborate. If you find that your neighbour does not consider a liqueur that is 19 per cent proof to be a 'proper' liqueur, you may decide that you need a ruling that prescribes an alcohol content of 20 per cent (or 25 per cent or 30 per cent or whatever figure you deign to arrive at) for all liqueurs within the EU. That way, you avoid arguments – but you also develop a 'one-size-fits-all' approach that threatens the natural variety of goods within the Community. You will generate understandably hostile reactions in the media (think of those strange articles about 'straight bananas' or compulsorily metric measurements for beer that occasionally surfaced in the UK). A far better approach would surely be to accept the differences between products and limit the area for harmonisation to common health and safety requirements. That was what the *Cassis de Dijon* ruling made possible, establishing the principle of 'mutual recognition' and limiting the area of harmonisation.

It was not an arrangement that would solve all potential disputes, of course, since there would be arguments about whether or not a restriction really fell under the health and safety heading. Once again, there is a case involving alcohol in this area, when Germany claimed that beers from countries that did not have the tough purity laws (*Reinheitsgebot*) governing beer production that Germany had were liable to be 'unhealthy'. The ECJ ruled in 1987 that any unhealthiness was created more by the alcohol content of the beer than by any additives that might have been included!

Despite continuing arguments about whether or not a product could be kept out under the health and safety heading, there is no doubt that the *Cassis de Dijon* ruling opened the door to easing the circulation of goods within the (then) European Economic Community without undermining the natural variety that it was otherwise the fervent wish of that Community to encourage.

Ensuring the free movement of goods is not only a question of opening up markets to competition. Measures are taken to ensure that companies do not reach agreements to fix prices (forming cartels – they can be fined up to 10 per cent of their annual turnover for doing this) and do not abuse a dominant position. This was what Microsoft was found to have done. Microsoft's Windows operating system held a 95 per cent share of the market, and was found by the Commission to have abused this dominant position by, among other things, withholding information that rival server software would have needed in order to 'talk to' Windows-based personal computers. Microsoft was judged to be squeezing out the competition. As a result it was fined half a billion euros in 2004 (the case then went to a lengthy appeal, which Microsoft lost, securing an even heavier fine).

The Commission also judges whether proposed company mergers (of which it must be notified if they have a large turnover) will impede competition, and may decide either to ban the merger or, among other things, to require one of the companies to sell off part of its business. The companies involved in any of these measures could have their headquarters outside the EU, but this makes no difference. They have to comply or else cannot do business in what is now the largest market in the world in terms of GDP. The power of the EU's internal market is such that its rulings have to be taken into account by any company wishing to be truly 'multinational'. Because decisions are taken at the EU level and not by individual member states, there is no opportunity to play one country inside the Union off against another. This is another reason why a single market is not an unambitious project. It gives the EU the power to require multinationals to conform to its rules in order to win access to its (huge) market. This might involve, as here, competition rules or it might involve environmental rules. This is a further example of the way in which economic might creates in turn *political* leverage. If you possess such a big and important market that multinationals are willing to conform to your rules in order to gain access to it, then you can use those rules, for instance, in order to require them to conform to stringent environmental standards (see Chapter 8).

From goods to services

The emphasis so far has been on the free movement of *goods*. However, the other three freedoms (services, persons and capital) are also crucially important. By the 1980s the focus of concern in the creation of the single market was moving from the free movement of goods to that of services. This was unsurprising in that an increasing percentage of EU GDP was coming from the services sector (it is currently about three-quarters), and there was little left to do in the goods area. However, this area proved to be even more of a minefield than that of goods. Various national champions bestrode the sector, in areas such as aviation, telecommunications and energy services, and lobbied governments hard in the cause of resisting liberalisation. They had some successes, but in a number of key areas were unable to do more than delay liberalisation, because the benefits in terms of lower prices were often substantial and the producer lobbies were eventually forced to yield to the interests of consumers.

It is difficult to see, for instance, how the era of cheap air travel in Europe could have taken off as it did in the 1990s without the liberalisation of services – before then the state-owned national carriers such as Air France and Alitalia had made sure that air transport was regulated and costly. The air market was controlled by two-sided agreements between national airlines. As McCormick points out,[4] it had sometimes been cheaper to travel from one European country to another via the USA. Though newspapers might be filled with a grumbling Michael O'Leary 'tackling' the Commission over its criticism of state subsidies for Charleroi Airport (which Ryanair is pleased to see called 'Brussels South' on the airport's website, since it gives the impression of being close to the capital) or for its criticism of the Ryanair website, which was less than transparent concerning additional costs (for example, airport fees, charges for luggage) beyond the headline 'fiver' for the flight itself, it remains the case that Ryanair could not have existed without the Commission's push to liberalise air transportation in the 1990s. Whatever the 'hidden costs' of flights or the difficulties of accessing airports in the middle of nowhere, it is fair to say that cheap air fares from operators such as Ryanair have been a godsend to consumers, such as the North European families who can at last afford to take their children to the only part of Europe (the Canary Islands) where they can be assured of escaping the cold and the cough-ridden environment of home for a couple of weeks in the middle of winter (admittedly at the cost of increasing their own carbon footprints). In Poland, for instance, where the airline market was protected from competition until Poland's entry into the EU in 2004, the cheapest ticket for a flight to London was about 200 euros. At the same time, most of the international flights were from Warsaw, requiring passengers to incur the extra cost (and time) of travelling to the capital. Such sums far exceed the cost of the cheapest flights now, whatever the impact of 'hidden extras'.

Another example, this time from the first decade of the twenty-first century, concerns the telecommunications sector, which had been opened up completely to competition from 1 January 1998. Over the next five years, the cost of domestic calls on fixed lines fell by over 10 per cent for residential users and over 20 per cent for business users, while the cost of most international calls fell by over 40 per cent. Later in the decade, attention turned to mobile phones (the first mobile phone call was made in 1991, but it was not till the next decade that their use became widespread), and a lot of publicity was given to reduced roaming charges for calls by mobile across national frontiers (in his State of the Union address in 2013 the President of the European Commission called for their abolition). The cost of making and receiving a call while abroad in 2012 was less than half what it had been in 2005.

In other service areas, liberalisation has proved to be much more problematic. Gas and electricity, for instance, have not seen comparable price falls and have even seen some significant increases in costs. As Chapter 8 points out, there are many incentives for completing an internal market in energy – scheduled by a European Council declaration of February 2011 for the end of 2014 but likely to be delayed. Since member states differ in their level of energy dependence, there have to be efficient means of transferring energy from one state to another. True competition depends upon fully interconnected energy networks (just as it depends upon fully interconnected transport networks).

If the liberalisation of services proved popular in terms of the benefits it brought to consumers, it ran into opposition in terms of the loss of benefits it supposedly brought to some employees (at least if they ignored the fact that they were also consumers). This came to a head in the first decade of the twenty-first century, a time when there was nervousness about the influx of ten new member states (eight of which were former satellites of the former Soviet Union and with weaker economies than those in the West). Fears of the impact of enlargement meshed with fears about globalisation in general to provoke an unexpected reaction when Commissioner for the Internal Market Fritz Bolkestein drafted a directive on services in the internal market (the measure became known as the Bolkestein Directive and was nicknamed the Frankenstein Directive – in the end the Commissioner would open discussions by saying 'I wish to remind the audience that my name is *Bolke*stein'). It was intended to be a relatively uncontroversial instrument for realising the Lisbon Agenda, launched in 2000 to make the EU the world's 'most dynamic and competitive economy' by 2010.

The directive was meant to deal with the sort of regulatory blockage now impeding the liberalisation of services and that had once impeded the single market in goods. Proponents of the directive believed that the service sector comprised a lot of small and medium-sized companies that could not afford the legal costs of entanglement in too much litigation. Controversy erupted around the so-called country of origin principle, according to which a company offering its services in another country would operate according to the rules and regulations of its home country. In the context of expansion to the poorer countries of the former Central and Eastern Europe, it was easy to stoke fears of the inevitable 'Polish plumber' relocating to France and working under (presumed to be non-existent) Polish labour laws. In fact, the directive would not have applied to social legislation and rules concerning health and safety at work. Moreover, where the recognition of qualifications was concerned, the rules of the country where the services were provided would apply.

In the end the directive was adopted in an amended form that dropped the 'country of origin' principle and limited the range of services to which it applied (excluding areas such as public healthcare and social services). It was never intended to be controversial. There did not seem to be any difference between requiring Belgium to admit margarine in cone-shaped containers and requiring the Autonomous Region of Sicily to permit opticians to be located within 300 metres of one another and to allow more than one optician for every 8,000 residents (this was a regulation applied by the regional authority and challenged in the European Court in 2011 – Case C 539/11).

But what was intended to be a tidying-up exercise became an occasion for mass demonstrations and ideological drumbeating. It illustrates how easy it was to tie together the free movement of persons with that of services in order to present a picture of 'invaders' willing to work for nothing, undercutting wages and hard-fought rights in the older member states and denying workers in the older member states employment. In fact, by the time the directive was finally passed it was explicitly said that it did not affect employment law. So the relevant rules on working time, minimum wages, holidays and the right to strike would be those in force in the country where the service was being provided. Arguably, the directive never intended to be any more controversial than making it easier for EU service providers to operate in another member state. But, as this chapter has claimed throughout, it is no easy task to create a single market, not least because all the changes reverberate through the entire economic and social systems of the member states. To develop such a market despite these reverbera-tions is no mean achievement.

The free movement of persons

As the last section pointed out, one of the reasons the Bolkestein Directive proved so controversial was the way in which it seemed to tie together the free movement of persons with that of services. Yet the free movement of the inputs to the economic process – persons and capital – was clearly as crucial to its success as the free movement of the outputs – goods and services. As argued in Chapter 2, what sense did it make to have a single market if it was not made easy for citizens of any of the 28 member states to live, to be employed, to open a bank account, to buy property, to pay their taxes, to have their children educated, to have access to medical care and to receive a pension anywhere in the European Community? But, as the furore over Bolkestein demonstrated, no one considering ways of encouraging the free movement of people, for instance, could be unaware of the fact that this would raise a whole lot of issues going beyond the purely economic. Inevitably this would introduce a degree of friction into further attempts to strengthen the single market, even if these attempts were justified in purely economic terms.

That there was nevertheless progress in the free movement of persons, particularly from the 1980s onwards, is in no small measure owing to the fact that, however politically sensitive such developments might be, they were generally recognised as economically beneficial. The establishment of visa-free travel between member states was one example (the first agreement in this area was reached in the Luxembourg town of Schengen in 1985). The 1985 agreement established the so-called Schengen area of visa-free travel that now encompasses 22 of the 28 member states of the EU and three countries that are not members of the EU (Norway, Switzerland and Iceland). However, the free movement of persons involves much more than being able to cross a border easily. It also raises questions of how easy it is to live (perhaps with a family) and work in another member state. Hence the need to consider some of the other issues mentioned above: procedures for opening bank accounts, dealing with 'double taxation', buying and selling property, having a school to send children to, having access to healthcare and the right to a pension. There might be legal questions too. Perhaps a marriage breaks up and a citizen of state A married to a citizen of state B, the two of them living in state C, have to consider questions of alimony. Which country's legal system should apply?

Trying to sort these issues out has nothing to do with 'straying outside economics' and trying to create a common education, health, legal, taxation or pension system throughout the EU. It is entirely to do with ensuring the interoperability that enables citizens of one member state to live and work in another one. Without such arrangements, the aim of a single market in which it is as easy to do business in another member state as in another region of the same state is unrealisable.

The free movement of persons becomes contentious when such interoperability is seen as producing an influx of (usually unskilled) workers in the better-off member states. The efforts to facilitate the search for work in other parts of the European Union is then seen as producing large numbers of people who are either going to 'take the jobs' of resident nationals or are no more than 'benefit tourists' trying to take advantage of a range of social benefits, including unemployment benefit. The issue is examined in more detail in the section entitled 'The question of labour mobility' later in this chapter

From the Single European Act to the single currency

Given the difficulties outlined in the previous sections, it is remarkable how much progress has been made in the last 30 years towards realising the internal market. In 1986, member states signed the Single European Act, the first revision to the Treaties of Rome signed 30 years earlier. It followed a white paper produced by the Commission, a paper that talked in grandiose terms about 'completing the single market by 1992'. This was entirely consistent with the logic of the EU's development: set out to do more than you can possibly achieve, and end up doing more than you might otherwise have expected. The internal market was not completed by 1992. The internal market has not been completed yet. Nonetheless, the 300 proposals in the white paper provided a benchmark for further development, and the Single European Act made clear that further economic integration was inevitable. Like all treaties, it required (and received) the unanimous support of all member states, including the UK, whose prime minister at the time was Margaret Thatcher.

Margaret Thatcher signed into being a treaty that at last broke the deadlock over Qualified Majority Voting (QMV), which had hindered progress since the Empty Chair Crisis and the Luxembourg 'Compromise' of the 1960s (see Chapter 2). When Thatcher arrived at a summit in Fontainebleau in 1984, the summit that is famous for finally settling the question of the British budget rebate, which had remained a festering boil for some years, she talked not only about 'getting her money back' but about a paper entitled 'Europe: The Future', which called for a common market in both goods and services. In her memoirs she referred to 'our' paper that was being produced for the summit and explains that 'I accepted that it should be liberally sprinkled with *communautaire* phrases.'[5] However, this is a little disingenuous – the paper was not just adopting a *communautaire* tone, it was pushing for more *communautaire* policies. It even called for an urgent examination of whether 'more can be achieved, or achieved more economically, by acting on a Community basis rather than nationally'. Point 6 of 'Europe: the Future' declared that 'if the problems of growth, outdated industrial structures and unemployment which affect us all are to be tackled effectively, we must create the genuine common market in goods and services which is envisaged in the Treaty of Rome'.[6]

The Single European Act, with its key provisions for QMV, was passed in 1986. From Thatcher's point of view, a measure was being introduced that would break down the barriers to free trade that still existed within the EEC. As Menon comments:

> Delors was adept at adjusting his language to suit his audience: the emphasis on social Europe that earned him a standing ovation at the 1988 Labour Party conference was far different to the stress on deregulation that helped woo Margaret Thatcher.[7]

This illustrates the way in which a proactive president of the Commission can find methods of pushing an agenda forward that are acceptable to national leaders from different parts of the political spectrum.

However, it is always possible to push that agenda forward in a way that underestimates the political fallout. Some of this might have been anticipated from the reaction of Margaret Thatcher herself. As explained, she was an enthusiastic supporter of the Single European Act, even though it in effect reduced the scope of national vetoes in key economic areas. She was prepared to accept such a move in the interest of service liberalisation. When it came to the idea of a single currency, in contrast, she remained implacably opposed, despite the arguments in terms of 'economic logic' concerning a single currency.

Indeed, nowhere are the problems of the single market more highlighted today than in the area of the single currency. This is not the place to go into the complex issue of the advantages and disadvantages of membership of the eurozone, or for that matter the best mixture of 'growth' and 'austerity' to hasten (it is to be hoped) the end of the eurozone crisis. What can, however, be said is that the formation of the eurozone is a perfect example of the way in which creating a single market is not an activity that can be carried out within a narrowly defined and supposedly uncontroversial 'economic' area. As pointed out in Chapter 2, there was an obvious logic to supporting a single market with a single currency, particularly in the light of the currency fluctuations that followed the end of the Bretton Woods system. Greater price transparency, the elimination of exchange-rate uncertainty and of transaction costs, and even the enticing prospect of creating an 'international currency' – all these factors seemed to be part of smoothing the way for a more efficient single market. But a single currency meant giving up control of interest rates and exchange rates at the national level (not that in practical economic terms that 'control' at national level is always very assured). In effect it meant that the members of the eurozone had to be working within a common macroeconomic framework so that a cut in interest rates, for instance, would not benefit the economy of one member state while harming that of another. Whatever 'a common macroeconomic framework' is taken to mean, it is probably more than some countries anticipated when they signed up to the euro for what appeared to be commonsense reasons associated with the advantages of a single currency to the workings of a single market. Moreover, it would be something imposed on them from without (if they were in need of loans following the economic crisis) rather than determined from within. The single currency had turned into visits from the Troika (ECB, Commission and International Monetary Fund (IMF)) telling them to shave pensions and public sector staff levels.

The limits of the single market

Viewed from the perspective of today, there are certainly many areas in which the single market is still not like the internal market of a single state. For instance, banking rules have not all been standardised and taxation rates have not been made common (there are agreed minimum rates for indirect taxes such as VAT and excise duties but not for other taxes such as corporation tax, which can go as low as member states wish them to). Member states adopt a strongly 'hands off' approach on tax issues, which is one of the reasons it was impossible to introduce a 'green' tax on energy products in the 1990s. In the end (see Chapter 8) other methods were eventually tried, such as the Emissions Trading System. In the context of the current financial crisis, the same reluctance is being shown by some member states towards a common Financial Transaction Tax, which was initially proposed at a level of 1 per cent on share deals and 0.1 per cent on derivatives. Of course there is a range of arguments on this issue, including fears that it will drive business elsewhere. Indeed, there is a range of arguments on each of these issues and there is more to each one than simple dislike of reaching a common position on tax. The point is simply to show that the single market remains, and perhaps should remain, incomplete.

If the above has provided a fair representation of some of the problems on the way to the creation of a single market, then the dilemma facing the EU where the future is concerned can be simply stated. If it is correct to assert that the creation of a single market is neither an unambitious alternative to hard policy development nor an activity that can be pursued without spillover into other areas, then should the policy of the EU be to do anything it needs to do in order to improve the single market? Or does it need to say that the desire since the 1980s to create a market as efficient as that of the USA (whether the USA market is really so efficient is another question) has led it to be *too* ambitious? Are there, perhaps, limits to the extent to which 28 separate states will be willing to create a market as integrated as that of a single nation-state?

In 1955, member states realised that there were areas in which they could share sovereignty and areas where they could not (for instance, the defence and foreign policy fields). After the failure of the European Defence Community, they ran for cover to the economic sphere (EEC, EURATOM) where sovereignty-sharing had already been successful. This chapter has argued that Fukuyama was wrong to see this as a 'wimp's option'. But, if that view is right, then should one not be careful how far one goes towards sovereignty-sharing even in the (supposedly relatively safe) economic sphere? Has the EU become too complacent about the 'hard' implications of a single market?

Even if it cannot achieve an internal market as strongly integrated as that of a single state, and even if in doing so it finds that there is an economic cost (the sort of costs that Jacques Delors ensured were made clear in the 1980s through Cecchini's 'The cost of non-Europe' – see Chapter 2), it might still be the case that limiting the range of economic integration is politically wiser than trying to push it too far. Better a less than fully integrated market than one that collapses.

It is not that the EU should confine itself to 'economic' rather than 'political' integration, as so many seem to be saying within the UK. This is impossible. It is more that the political costs of economic integration may at some point become unacceptable. The EU will never be a single 'superstate'. It will also, arguably, never have a market as integrated as that of a single state. But such limitations do nothing to take away from its extraordinary achievements in the field of economic integration so far. It has created the largest economic bloc in the world, giving it significant clout in many areas (illustrated in this book). It has done so because of the willingness of member states to absorb the political and social tremors that such economic integration is bound to bring. But, for precisely that reason, it would seem sensible to accept that there are limits to integration even in the economic sphere. If that were better recognised, fewer people would consider that behind all the current talk of 'banking unions' and (inevitably) changes requiring a new treaty lies a surreptitious desire to create the Kingdom (or Republic) of Europa. It is nothing like that. They are just people trying to get out of an economic hole they have dug themselves into.

Example: The question of labour mobility

In 1983 the first series of what became a cult British comedy series, *Auf Wiedersehen, Pet*, was aired on ITV. It was the story of seven out-of-work builders from various parts of the UK who went to look for work in the city of Düsseldorf in what was then West Germany. It focused primarily on three men from Newcastle upon Tyne. Hence the title, with *Auf Wiedersehen* being the German for 'farewell' and 'Pet' a Geordie term of endearment for the wives, girlfriends, friends and family members being left behind as the brickies seek work and a new life abroad.

Thirty years later, an event was held in the same city as part of the EU Youth on the Move programme. Information could be had by sending an email to Youth on the Move, Jobmesse® Düsseldorf 2013. The blurb began by asking: 'Was kann Europa konkret für Dich tun?' Literally translated this means 'What can Europe actually do for you?' It went on: 'Suchst du einen Job in deinem eigenen Land oder möchtest du dein Glück im europäischen Ausland versuchen?' ('Are you looking for a job in your own country or do you fancy trying your luck in another one?'). It pointed out that, through the Youth on the Move initiative, financial and practical assistance was available and invited those interested to write for more information or to attend the Jobmesse (jobs fair) in March. But how likely were people in the UK or

Figure 7. The city of Düsseldorf in Germany.
Note: Düsseldorf was the location of the cult TV series Auf Wiedersehen, Pet in the 1980s.

elsewhere to take up the offer and seek work abroad like the characters portrayed in a famous television series from 30 years earlier?

Many people know of (or can still recall) the famous remark by former UK Conservative minister Norman Tebbit in 1981: 'I grew up in the '30s, with an unemployed father. He didn't riot. He got on his bike and looked for work and he went on looking 'til he found it.' Norman Tebbit repeated his advice 30 years later in a talk to students in Merthyr Tydfil, in Wales, an area of particularly high unemployment, particularly after the closure of the Hoover factory in 2008. 'People are willing to do it in Poland, in Hungary, in Lithuania,' he commented, 'why are they more willing to do it than we are?'

Tebbit's 2011 reiteration of his idea of job mobility provoked several hostile comments from people who saw why Tebbit Senior should go biking from one end of London to another looking for a job, but not why Janusz should go from one end of Europe to another. Janusz would most probably not be using a bike. Instead he would take advantage of two products that, as this chapter has already discussed, have been made considerably cheaper following deregulation: the cheap airline and the mobile phone. Ryanair or Wizzair could take him cheaply to the UK, after which text messaging would allow him to set up appointments and make contact with the existing Polish community in the UK. And why not? Labour mobility is fundamental to the idea of a single market. At a time of economic crisis, when some parts of the EU are clearly affected more than others, it is essential that people are able to 'do a Tebbit' and go where the jobs are, just as they would in the USA, whose junior 'Tebbits' would think nothing of going thousands of kilometres to find work.

Indeed, there is something almost quaint about government efforts in the UK to promote labour mobility. In 2010 the work and pensions secretary, Iain Duncan Smith, once again in relation to the situation in Merthyr Tydfil, recognised technological progress insofar as it had progressed from the bike to the bus. He pointed out that Cardiff was only one hour by bus from Merthyr, and jobseekers would find 100 or more jobs advertised in the Cardiff jobcentre. Presumably his advisers suggested that he avoid anything as radical as a bus ride to Bristol (that being 'across the border' in England), and the notion of getting onto a plane and looking for work in the rest of the EU was completely unthinkable. In 2006 the EU had had its 'European Year of Workers' Mobility'. Four years later the Conservative–Liberal Democrat coalition government in the UK was tentatively suggesting a bus to another part of South Wales.

European Commission reports have consistently highlighted the benefits of worker mobility (in terms of moving to another member state) and the fact that it is currently at very low levels. Aware of concerns among the older member states (the EU-15 that were part of the EU before 2004) that they might be overwhelmed by workers from the member states joining in 2004 (the EU-10) and 2007 (the EU-2), the Commission produced reports in 2008 and 2011 on the impact of the two waves of enlargement. Though claims that worker mobility had added to levels of overall growth, had not depressed wage levels and had not caused an increase in unemployment will undoubtedly remain open to dispute, what will not be disputed are figures that show that, between 2004 and 2007, the proportion of those with the EU-10 as their home country living in the EU-15 had risen from 0.2 per cent in 2003 to 0.5 per cent in 2007. This was hardly an 'invasion'. A report focused on the EU-2 (Bulgaria and Romania) in 2011 found that the proportion of those with the EU-2 as their home state had risen from 0.2 per cent to 0.6 per cent. In the case of every member of the EU-15 bar Ireland, the percentage of residents whose home state was outside the EU was greater than the percentage of residents whose home state was one of the member states of the EU. Whether or not worker mobility is a good thing, it could hardly be said to have taken off.

On the other hand, even statistically small figures are significant in absolute terms. If 0.5 per cent of those living in the UK (for instance) are from Central and Eastern Europe, that is 300,000 people – enough for a city. Since they will want contacts with – and support from – fellow expatriates, they may well congregate in particular areas where they will be highly visible (as indeed was the case with an earlier wave of immigration from the former Empire). There can be no denying this. There can be no denying, either, that this can be hard to deal with (access to services, language difficulties and so on).

The real problem with the attitude of many in the UK (and of course it is not alone in this) is not so much exaggerating the 'invasion' or even seeing that it could cause difficulties but the one-way view of migration it reveals. Enlarging the EU (and with it the single market) is always seen in terms of 'more of them' coming to 'us' rather than more opportunities for 'us' to go and live among 'them' – more places for those who take Tebbit Senior's advice seriously to fly off to in search of work.

The single market can operate most effectively if people are willing to look for jobs everywhere. From an economic point of view, the problem is not that too many people are going from one place to another, but that too many people never think of going anywhere. This is not to say that people should be made to go, for instance, to Finland if they fail to find work in Merthyr Tydfil (there were surely places that even Tebbit Senior might have turned down – one suspects that it might have included the whole of the North of England). Nor is it to say that there are not important benefits to staying put in terms of maintaining the collective memory of a community or looking after aged relatives.

But we are talking about *options*. EU citizens living in a member state that is different from the state of which they are a national constitute only 3 per cent of the EU labour force. Is that really the sort of figure to be expected, given the number who might be willing to seek work in other member states – or even enthusiastic about doing so? As the Organisation for Economic Co-operation and Development (OECD) pointed out in its 'Economic Survey of the European Union' produced in March 2012: 'High unemployment, particularly among young people, and low labour mobility [in some regions] coexist with skill and labour shortages in other regions.'[8] To facilitate greater mobility, the Directorate-General (DG) for Employment, Social Affairs and Inclusion created a pan-EU job search network called EURES (in fact it covers the European Economic Area, that is to say the EU plus Norway, Iceland and Liechtenstein; it also covers Switzerland). In one form or another EURES has been in operation since 1993. The network is designed to make it easier for jobseekers to contact employers looking for particular skills. The job mobility website receives about 4 million visits per month and keeps a daily record of vacancies, CVs and registered employers. To take a date at random, on 3 May 2013 the figure was 1,348,508 job vacancies, 1,110,057 CVs and 30,641 employers.

As the OECD report pointed out, the EU is characterised both by severe pockets of unemployment and by pockets of skills shortages. Indeed, the number of vacancies in the EU has been on the rise since mid-2009 (a point often forgotten when the focus is on jobless totals). The job mobility website sets up about 200,000 contacts per month between jobseekers and employers, achieving about 5,000 placements per month. In addition, it supports and coordinates various events and job fairs throughout Europe, and a team of EURES advisers has been set up and is being rapidly expanded in order to provide information to jobseekers and employers through personal contact. By the middle of 2013 there were about 850 EURES advisers across Europe, but the number is constantly increasing. The number working in the UK in mid-2013, in contrast, was only 15.

As already made clear, there are perfectly understandable reasons why people will have commitments or physical limitations preventing them from moving a thousand miles away to look for work. On the other hand, it is young people who are most likely to be able and willing to travel, and at the same time it is young people who are suffering most from lack of work. Statistics vary, but youth unemployment is clearly higher than the rate for other age groups and in some member states it is (at least) nudging 50 per cent. Eurostat figures for October 2011 showed unemployment for 15–24 year olds in Spain at 48.9 per cent. The level has since risen. This means that a young Spanish school leaver is actually *likely* to be out of work. Hence EURES particularly targets the young.

A number of initiatives to promote youth employment have sprung up around the Europe 2020 Strategy, but the most useful practical programme is 'Your First EURES Job', part of the Youth on the Move initiative designed to make it easier both for employers to recruit from other countries and for young workers to move there. It began with a pilot programme for 2012–13 targeting 5,000 young jobseekers from Germany, Denmark, Italy and Spain, but it has plans to expand that number considerably. Support meant a contribution towards inter-view costs and removal costs for going to live in another country. At the same time, financial support was given to employers in small and medium-sized enterprises (SMEs, or businesses with fewer than 250 employees) through contributions towards training costs (including language training). To some extent the model for EURES is the Erasmus and Leonardo da Vinci programmes for academic and vocational training exchanges at the tertiary level, but it needs to be borne in mind that a student on an academic exchange is probably spending a relatively short period in another country. An apprentice, on the other hand, is by definition someone engaging in long-term training. There is a difference between a semester studying abroad, and a decision to live and work in another country – perhaps not forever but for a substantial period of time during which all sorts of issues will come to the fore (buying property, becoming proficient in a language, perhaps even putting children through school) that may not concern a student or volunteer taking part in a programme lasting a few months.

Support therefore needs to include provisions such as language training. When Vivat, a German company providing residential housing and facing a nursing shortage, looked to EURES for help in finding nurses on permanent contracts, it was able to recruit a number of nurses from Spain. However, it recognised that it had to help them with matters such as housing, insurance and translations of documents. It also put them on 80 per cent time so that they could spend the other 20 per cent learning German. This was worth it if the company was going to find good staff on long-term contracts, but it required accepting that they would need support in order to integrate.

Of course there are many difficulties in moving between states that do not arise when moving within them – for persons as for goods, capital and services. These were mentioned earlier in the chapter. Working in another state will probably involve knowing (and perhaps learning) another language, although this is less daunting in states where, unlike in the UK, learning a second or even a third European language is a fundamental part of the curriculum. In a French-speaking Belgian school, for instance, Dutch is compulsory from the age of seven and English from the age of nine (with some variations). Nevertheless, despite all the 'scientific' claims about it being too late to learn languages later in life, it is perfectly possible for adults to acquire proficiency. It will mean a degree of 'culture shock', though this can be seen in a positive way as an opportunity to benefit from the cultural richness of the EU.

One important thing EURES does is to help match skills in one country to the needs of another. When LEGO sought to increase the number of engineers and technicians working at its headquarters in Billund in Denmark, it was advised to concentrate on toolmakers in Portugal. Portugal has a thriving plastics industry and produces many engineers and toolmakers in this area of work. Recruitment consultants therefore travelled from Denmark to a European Jobdays event organised by EURES in Lisbon in October 2012 and hired several toolmakers. This was far more effective than simply posting jobs on a website.

Job mobility may concern relocating entirely from one country to another, or it may mean living in a different country from the one in which you work. About 600,000 EU citizens are in this situation of commuting across borders, which often raises legal, administrative and fiscal problems. EURES has formed cross-border partnerships to help make it easier to work in a country other than the one you are living in. Of course, the number of cross-border workers will vary from country to country. Though most of the UK is an island, it does have two important cross-border partnerships. One concerns all the counties of Northern Ireland and the border counties of the Republic of Ireland; the other involves the county of Kent, West Flanders (part of Belgium) and the Calais district of France.

There is a tendency to suppose that the reluctance to relocate for jobs – or for better jobs – is something that applies only to unskilled or low-skilled workers. But the drive to increase numbers able and willing to get 'on their bikes' and relocate to another country does not simply concern cleaners and bricklayers. Skyline Communications is a Belgian company in desperate need of qualified engineers. Using EURES it has attended a number of jobs fairs across Europe and the results have been significant. In 2012, for instance, Belgian employers recruited 79 Portuguese engineers. In Flanders (northern Belgium), the regional authority provides language classes (Dutch) and assistance with schools and housing. The aim is to have people working there long term.

As the *Wall Street Journal* reported on 13 April 2011,[9] it is often engineers, architects, accountants, doctors and lawyers in the EU who find it difficult to have their qualifications recognised outside their home country. The article reported that Germany had 36,000 engineering vacancies and 43,000 IT vacancies, and quoted the Director of the International Economics programme at the Carnegie Endowment for International Peace pointing out that 'professional services is the most protected service in the world'. 'Is a dentist in Spain as qualified as in Germany?', Mr Dadush asked rhetorically. Clearly, mutual recognition requires a degree of trust and a clear indication of standards being met in each country.

Dentistry provides a useful example where the language issue is concerned. Since 2010, the European Commission has produced *FMW*, a roughly biannual online journal on the free movement of workers within the EU. The first edition, published in November 2010,[10] discussed a case brought to the ECJ for a ruling concerning one Mr Haim, an Italian dentist who sought to practise dentistry in Germany. The Court found that it was reasonable for an Italian dentist in Germany to be required to have a 'proportionate' linguistic ability in German – that is to say, enough to be able to deal with patients and with the relevant administrative authorities, but not fluency. The Court also pointed out the advantage of an Italian dentist for patients whose mother tongue was Italian (think of those British holiday-makers or retirees in Spain desperate to find a doctor who speaks English). The more there is a real mix of languages throughout Europe, the more the fact that someone speaks a different language from the official one (if there is an official language) can seem an advantage rather than a burden. A mix is best of all, whether at the skilled or unskilled level, whether seasonal or longer term. Many of the jobs advertised on EURES (such as the Sheraton Frankfurt Airport Hotel in Germany looking for multilingual staff or the travel company Wintour looking for sports coaches and children's entertainers for the coasts of the Mediterranean) are specifically looking for people to work in a multilingual environment.

In fact there are many examples of this in tourism, though jobs in this sector may well be temporary. TMC tourist services, for instance, is based in Denmark, but the package holidays it organises around the Mediterranean involve many Russian speakers. Via EURES the company recruited a lot of staff from Estonia, where Russian is the second language. In the tourism and travel business, English will be the most important language to possess, providing UK citizens with a good start, but it will not make it unnecessary for them to learn anything else. They do not need to be proficient before they come, however; sometimes the problem is persuading them that they can do it. But, as Bomber remarked in *Auf Wiedersehen, Pet*, 'it's easier to learn German than understand Geordie'.

EURES is not the 'solution' to the EU's unemployment problem. It might be if there were a perfect match between available labour and vacancies, but that is not the case. There are shortages in areas such as information technology, as we have seen, as there are in the area of new methods associated with the drive for environmental improve-ment, for instance through the development of forms of renewable energy (see Chapter 8), but these are broadly speaking skilled areas. This is no good if there are an increasing number of unskilled jobseekers, which figures suggest there will be. Though it is true, as pointed out, that there is important work to be done in matching people to vacancies in skilled areas such as law and engineering, it is also the case, as the Europe 2020 strategy itself admits, that there is likely to be an increase in unskilled jobseekers by 2020. Successful 'jobs fairs' that recruit budding software engineers who speak three languages are not going to be a way of dealing with those whose skills are not at that level.

In some cases, jobseekers will simply go to another member state in search of work without having been recruited for a specific job. If they do so, they have the right to live there while they search for work and to have their unemployment benefits paid in the country they are visiting for a fixed period (initially this is three months under current regulations, with the possibility of an extension up to a maximum of six months). Needless to say, the question of benefits provoked a storm in the UK in 2013, when the country was accused of having additional 'residency tests' (with more planned) that had prevented some EU residents from obtaining benefits to which they are rightfully entitled. The EU position (which the UK signed up to) is that such provision should take the same form in each member state, since it exists to provide support for enterprising jobseekers looking for work anywhere within the single market. These measures are unavoidable if that market is to work effectively, in terms of both generating new jobs and finding people to fill the vacancies that already exist. At the same time, a great deal can be done to promote jobseeking without the need to go abroad in order to search for work – for instance through the increasing use of Skype for job interviews.

Conclusion

The chapter began by focusing on the history of the single market and argued that it was not in any way unambitious for a group of states to focus their sovereignty-sharing efforts in this sector. Not only is this area the main determinant of the political fortunes of national leaders, but that in turn means that it is the main concern of their citizens. Making the single market work in such a way that it is seen to benefit everyone is hard work, and the task remains incomplete. Perhaps it ought always to full short of the sort of economic integration that can be achieved by a single state. But even if such a limitation is accepted, it remains a huge endeavour.

The chapter then looked at one aspect of that single market, the free movement of persons in the context of the search for work at a time of

Figure 8. The limits to labour mobility?

rising unemployment. It touched on various programmes to help jobseekers (especially young ones) find employment in other member states. It did not (and this book does not) address the issue of why there is a crisis in the eurozone and what mixture of 'austerity' and/or 'growth' measures will help to solve it. It simply suggested that one mark of an effective single market would be a culture in which it was acceptable and even normal to 'get on yer bike' and look for work in other countries.

In Figure 8, the male model in the poster on the right announces to French tourists: 'Je reste en Pologne', to reassure them that he is a plumber staying in Poland, and invites them to visit his country in their thousands ('Venez nombreux'). The woman in the poster on the left reassures them that she is a Polish nurse staying in Poland where she too is 'waiting for you' ('Je t'attends'). It was a good-humoured response to French myopia, not to mention a response to Polish fears about their skilled workers all emigrating west (the sending countries fear what they are losing, while the receiving countries are afraid of what they are gaining). Of course it could equally well have been in English or German and a comment on their own fears of invasion.

When new member states join the EU – most recently Croatia in July 2013 – this will mean not only the 'threat' of an influx of workers into the older member states but also a new opportunity for jobseekers in the older member states to seek work (for instance) along Croatia's Dalmatian coast. The illustrations in Figure 8 are a gentle reminder that there are still Polish nurses and plumbers who are staying in Poland, where they can (among other things) cater for French tourists, but a properly developed single market would make it equally natural for the nurse waiting for those tourists to be French, while the male model offering to fix the plumbing in their hotels turned out to come from Paris. Such practical exchanges would not solve the economic problems of the EU, though they would help in the work of matching skills to vacancies. But they would at least cut through some of the acrimonious debate over national policies by pointing out that an increasingly mobile workforce is prepared to go are the jobs were. Not everyone can do that, but the young, the ones who need the help most, are those who are most able to do so. Since it is they who will determine whether the EU has another 50 years of existence, it would help if they felt that the ease of crossing national borders that is at the heart of the 'project' were something that could help them in their own lives.

5

Agriculture and aquaculture

There are many ways in which the Common Agricultural Policy (CAP) provides a perfect introduction to the European Union (EU) at work. In the first place, it raises fundamental economics questions concerning the nature of a managed market and, in particular, the way in which the EU organises a market in agricultural products. In the second place, it is a very important part of the work of the EU and involves a significant slice of its budget (today about one-third, though in the past it has been much more). Third, it is a policy that, in the jargon, involves 'actors' at many different levels. On the one hand, the EU comes under international pressure 'from above' – from particular nations such as the USA and institutions such as the World Trade Organization (WTO) – and, on the other hand, it faces pressure 'from below' involving particular countries (France is often singled out, but Germany and the United Kingdom have been just as robust in seeking to exercise influence). Fourth, the CAP throws a great deal of light – in a very practical way – on questions that are often discussed in a (sometimes) stiflingly academic manner concerning who really has power in the EU (a debate that usually leads to some conclusion claiming, for instance, that the Commission is 'really' steered by the member states). Fifth, the CAP is controversial and much discussed. People tend to know about 'butter mountains' and 'wine lakes', not to mention tales of farmers being 'paid to do nothing' under various attempts to reform the CAP.

A managed market

Though there are political philosophies that advocate non-interven-
tion in the market by governments, this is a rule more honoured in the
breach than in the observance. All governments manage or attempt to
manage markets in certain sectors.

The CAP is undoubtedly a way of managing part of the market, but
it is important to point out exactly what this 'managing' means. There
are all sorts of ways in which a government might seek to intervene in
the area of food. It could, for instance, decide to control prices by
insisting that shops do not charge more than a certain amount. It could
try to ration consumption. It could limit exports by fixing quotas or
banning exports altogether. It could order farmers to sell all their food
to the government, and then distribute it to those whom it favoured.
All these methods have been tried in the past, and outside the EU some
are still being tried. By and large they are bureaucratic, wasteful and
counterproductive. They generate the images with which we are
familiar from socialist societies in particular: the queues for food, the
armies of bureaucrats who distribute and manage ration books, the
growth of black markets, the failure to export and often a desperate
desire to import or receive food aid instead, and in extreme cases the
deliberately planned starvation of groups or even countries (as in
Stalin's treatment of Ukraine).

These sorts of intervention can hardly be referred to as 'managing'
the market, because they essentially undermine it and prevent it from
functioning in the proper way. The CAP is different because it accepts
that the market in agricultural products should function according to
the laws of supply and demand that govern prices. It manages that
market by having a mechanism for increasing demand at a point where
prices threaten to become too low, but that is not the same as 'denying
market forces'. Price controls, for instance, seek to prevent the laws of
supply and demand from having their proper effect on prices. The CAP
accepts that prices will be governed by these laws and then makes sure
that demand increases when prices threaten to become too low.
Language used to describe the CAP often misses this point.

Particular circumstances after World War II also need to be taken
into account. There were severe food shortages after that conflict, and

towards the end of the war itself there had been famine in the Netherlands and Greece. So it was natural enough to want to find ways of boosting agricultural production. There was also a fear of large numbers of people being displaced from rural areas to the devastated towns, and that rural discontent might lead to a revival of political extremism. These were factors that influenced the decision to support the incomes of farmers, but it also needs to be emphasised that farming at any time is a risky business, in that price volatility is bound to follow from the natural unpredictability of harvests owing to fluctuating weather conditions (irrespective of the longer-term effects of climate change). Moreover, farmers cannot respond quickly to changes in the market. If it suddenly becomes clear that it would be more lucrative to be planting orchards than growing wheat, it will take several years to grow an orchard (by which time prices may have changed again). Farmers need to plan years ahead and they cannot quickly change their plans. Stable prices are therefore very important for them. To this extent the CAP was not simply a product of particular political and social circumstances (though they had an influence) but represented a recognition of what farmers needed in order to have the confidence to invest in agriculture.

Of course the decision to support farmers as the source of Europe's food meant a decision not to buy from outside the Community. There were plenty of people willing to sell food to European countries after World War II, though this would have been costly and initially might have aggravated dollar shortages while diverting precious funds from investment at home. However, it would be false to suggest that importing food was either impossible or unaffordable. It was neither, but a deliberate decision was taken to discourage such actions through a common external tariff. A political decision to avoid reliance on others as a source of something as vital as food was also part of the decision to ensure that agriculture revived in Europe after World War II. It is difficult to be confident of your independence when others can ensure that you cannot eat (one can note similar concerns in the twenty-first century over the EU's increasing dependence on external sources for supplying its energy needs).

Hence the CAP is the product of a double development (see Chapter 4), namely the abolition of internal customs duties combined with a common external tariff. There was no point in having a guaranteed minimum price for wheat throughout the European Economic Community (EEC) if Italy (for instance) was able to import it from Canada at a lower price and then perhaps sell it on to France.

Once the system was in place, it arguably worked very well at giving farmers the confidence to produce. Those who criticise its effectiveness tend to concentrate on failings such as the particular products that were supported in this way (mostly those that concern the north of Europe such as beef, lamb/mutton, milk, wheat and sugar), and the particular levels at which the floor prices were set (arguably too high, thereby making the CAP very expensive indeed over time). Such criticisms are not without justice, but they do not question the system itself, that is to say the idea of guaranteeing a minimum price so that farmers can feel secure committing themselves to expanded production levels.

The CAP ran into difficulties by the 1970s because (as its supporters liked to express it) it was a victim of its own success. Farmers were encouraged to produce more and so they did, arguably with little attention being paid to environmental considerations or animal welfare (as the example of organic farming and fishing considered later in this chapter shows, these considerations became much more important in later years). A huge surplus of food was building up, and embarrassing tales of butter mountains and wine lakes in the EU were juxtaposed with pictures of starving children in sub-Saharan Africa. And all this was costing more and more money. In order to maintain the floor prices, the EEC had to instruct governments to buy any products that were approaching the floor, for which it reimbursed them. The EEC then had to store the produce, and this often added considerably to the costs – a butter mountain has to be kept at −20°C in a refrigerator capable of containing a mountain, which is hardly a cheap option.

At first the method for dealing with overproduction was not to reduce the incentives to produce more but to find some way of using the surplus profitably (or less unprofitably than merely storing it). Perhaps, where butter was concerned, it could be sold at home, by persuading manufacturers of biscuits and cakes to buy more. Perhaps some of it could be given away; at one point it was distributed free to pensioners. Such policies were tinkering with the problem at best.

It could be sold abroad, but only at the world market price, which was lower than the price at which the EEC (and later the EU) had purchased it from the farmers. This meant that whenever the EU sold a ton of wheat or butter outside the Community it was selling it at a price that was lower than what it had paid the farmer, thus incurring a loss on every ton sold. This loss had to be covered at the end of the budget year by the governments of the member states, which were understandably sceptical about such arrangements and eventually refused to dig deeper into their pockets.

Not only was there a budgetary cost to the export of surplus food, but there were complaints that, because the EU was selling food at less than what it had paid for it, it was therefore 'dumping' its surpluses onto the market of other countries (usually developing nations). This accusation came from countries – such as Canada, Argentina and Brazil – that found themselves displaced from these markets. Agreements reached in 1995 under the auspices of the WTO placed a limit on the quantity of products that could be 'dumped' onto the markets of other countries.

A further problem of dumping was that it undermined the farmers of developing countries. When a trading company won a contract from the EU to remove surplus produce from EU territory, it would ship the produce from the EU to a developing country, where it would sell it – usually at less than the market price. In this way, the farmers of the developing country were, in effect, driven out of their own national market by imports that were rendered artificially cheaper.

We have seen that within the EEC a common external tariff to keep out imports from abroad was essential for enabling farming to develop inside the Community. So why should Egypt or other developing countries not seek to keep out cheap imports from the EU in order to support *their* farmers? What was sauce for the protectionist goose was also sauce for the protectionist gander. The EEC eventually recognised that this 'dumping' option was not acceptable.

Alternative strategies had to be found for tackling the problems of overproduction. One introduced during the 1980s was that of imposing quotas – that is, a ceiling on how much could be produced. This was done in the case of milk and (its supporters claimed) proved to be successful with farmers, the food processing sector, consumers and governments. But it was not extended to the agricultural sector generally. Then in 1988 a controversial 'set-aside' system was introduced, where farmers could take land out of production and receive a 'set-aside payment'. This was an arrangement that critics immediately pounced on as 'paying people to do nothing'. Something else would have to be done.

An arguably better option to deal with overproduction was proposed for the 1990s, namely a lowering of the floor price. Intervention to keep prices above a certain level would remain, but the level itself would fall. This would inevitably mean a drop in overall production, because farmers would calculate that it was no longer worth cultivating fields where fertility was low and so they would plough less land. The setting aside of land would naturally flow from the lowering of the floor price itself. If this were so then, even without set-aside payments, farmers would assess that cultivating less fertile land, which it had been profitable to cultivate under a higher floor price, would no longer be worth their while.

However, proposing to lower the floor price was bound to meet with powerful resistance from the farmers themselves. This was a problem that led to some very tense negotiations in the early 1990s.

The MacSharry reforms

Instrumental in steering through reforms was Ray MacSharry, the Irish commissioner for agriculture. Though it is always important to remember that commissioners are required to work for the benefit of the whole EU, and not just to promote the interests of their own country, it is clear that a commissioner will be influenced by the situation in his or her own homeland. With its (relatively) large agricultural sector and tragic events in its history such as the nineteenth-century famine, which produced a million deaths and the migration of a million others, it is unsurprising that the Irish Commissioner should have been a supporter of the principles underlying the CAP. However, support for the policy in principle did not mean that he was not alive to its limitations in practice.

MacSharry's success in reforming the CAP would have been impossible without the broader international context. The 'Uruguay

Round' of GATT (the General Agreement on Tariffs and Trade, forerunner of the WTO) had opened in 1986. For the first time, agriculture played a major part in international trade negotiations, an inclusion that inevitably meant that countries would use agricultural reform as a condition for reform in other areas. The EEC found itself confronted by the so-called Cairns Group, made up of other food exporters such as Argentina, Australia and New Zealand, which demanded that agricultural markets be liberalised. The result was stalemate.

However, the stalemate was enough to convince Germany in particular of the need for reforms, because, as a huge exporter of manufactured goods, it did not want to see other parts of the Uruguay Round put in jeopardy. As it was, German acceptance of the MacSharry reforms was just enough for them to succeed, despite their many opponents in the European Council. France was – unsurprisingly – generally opposed to reform (though the cereal growers favoured it) and the other countries had particular objections that could easily be exploited to prevent change. The UK and Germany thought that large farmers were not getting enough compensation, whereas the Mediterranean countries and Ireland felt that the small farmers were not getting enough (the meeting was chaired by the Portuguese, who held the presidency at the time). The final agreement was published under the heading 'Summary record of the Council of Agricultural Ministers (Brussels, 18 to 21 May 1992)', showing that the discussions had lasted two days (hardly very long when one considers that the Uruguay Round lasted nine years and the Doha Round also known as the Doha Development Agenda, if it is completed at all, will have lasted even longer).

Reform had been difficult because, even when it had been accepted that the floor price had to fall (cereal guaranteed prices were reduced by 35 per cent and beef guaranteed prices by 15 per cent under the reforms), farmers were bound to find life more difficult and it was generally agreed that they would need to be compensated. MacSharry accepted this and sought to compensate farmers for lower floor prices with a system of direct payments. This was a radical change, but it was not necessarily a cheap one. The question from the first moment that direct payments were introduced was *how* to manage this process of compensation and *who* should be compensated. In the end, MacSharry's reforms passed because the direct payments were set at a level that did not (immediately) reduce the overall budget of the CAP. However, what they did do was begin to tackle the problem of over-production, and in time this was bound to lead (and has led) to a reduction in cost of the CAP (at least as a proportion of the EU budget).

The problem of the budget

As mentioned in the previous section, although the MacSharry reforms were a good way of dealing with overproduction, they did not do much to reduce the size of the CAP budget. What was saved in terms of reduced floor prices was more than made up for by the direct payments (which were always higher than the Commission had originally proposed after the Council had reacted to the entreaties of agricultural interest groups). By the end of the century it was clear that there would be up to ten new member states joining the European Union, some of them with very large agricultural sectors and at the same time with low rates of productivity. In all there would be a doubling of the farm labour force and a 50 per cent increase in agricultural land. How could the CAP possibly be afforded after their entry?

Where the Cohesion Funds were concerned (see Chapter 6), it had been possible to add to the money available in order (at least partially) to cope with the demands of new members such as Spain and Portugal in 1986 or the Central and East European countries in 2004, without reducing the level of support for existing member states. But regional spending had started at 5 per cent of the EU budget and had risen to what it is today, about 45 per cent. The CAP had at one point taken up nearly three-quarters of the EU budget and – it was almost universally agreed – had to fall.

Hence further changes to the CAP had to be made. First there was the Berlin Agreement at the European Council held in Berlin in 1999 and incorporated into Agenda 2000, which was clearly focused upon coping with future enlargement – it described itself as a strategy 'for strengthening and widening the Union in the early years of the twenty-first century'. However, this did not reduce overall spending on agriculture and therefore its ability to address the problem posed by enlargement was limited. Existing members were not taking smaller slices of the cake and there were about to be more people eating (and no realistic hope of a bigger cake). The result was that when the new member states joined in 2004 they found that they had to receive smaller slices. The system of direct payments would be 'phased in' starting at 25 per cent of the level that would have been allocated to them if normal rules had applied. The candidate countries protested and won a little bit extra, but in effect had to accept that they would be joining on unequal terms with the others.

Going green?

There was a further reform in 2003, just before the enlargement of the EU to 25 states. This is known as the Fischler reform (Franz Fischler was the agriculture commissioner at the time), and was important for its introduction of the 'single payment scheme', which began the process of decoupling direct income payments from production. That was of great significance – in its own way as significant as MacSharry's reforms. Support became increasingly independent of any obligation to produce. This certainly helped to avoid problems of over-production, but it obviously raised the question of what, in that case, support *would* be based on. However, some very radical and far-reaching answers could be given to that question. Why not support more environmentally friendly farming? Why not support farming methods that took more account of animal welfare? Why not use the fact that the *quantity* of food produced was less important in order to boost the *quality* of food? The need to support farmers while no longer requiring them to produce at all costs could therefore become an opportunity for ushering in a range of new and advanced farming methods. One of these methods, organic farming, is the subject of more detailed examination later in this chapter.

Moreover, a very important statistic could be used to support the advantages of such a change of emphasis. Essential in their work, symbolic in their function and effective in their organisation though farmers may be, their number in the EU has declined, is declining and will continue to decline (currently it is at most 15 million), whereas the number who live in rural areas, while also coming down, stands at about 250 million, and the number of people concerned about the environment is probably even greater. By expanding its remit, the CAP could also expand its constituency of support.

It was therefore a very important development when at the time of Agenda 2000 it was decided to create a specifically designated area of the CAP (known as its 'second pillar') concerned with rural development. At the same time, the Directorate-General (or department) of the European Commission dealing with agriculture expanded its name to DG Agriculture and Rural Development, allowing it to be perceived as involving itself in a range of matters concerning the rural environment as a whole. The 'rural development' pillar was boosted considerably in 2005 when the Council agreed to divide the financial support for the CAP into two separate funds: the European Agricultural Guarantee Fund (EAGF) and the European Agricultural Fund for Rural Development (EAFRD). Funding could now be earmarked for dealing with wider environmental considerations.

Under the heading 'rural development policy', measures could be taken to offset carbon dioxide emissions by reforestation or to promote rural employment, for instance by encouraging 'agri-tourism' or training in rural crafts and preserving the 'rural heritage'. 'Rural development' could be linked to the energy field too, through the conversion of animal waste into biogas, thereby delivering renewable energy. The CAP was able to reinvent itself as a heading under which important employment, energy and environmental initiatives were taking place, while farmers became the 'custodians of the countryside' rather than (as some critics of the early dash for productivity suggested) its despoilers.

On the other hand, there are two important caveats. First, it has to be remembered that the budget under this 'green' pillar was and remains small, though it has the ability to grow over time (it grew under the 2008 'Health Check') and, despite being a small proportion of the budget, it still runs into billions of euros.

The second caveat may prove more important. The demarcation between the two pillars is not as clear-cut as it might seem. It needs to be stressed that member states continue to implement very different rural development policies. Belgium decided to spend half of its second pillar payments for 2007–13 on enhancing farm competitiveness (not necessarily a means of protecting the environment) and only 38 per cent on preserving the rural environment. Ireland decided to spend 10 per cent on improving farm competitiveness and 80 per cent on protecting the rural environment. Being classified under the second pillar does not necessarily guarantee that funds will be used for the sorts of purposes that are seen as part of a 'green agenda'. Moreover, there has been a tendency to see the second pillar as a useful place to raid in order to deal with shortfalls elsewhere. This is almost inevitable when there remains the problem of new member states not receiving their fair share of funding (or not feeling that they are receiving it, since there are many different ways of calculating a 'fair' distribution). Member states that joined the EU after 2003 (13 out of 28) can transfer up to 20 per cent of their rural development funds from the second pillar in order to top up their payments under the first pillar.

Other measures could be taken that would increase the number of measures supporting a green agenda beyond the funding available under the second pillar. If there was a danger of taking some of the green out of the second pillar, might there not be measures that would achieve the reverse? The key term was 'cross-compliance', meaning that direct payments would be linked to practices that might not increase output but had other benefits, for instance forestation and animal welfare. If this policy took hold, then could not the first pillar itself be given something of a green tint? Once again controversy arose in 2013 when it was argued that such a scheme would give rise to 'double funding', where farmers would get paid twice for the same thing under both pillars. Clearly, whatever system is produced for deciding how to allocate direct payments, the perception remains strong that at least some farmers are simply paid too much, whatever the criterion chosen for making such payments.

Who is a farmer?

Greater transparency has helped to highlight who exactly receives support from the CAP. Lists of the main beneficiaries were progressively published in the member states from 2004 (in 2007 the Council agreed to the full disclosure of all recipients of financial support under the CAP, and the data have been made available in all member states since the end of 2009). From as early as 2005 it was possible to discover from reading the *Guardian* (7 April 2005) or from consulting an Oxfam press release that, in the case of the UK, payments of about a quarter of a million euros each were made to the Queen of England and to a range of dukes including the billionaire Duke of Westminster (the Prince of Wales received about half this amount) – the payments being made to them as landowners, even though they could hardly be described as farmers. As Desmond Dinan puts it:

> Analysis of the date shows that, over the years, large CAP payments have gone to rich investors, wealthy aristocrats and large conglomerates, and have funded golf courses, theme parks and the like.[1]

The publication of the data showed that where the CAP was concerned there was an argument *between* countries about who should get what (an argument where the UK was vociferous in its calls for 'fairness') and an argument *within* countries about who should get what (where the UK was notoriously silent). In her discussion of the CAP, Eve Fouilleux provides an interesting table of the distribution of total direct aid for select member states in 2006.[2] It shows that the total for the UK was slightly less than half that for France (3.5 billion euros as opposed to over 7.5 billion), but whereas only 1 per cent of what the French received went in tranches of more than 200,000 euros, some 10 per cent of what the British received went in such tranches. Of course this should not be taken to mean that there are not many very large beneficiaries in France. The top 20 per cent of French farmers received about 15 times as much as the bottom 20 per cent, and in the EU-27 as a whole (the figures come from before Croatia's accession to make it 28) about three-quarters of the money went to one-quarter of the farms – the largest. Nevertheless, support for the wealthy few is most egregious in the case of the UK, and it seems intent upon continuing to be in this position.

As the quote from Dinan above makes clear, there is a problem about defining a 'farmer'. In an attempt to avoid subsidising golf courses or airports, the Commission raised the idea of restricting payments to 'active farmers', but what is an 'active' farmer? As Clémentine D'Oultremont points out, the broad definition of an 'active' farmer retained by the Commission includes anyone whose annual income from direct payments represents more than 5 per cent of their annual income from non-agricultural activities. This would mean that the Queen of England, who receives about 6 per cent of her annual budget from direct payments, must be viewed by the Commission as an 'active farmer'.[3] A further problem for the EU is that it is required under WTO rules not to link support to production. Thus it feels that 'active' farmers cannot be helped because it might suggest an unfair subsidy, and helping 'inactive' farmers might appear to be no more than a way of boosting land values and defraying the costs of royal weddings and jubilees.

A good or a bad thing?

Much is made of the undue influence exerted by powerful lobbying groups representing farmers such as the Committee of Professional Agricultural Organisations (COPA). It is certainly the case that farmers are very well organised and show a capacity for concerted action that puts to shame many other interest groups which perhaps lack the resources to paint parts of Brussels white (with milk), bring traffic to a standstill with hundreds of tractors or get a cow into a meeting in the highly security-conscious Berlaymont building, head-quarters of the Commission (presumably the cow had an official badge round its neck and showed no trace of metal when passing through the scanner). But many other organisations have powerful lobbying groups that are much less successful. It is difficult to see how farmers could have the influence they do without a general acceptance that they have a difficult and time-consuming (as well as essential) occupation that needs to be supported through action to address the problem of price volatility. There may be some truth in claims that there is a 'romantic' view of sons and daughters of the soil being inseparable from the soul of the nation in some countries, but there is a perfectly down-to-earth reason why those who labour under difficult conditions on the earth (like those who labour under the earth) are especially valued. Just as the miners were respected by those who knew that they could not keep their toes warm in front of the fire without the laborious and dangerous work of others underground, so those who work on the land are respected by people who know that, whereas almost everything else they have can be counted a luxury, food cannot be.

Nevertheless, as suggested earlier in this chapter, although there is sympathy for farmers in general and with the idea that they should receive support, there is a great deal of criticism of the way in which that support is handled and in which farmers (if they are farmers at all) receive it. The headlines about overproduction have largely gone away because Europe now is roughly in balance, producing approximately what it consumes. But the sense of unfairness in terms of who benefits and why from the CAP has not gone away. As the arguments in 2013 between national leaders over the 2014–20 budgetary framework made clear, the CAP is in danger of becoming an agent of redistribution rather than of policy. Too much analysis of the EU budget is focused on questions of how much each country 'gets', and the parcelling out of the funds in 'national envelopes' that each country then decides to apply in its own way only intensifies this perception. Compensation for farmers who lose out becomes compensation for countries that lose out. Reforms are delayed or do not take place simply because countries estimate that their slice of the cake will get smaller. The member states have solved their problem of overproduction without finding a proper method of determining who should be paid to produce.

As a result, the form that direct payments should take has never come right and does not look likely to improve in the foreseeable future. Criteria for deciding 'who gets what' have ended up supporting those who do not need it or supporting farmers for the wrong things or even supporting people who can hardly be called farmers at all. The result has been terrible publicity for what is in essence a good policy.

Probably the most positive outcome of the drive to solve the problem of overproduction was the impetus it gave (to some extent unintentionally) to measures that concentrated upon quality rather than quantity. A focus on support for greener measures in the agricultural field therefore provides a possible way forward for a dwindling, often unloved but vital section of the Community. One specific area that deserves attention is discussed in the next section.

Example: organic farming and fishing

Organic farming

Some EU policies are part of the agenda from the beginning; others enter the limelight almost by accident, as spin-off from some other policy or as a way of coping with unexpected circumstances. This chapter has tried to show how, in the early years of the CAP, the guaranteed floor price encouraged farmers to produce as much as possible by any means possible (not least because the floor price was set at too high a level). By the 1980s, it was clear that, quite apart from the costs of overproduction in terms of storage and subsidies, there was a severe environmental impact. If farmers were simply being paid to produce more, then they were unlikely to worry about how they produced it. The damage could take various forms, including soil erosion where there had been intensive crop production, pollution through the (over)use of pesticides, water pollution (from nitrate fertilisers) and unwanted changes to the rural landscape. For instance, a farmer might seek to remove hedgerows in order to create larger fields; conservationists concerned about plant, bird and insect species might take the opposite view. Another example would be the 'reclamation' of wetlands, which from another point of view represented 'destruction' (of bird habitats, for instance) rather than reclamation.

Such considerations would hardly in themselves have been likely to provoke action, even though the environment was steadily becoming a more important issue. But, for an EU struggling to find a way of ending overproduction without disappointing farmers, there were distinct advantages in supporting alternative and less 'productivist' farming methods. I was careful to point out above that the 'greening' of the farming sector in recent years can be overstated and continues to be a source of controversy. Nevertheless, the circumstances described above meant that it could proceed much further than it otherwise would have done. This section looks at one particular area in which progress has been made, namely organic farming. Because the health of the consumer is also dependent upon the well-being of the life of the seas and rivers as well as of the soil, there will also be a discussion of organic aquaculture.

The appeal of organic farming

It might seem that the interest in organic farming is simply a fad or the concern of a fringe group. Statistics suggest otherwise. In the EU as a whole there are currently over 200,000 organic farms covering some 5 per cent of agricultural land, and the number has been increasing by about 25–30 per cent a year for the last two decades. Even in parts of the EU where it has not been common (for instance Flanders, where organic crop production involves some 0.6 per cent of the total land used in agriculture and organic fruit production some 2–3 per cent), there is still a steady increase year-on-year.[4] The world's largest organic farming fair is held every February in Germany, and attracts increasing numbers of exhibitors and visitors (the 2013 fair in Nuremberg had over 40,000). The range of its displays anticipates the areas in which organic farming is likely to develop rapidly in the future (for instance, organic wines so far have been defined only in relation to the way the grapes are harvested but are now to be defined in terms of the processes used post-harvesting as well).

Unsurprisingly, given its association with several controversial policies, DG Agriculture and Rural Development makes a regular assessment of the way people access its website and was surprised to discover that the section on organic farming was the most visited (and clearly not because it was the most contentious!). Why has organic farming seen such consistent growth in recent years?

The explanation lies in the fact that organic farming has benefits in several different areas. Five clearly stand out.

First, *health*. Concerns about this have been rising for at least a generation. The 1990s, the decade when the European Food Safety Authority appeared, was also a decade when a number of 'health scares' raised public concern about food safety. In the 1980s there had been an outbreak of BSE (bovine spongiform encephalopathy, more commonly known as Mad Cow Disease) in cattle in the UK, but in the following decade fears were raised about the transmission of the disease from cattle to humans, with an outbreak of a variant of Creutzfeldt-Jakob disease, from which more than 150 people in the UK (and about 50 outside it) have so far died. The development prompted a number of bans by other member states on the import of British beef in 1996 (a few continued for several years afterwards – the French one till 2006, the Russian one till 2012). If the disease had been a 'natural' illness afflicting animals, the cases of which had unfortunately been concentrated in the UK (there have been a few cases elsewhere too), it might have been accepted that this was merely a case of bad luck. But though scientists continue to disagree over the causes, the likelihood is that the illness was a product of certain farming methods, most notably the feeding of cattle (which are herbivores) with protein supplements essentially made up of ground meat and bones, the leftovers of the slaughtering process. Infected protein supplements were also being given to very young calves. A natural protein supplement used elsewhere in the world, soybeans, was considered too expensive (and does not grow well in Europe). The illness therefore generated the feeling that many farmers were employing dangerous and 'unnatural' farming methods in order to boost their profits. Unsurprisingly, since 2008 farmers have been required to provide 100 per cent organic feed to cattle in order to be able to market their products as organic.

The use of organic feed is linked to the second area where organic farming is important, namely *animal welfare*. This involves a range of practices from access to open pasture to short transportation times and rules for procedures such as the docking of tails and control of beaks and horns. Safeguarding the welfare of the animal means not maximising production levels at all costs. For instance, organic feed rules out artificial growth boosters (these are actually excluded on any EU farm, not just organic ones); in the same way, rules concerning low stocking rates to avoid crowded conditions will limit the number of animals that can be farmed. The result is fewer but more contented animals and (its supporters say) better-quality food.

Better quality is the third attraction of organic farming. Inevitably this is to some extent a subjective feature. It is likely that food produced without chemical pesticides, giving more time for plants and livestock to grow to maturity and then be processed without the use of additives, will appeal from a culinary point of view, but you cannot 'prove' that free-range eggs taste better.

Fourth, organic farming is important in the area of *environmental protection*. Greater biodiversity is a natural consequence of organic farming methods. Using livestock manure as a fertiliser will increase the numbers of micro-organisms, not to mention creatures such as earthworms, spiders and beetles. Organic farming helps to prevent soil erosion and at the same time increases its level of water retention capacity, thereby reducing the impact of drought. Maintaining hedgerows (rather than destroying them to create larger fields) or even planting new hedges and trees is another way of maintaining biodiversity, as well as increasing the visual appeal of the agricultural landscape (though this is obviously not a practice limited to organic farmers).

Fifth, in the area of *jobs and employment*, organic farming can contribute to reversing rural depopulation trends and maintaining a skilled workforce in the countryside. Restrictions on synthetic pesticides and fertilisers and feed additives for livestock mean that organic farmers need to be able to anticipate problems that might otherwise be ignored with a 'quick synthetic fix'. This illustrates one common myth about organic farming, namely that it is 'unscientific'. Organic farming does not mean returning to the hand-plough and oxen. It is true that it may sometimes use 'natural' alternatives to certain modern methods, as when livestock manure is employed as a fertiliser. But organic farming often means *more* use of modern technology, for instance where mechanical weeders are used in place of herbicides. Moreover, it is certainly not hostile to modern science. The fine-tuning required to organise crop and pasture rotations using organic farming methods arguably requires *more* scientific analysis (for instance of the soil or of ways of encouraging natural resistance to pests and disease in crops). A lower degree of scientific competence is required on the part of those willing to bypass the necessary research through resorting to the blanket use of additives and pesticides.

Organic farming creates jobs through the particular skills it requires and increases opportunities for rural communities to continue. Rural depopulation is a problem and, because the average age of a farmer is over 60, this is likely to increase if these communities are to survive.

Figure 9. The EU label for organic produce.

The average age of organic farmers is lower and organic farms, according to a survey by the UK's Soil Association in 2006, provide on average 32 per cent more jobs per farm. Organic farms tend to be smaller and are more likely to have apprentices and trainees working for them, precisely because the scientific knowledge and practical skills required are higher than in the case of other farms.

EU support for organic farming

The most important contribution of the EU to organic farming is the application of a common standard throughout the Community, which is the necessary condition of any article being approved and so of being able to use the logo featured in Figure 9. Details can be found in the Organic Farming section of the Commission's website for DG Agriculture and Rural Development: 'Foods may only be marked as organic if at least 95% of their agricultural ingredients are organic.'[5]

Of course the precise nature of the regulations changes and they may or may not be as rigorous as some would like. The UK Soil Association, for instance, claims that its criteria for judging farming methods to be 'organic' are even more stringent than those of the EU. The point, however, is that even if the EU's regulations could be strengthened, the rules of the single market mean that a single classification can be effective throughout a market of half a billion consumers. It is a single classification that covers the range of issues described earlier – rules concerning the sorts of pesticides and fertilisers permitted, rules concerning the size of housing and exercise areas for animals, rules for animal feed and additives. It also involves a ban on the use of genetically modified organisms (GMOs) and any other products produced from them. Since 2010, any product that is produced as organic has been required to use the EU logo as a mandatory way of making it easy for consumers to recognise a product as organic. Moreover, the range of products covered by the 'organic' label has been steadily increasing. In 2012, for instance, rules for the production of organic wine were agreed. These included the use of organic methods not only for the grapes themselves but also in the post-harvesting process where, for instance, sorbic acid and desulfurication will not be allowed.

Anyone wanting to break into the organic food market from outside will be required to conform with those conditions too. Special control bodies have been created in third countries by the European Commission in order to do this, since methods are bound to vary from one country to another and it is not always easy to tell whether they are organic. Those who do not farm in a manner that satisfies these bodies will not be able to sell their produce as 'organic' within the Community. The EU is a big enough market to force other countries or regions wanting to have a share of the organic food market to increase their standards, and can arguably exercise its influence on other countries in order to make them 'raise their game' (see the discussion in Chapter 8 of how higher emissions standards will affect car manufacturers). In some cases, mutual recognition makes the process easier. In February 2012, for instance, the EU and the USA recognised each other's standards and control systems as equivalent. The US Secretary of Agriculture accepted that EU rules were equivalent to the USA's own National Organic Program. On the basis of this mutual recognition, trade in organic products between the two increased, facilitating the export of EU 'organic' products outside the Community.

The second important contribution that can be made at the EU level concerns funding, which has been available since the reform of the CAP in the 1990s. There are bound to be start-up costs for organic farmers, particularly if they are converting from other farming methods. Conventional farmers must undergo a conversion period of at least two years before they can begin producing agricultural goods that can be marketed as organic. Some farmers will want to produce both conventional and organic produce, and if they do this they must clearly separate these two operations throughout every stage of production. Here again, there will be costs involved, so that even though this is a growing market sector it will take time for profits to accrue for those who enter it.

Organic methods in aquaculture

People tend to think of organic farming in terms of plant and animal life, but it is increasingly recognised that the same principles apply to organic aquaculture.

Aquaculture (essentially the farming of fish, crustaceans, molluscs and aquatic plants) is something that the EU has so far failed to invest in: 60 per cent of the world's aquaculture comes from China and just 3 per cent from the EU. In the agricultural sphere, as this chapter has already pointed out, the EU has always placed emphasis on maintaining the independence that comes from self-reliance. In fact, something like two-thirds of the EU's crustacean and fish product consumption comes from imports. At the same time, demand for fish is likely to grow, not least because of the perceived health benefits both in terms of the heart, eyes and brain and in terms of the overall campaign against obesity.

The Common Fisheries Policy of the EU is usually discussed in terms of issues such as Total Allowable Catches and the problem of discards. The focus is upon limiting the numbers of sea creatures that are caught. Aquaculture represents a different (though not incompatible) approach to managing stocks, namely how to boost the supply of fish and crustaceans. Moreover, whereas limiting catches threatens to reduce jobs, investing in aquaculture creates them, both directly in terms of work in the aquaculture business, currently employing about 80,000 people in the EU, 90 per cent of them in small and medium-sized enterprises, and indirectly in their effect in boosting stocks, for instance through lobster hatcheries – one of the projects that has been supported by the EU in Cornwall (see Chapter 6).

From 2007 the labelling of organic foods within the EU was extended to include seafood, which is expanding from a niche to a mainstream market; in France alone, organic seafood consumption rose over 200 per cent between 2007 and 2008, making it worth 17 million euros. By 2008 there were over 100 organic aquaculture operations in the EU, accounting for about half of the 50,000 tons produced globally. Then in 2009 binding rules for aquatic production (both organic and non-organic) were agreed by member states (by QMV – the advantages of Qualified Majority Voting in this area are as clear as they were in the agricultural area when pushing through the MacSharry reforms).

Many of the rules concerning organic aquaculture are similar to those that apply to organic farming. There are limits on stocking density, rules concerning fish feed and the banning of methods such as artificial hormones to boost spawning. The advantages are similar too: better taste, better treatment of animals, respect for biodiversity and job creation. It is true that organic seafood is more expensive than non-organic (salmon produced by organic methods is about 50 per cent more costly), but part of the reason for this is the fact that organic aquaculture is more labour intensive, and the creation of jobs is a vital concern for the Community. However, probably the main incentive concerns health.

It is generally recognised that dangerous substances can get into the food chain where sea creatures are concerned and that these can be a threat to health (for instance mercury and cadmium). What is less often recognised is the fact that the agrochemicals, antibiotics and formulated feeds used in aquaculture can also be dangerous and may prove a long-term health hazard. Growing resistance to antibiotics, which has been a problem raised frequently by doctors in recent decades, is a result not just of too many antibiotics being prescribed but of what goes into our food.

That the EU generates half the world's supply of seafood produced through organic aquaculture, despite its lagging behind so much in aquaculture as a whole, testifies to its capacity for innovation and to the advantages – in this area as in that of organic farming – of EU-wide legislation prescribing the conditions to be fulfilled for organic labelling. Where producers know that consumers are willing to pay more for organic products, and that they are part of a huge single market within which strict rules apply as to what can be called organic, they have an incentive to satisfy a demand that they can see exists.

Conclusion

This chapter has been as sceptical about the current state of the direct/single payment scheme as it is clear about the correctness of the principle underlying the CAP. There were perfectly good reasons for supporting farmers after World War II. The EU is forever wishing that it did not have so much political vulnerability in the energy sector through being dependent on outside suppliers, but it does not have such problems in the even more important food sector. The support was right in principle even if badly managed in practice. Though farmers ended up producing too much, one of the spin-offs of getting them to reduce their levels of production has been to encourage more environmentally friendly methods such as organic farming.

There will always be those who persist in saying that such methods are inefficient. But what does 'inefficient' mean? Farmer A produces 200 tons of wheat per annum and farms 10 hectares. Farmer B produces 200 tons of wheat per annum and farms 5 hectares. So who is more 'efficient'? The answer may seem obvious: Farmer A because he or she produces more. On the other hand, suppose Farmer A uses a big gas-guzzling tractor and fills the soil with heavily nitrogenised fertilisers, whereas Farmer B uses organic methods, has no tractor (being one of many farmers who uses a horse) and fertilises with horse manure. Farmer B can claim to be more 'efficient' in terms of doing more for 'sustainability'. Farmer B does nothing to take away the richness of the soil for future generations, and leaves less of a carbon footprint by the way in which he or she tills the soil. This is also a very 'efficient' way of farming. It just depends where you put the emphasis and how you define the term. In the early years of the CAP, efficiency meant behaving more like Farmer A; in the later years of the CAP it has come to mean something closer to behaving like Farmer B, although it must never be presumed that organic farming means 'doing away with technology and machinery' – in many ways it is just the opposite. Has there been a loss of 'efficiency' since the beginnings of the CAP, or has there just been a change in the understanding of what 'efficiency' means?

If there is a better understanding of what 'efficiency' means today than there was 20 years ago, this is partly because of the need to find ways of supporting farmers that do not lead to costly overproduction. In the agricultural sphere, innovative approaches to production have partly reflected the way in which the direct payments system has been inadequately reformed. On the other hand, these methods (such as organic farming and organic aquaculture) can be defended in their own right, as offering a range of advantages from greater health and environmental benefits to job creation.

People no longer feel that they must support farmers at all costs in order to provide them with the most basic of all necessities, food. But even as they cease to be so concerned about the need for food as such, people have grown proportionately more concerned about the quality of the food they are receiving, its impact on their health and the implications for the state of the countryside as a whole (even in the highly urbanised EU, half of citizens live in rural areas). Becoming 'custodians of the countryside' is not a bad way for farmers to obtain public support in the future, but it has to mean that agricultural spending moves further in a direction that it has so far only just begun to explore.

6

A Europe of regions

Multi-level governance

The European Union (EU) is not just a union of 28 states; it is also a Europe of hundreds of regions. In the familiar jargon of multilevel governance, there are not only European and national 'actors' but also sub-national actors and regions, as well as sub-regional partners, including provinces and localities that may well have an important influence on the politics of the European Union. This is a reminder that power has to be seen at many levels, from the international to the local.

The United Kingdom (UK) is an example of a state that feels pressured from both above and below. One moment Westminster is looking suspiciously at Brussels, wondering about the 'surrender' (the preferred word to 'sharing') of more sovereignty; the next moment it is worrying about the effects of devolution as the Welsh Assembly aspires to be a parliament and the Scottish Parliament aspires to more powers of its own or even to be the parliament of an independent state. But similar complexities abound in other parts of the EU. Some countries, such as Belgium and Germany, have federal systems that allow for a considerable degree of autonomy at the regional level. For instance, Germany's 16 *Länder* (regions) send delegates to the country's Bundesrat, its federal council, which has the power to accept or reject laws that affect state competences (and in the course of the Bundesrat's history the definition of what affects state competences has been gradually extended) or that introduce a change to the constitution (see Chapter 3). These *Länder* are jealous guardians of regional competences and often take up seats in the Council of Ministers as well as the Committee of the Regions in Brussels.

When the principle of subsidiarity was introduced in the Maastricht Treaty, the UK saw this as the first step in being able to claw back competences from European to national level. The German *Länder*, on the other hand, saw subsidiarity as a means of guaranteeing their regional autonomy. Since 'subsidiarity' essentially means that policies should be realised at the lowest level consistent with effective implementation, both interpretations are tenable, though it is interesting that, in Germany, subsidiarity was seen as consolidating regional power, whereas the UK (despite its growing concern with the 'devolution issue') saw it in terms of 'repatriating' powers to the national level.

The beginnings: regional pawns in national politics

The attempt to deal with pockets of poverty at the regional level dates back to grants for retraining and conversion in depressed industrial areas. These grants were initially made by the Coal and Steel Community in the early 1950s. However, the presumption during these early years was that regional imbalances would be dealt with by *nations*. Commission proposals for a Regional Development Fund in the 1960s were not very favourably received, partly because the poor regions were virtually limited to the south of Italy. Things changed with the first enlargement of 1973, which brought in Ireland and the UK (though rich overall, the UK had significant pockets of poverty, particularly in Wales and Scotland). At this point regional spending began to grow, but it tended to be subservient to the demands of national politics. When a European Regional Development Fund was created in 1975, it was national issues that were at the forefront, particularly the question of how to compensate new member states (especially the UK, which was 'renegotiating' the terms of its membership under the newly elected Labour government led by Harold Wilson) for being net contributors to the Community budget.

The money in the Regional Development Fund was still a far smaller proportion of the Community budget than it is today, but what is revealing is the way in which it was given out in national quotas under the management of the Council of Ministers. Though the regions were supposed to be the beneficiaries of the fund, they were hardly in the picture at all so far as determining how the money would be spent was concerned.

In the following decades, regional spending continued to be a means of assuaging discontent at the national level. In the 1980s it was a way of dealing with existing members that feared they might be receiving less regional funding after new members had joined. Greece, Italy and France threatened to veto enlargement of the European Communities to include Spain and Portugal (these two countries acceded in 1986), for fear that this would add a large number of poorer regions that would seek access to the fund. One reaction was to create an acronym (IMP – the Integrated Mediterranean Programmes) and promise that there would be money attached to it. But the simplest way of allaying their fears, if there were more people clamouring for a place at the table, was to increase the size of the table. So funding at regional level began to grow.

Regional policy contributed not only to the process of enlargement but also to the process of economic integration that went with it, specifically in the form of the Single European Act and its goal of completing a 'single market' by 1992. Once again, the general approach was one of using regional spending in order to help those that found it difficult to cope. The free market principle of removing barriers to trade was accompanied by measures to help those that would (it was accepted) be vulnerable once those barriers were down. Thus the rigours of the single market would apply, but there would be a cushion for those regions with natural handicaps and those whose post-industrial transition made it difficult for them to compete. This was the policy pursued by Jacques Delors as president of the Commission in the late 1980s. He highlighted a report by Italian economist Tommaso Padoa-Schioppa published in 1987 which argued that market liberalisation would aggravate regional imbalances, in order to push for more regional spending. By 1992 (the year that had been set as a target for completing the single market), what were by then called

Structural Funds were taking 25 per cent of the EU budget, and Delors was talking about a 'second Marshall Plan' for Europe.

In the 1990s the use of regional funds as a lubricant for further enlargement continued. The first three members to join in the post-communist era were Austria, Finland and Sweden. In anticipation of the latter two joining (and perhaps in the expectancy that Norway's second referendum on joining the European Union would yield a 'Yes' vote; instead it yielded a slightly less emphatic 'No' than the one 20 years earlier), a new category was created for regional funding based on sparsely populated areas.

At the same time, a number of existing members were beginning to concern themselves with the implications of adopting a single currency. Spain, Portugal, Greece and Ireland were threatening to veto the Maastricht Treaty. The provision of more generous regional spending in the form of a Cohesion Fund helped to ease the creation of Economic and Monetary Union, just as a decade earlier the provision of Structural Funds had placated those who feared the completion of the internal market.

The importance of regional policy as a way of acclimatising member states to difficult changes could be seen at work again at the turn of the century, when the EU struggled to manage the impact of ten new members joining the Union in one fell swoop. Concern was voiced by the 15 existing members of the EU, which anticipated up to 80 million new citizens, the vast majority of them from poorer regions. At the same time, the new member states expected to be helped up the ladder by the funding that had helped existing member states. EU leaders (now 25 of them) met in Dublin to mark the accession of ten new members on 1 May 2004, during the Irish presidency. Though the location was a coincidence of timing, the new members were very aware of the example of Ireland, once one of the poorest parts of the Community and more recently one of the most prosperous. Though there were many reasons for that transition from poverty to prosperity in the second half of the twentieth century (and of course during the recent economic crisis new problems have arisen), the example of the 'Celtic tiger' was one that many of these new states hoped to emulate.

When decisions on the new seven-year budget for 2007–13 came to be made in the following year, the size of the funding agreed for what was now called 'cohesion policy', though less than the Commission wanted, was a considerable sum, amounting to about 50 billion euros per year. Indeed, by 2011 the various funds aiming at redressing regional inequalities had become the largest slice of the EU budget, at last exceeding the other large claimant upon EU funds (and traditionally the one that took most of the money), agriculture (or as it was now called agriculture and rural development).

Throughout the decades, then, regional spending has proved a useful tool for the purpose of steering recalcitrant states through the choppy waters of enlargement and economic integration. But can this really be done – particularly as regional spending has been rising to become the largest item in the EU budget – without measures to increase the importance of the regional level within the institutions of the EU itself?

The development of the decision-making framework

Even if actions in the field of regional spending were sometimes no more than a case of buying off the discontented at national level, they needed a framework. The Single European Act, signed in 1986 in the year that Spain and Portugal acceded, made regional policy a Community competence and declared that reducing disparities between regions was part of the process of 'strengthening social and economic cohesion'. At the same time, the steady provision of more funds for regional spending was accompanied by a building up of the regions as 'active players', particularly through the creation of a new institution, the Committee of the Regions, by the Maastricht Treaty (ratified in 1993). As one of the two major consultative committees (alongside the much older Economic and Social Committee), it has a merely consultative role (in areas such as health, culture, education and trans-European networks), but institutions that have to be consulted do exercise power in terms of being able to highlight issues and delay decisions. The 2007 Treaty of Lisbon makes it legally binding on the Commission, the Council and the Parliament to consult the Committee of the Regions when making laws that have a regional impact. Moreover, successive treaties have extended the areas where such an impact is seen to exist and therefore where the Committee has to be consulted. The 1997 Treaty of Amsterdam added the environment and transport to the list, and the Lisbon Treaty added energy and climate change.

The Committee of the Regions now has 353 members who serve a five-year term (nine were added in July 2013 with the accession of Croatia as the 28th member of the EU), with an equal number of 'alternate members', essentially understudies who can stand in when full members are unable to attend. They are nominated by member states – each country chooses how it selects its members, and it is expected that they will reflect a regional balance. They have to be people holding elected office or accountable to an elected assembly, and, if they lose office in their home city or region, they automatically cease to be on the Committee of the Regions.

The new Committee had aspirations for an important role in the allocation and implementation of Structural Funds, ensuring that there was not only a larger pot of money for the regions but a greater push in the direction of involving sub-national institutions in Community policy making. This continues to be emphasised today. After all, talk of a 'more integrated' approach (the buzzword as the difficult decisions over funding for the 2014–20 budgetary period were taken in 2013) could be interpreted in many ways. Not that the idea of being integrated was anything new – integrated, three-fund single programming documents had existed in 1994–9 but were scrapped for 2000–6. The constant desire to innovate is often satisfied only by making the pendulum swing back and forth; thus innovation is achieved only on condition of there never being any real change.

One way of understanding 'more integrated' is to talk about how all the different programmes under which regional funding takes place – the European Regional Development Fund (ERDF), the European Social Fund (ESF), the Cohesion Fund, the European Agricultural Fund for Regional Development (EAFRD) and the European Maritime and Fisheries Fund (EMFF) – need to be applied within a 'Common Strategic Framework' (CSF). But how is this going to happen? A CSF will add up to very little if it does not involve implementation through a partnership between the EU, member states and regions. Hence this 'more integrated approach' everyone is talking about must mean more regional involvement.

Politically, it may prove a useful way of pressurising national governments from above and below at the same time. As said at the beginning of this chapter, 'subsidiarity' might mean more say at the national level to a UK government and more say for the regions to a German government. The growing power of 'sub-national' actors has therefore opened up a second front, challenging member states from below as well as from above. If member states choose to complain about the 'democratic deficit', the supranational institutions can offer to bring the regions into play more overtly, as those that are 'closest to the people'. Moreover, once the regions are involved through the creation of bodies such as the Committee of the Regions, the system develops its own dynamic. Those with a strong sense of identity at the sub-national level (such as Wales, Scotland or Catalonia) find that they are able to express and develop these regional identities on the European stage.

The Treaty of Maastricht was careful to say that at meetings of the EU Council each state would have a 'representative at ministerial level', but this could in theory allow a minister for a regional government to represent the state at the meeting. For 'federal' states such as Austria, Germany and Belgium this is the norm, but other states have used it on occasion too – the UK, for example, with its own particular form of 'internal union'. For instance, Wales led for the UK in the Council of Culture Ministers under the last UK presidency and Welsh can now be used in Council so long as the Welsh government covers the cost. Slogans such as 'unity in diversity', which can be applied in order to call for a respecting of national differences at EU level, can also be used in order to call for a respecting of regional differences at national level.

The current situation

In 2013, decisions were finally reached on the multi-annual budgetary framework for 2014–20. Though there were a lot of headlines about the first ever overall cut in the EU budget, there was a great deal of continuity with the 2007–13 budgetary framework. The pie had become (very) slightly smaller, but the pieces were still divided up in much the way they had been. EU expenditure continues to be dominated by what Menon calls 'two essentially redistributive programmes – Cohesion Policy and the Common Agricultural Policy'.[1]

As we have seen from tracking the development of regional spending, when 28 heads of state get together to decide a budget, they tend to look at it in national terms so as to see 'what's in it for us'. They examine the list of beneficiaries from direct payments under the Common Agricultural Policy and they look at the list of poorer regions in their country and work out how much they are going to get. The result is that they tend to reject or underfund proposals that do not make it clear 'who benefits'. The Commission is desperately keen to see the Europe 2020 Agenda (and the Lisbon Agenda before it) advanced by spending in areas such as research and development (R&D), but if this means a pot of money for which scientists, for instance, have to bid competitively, there is no clear understanding in national terms of 'who benefits' and it is not an area of the EU budget that can get carved up between national clients (see Chapter 8).

The result is that there continues to be, for 2014–20, a relatively large pot of money in two areas dealt with in some detail by this book (regional policy and agriculture) but much less in areas such as research, innovation and technological development. Though the money allocated in these other areas did amount to an increase, it did not affect the way in which the budget continues to be dominated by the two 'giants'. The political price that the UK (in particular) paid for being able to go home in early 2013 saying it had made cuts was a failure to make any dent in the overall pattern of EU spending.

Certainly this book argues that the two dominant budget areas reflect some very important and necessary spending. But there is no doubt that other budget areas receive insufficient funding and that the EU has been unable to change its priorities for funding sufficiently to give the Europe 2020 Strategy a reasonable chance of success. Perhaps for this very reason the jargon about supporting innovation, entrepreneurship and creativity has been loaded onto regional funding as a way of compensating for the lack of financial support elsewhere. Cohesion Policy is therefore talked about as a key 'delivery mechanism' for the Europe 2020 Strategy and the creation of an 'Innovation Union' – but this is partly because other delivery mechanisms, which cannot be parcelled out among member states in the way that 'help for poorer regions' can be, have been left undeveloped. It is clear that, having decided to continue under-funding areas such as R&D, the EU will seek to mitigate the effects of this by making as many projects as possible in its various regional spending programmes research-and-development oriented. The shape of the spending in Cornwall and the Scilly Isles (see the example below) already reflects this approach and this will influence the way in which the EU implements its programme for 2014–20.

Two very important principles continue to apply to the programmes funded under what is now the CSF. One is 'additionality', which means that the region (with government departments) must always supply a proportion of the funding (25–50 per cent). Waste and corruption are much less likely when the region itself is a 'stakeholder'. The other important principle is that of multi-annual funding, which allows the Commission to release money in tranches and have regular assessments. It is crucial for this purpose that there is a seven-year multi-annual financial framework facilitating projects that involve funding over the best part of a decade. Seven-year budgetary programmes allow the EU to plan ahead more than member states can with budgetary frameworks limited by the four- or five-year lifetime (at most) of a government. Though the process of agreeing such a budgetary framework for 2014–20 took several gruelling meetings between heads of state in 2012 and 2013, and then required the consent of the European Parliament, throwing up a lot of headlines about whether agreement would finally be reached, the result once the dust had settled was (however disappointing) a spending framework to take the EU up to 2021. This meant that it could go ahead confidently with projects that might take up to seven years to complete.

The 2014–20 budgetary framework is heavily dosed with jargon about 'synergies', 'multilevel competence' and 'complementary inter-vention'. As mentioned earlier, regional funding may have begun (and to some extent has continued) as a fund for smoothing the feathers of those who were discontented at the national level, but in terms of implementation it has no alternative to bringing the sub-national 'players' into the picture.

As to the nature of the programmes supported, much can be learned from looking at an example – hence the discussion of Cornwall and the Scilly Isles in the next section. There are three categories within the 2014–20 budgetary framework. There are the 'less developed regions', where GDP per head remains at less than 75 per cent of the EU average. Cornwall and the Scilly Isles currently remain in that category. Then there are regions where GDP per head lies between 75 and 90 per cent, and which are classified as 'transition' (to greater levels of development, one hopes) regions – quite a bit of the North of England comes into this category. After all, the whole point of such funding is to enable poorer regions to approach the EU average. The rest are labelled 'more developed' regions. However, the focus in the example in the next section will remain exclusively on England's least developed region.

The Commission is always keen to prevent the perception that these programmes are simple 'handouts', as if an EU lorry full of life's essentials were to drop vital necessities off in poorer areas like the arrival of a food convoy. The emphasis (particularly in the light of the cuts made in areas that might otherwise stimulate such developments) is upon building competitiveness, helping the workforce to adapt to new economic conditions and supporting local businesses. The belief seems to be that, with a little bit of carefully targeted investment, poorer regions can achieve lift-off, and the new budgetary framework, for reasons already discussed, represents if anything an intensification of the 'innovation, investment, research and development' theme. Life is not always that simple. But Cornwall is an example of how it can be at least partially successful.

Example: Cornwall and the Isles of Scilly

There was a time when this extreme south-western part of the UK was a driving force of the British industrial revolution. Silver (and later tin) mining in the area date from the early modern period (when mining benefited from the ability of gunpowder to blast open granite rock and facilitate opencast mining), but production of tin and copper (and to some extent lead) reached its apogee in the nineteenth century, when at one point there were 600 steam engines working in Cornwall. Steam engines, it needs to remembered, were initially developed in order to pump water out of mines and the people who developed them were often mining engineers. It is arguable that the first steam locomotive was pioneered by a Cornish mining engineer, Richard Trevithick, though the 'puffing devil' did not manage to do much more than take a take a few people through the streets of Camborne on Christmas Eve in 1801.

Another famous scientist/inventor from Cornwall during this period was Humphrey Davy, known above all for his invention of the miners' safety lamp, which by surrounding the lamp's flame in gauze prevented it from igniting the methane gas that used to gather inside the mines. Scientists such as Davy and Trevithick in turn attracted many industrialists from outside the region; for example, the Scottish engineer William Murdoch was attracted by what at the time was seen as the area's 'cutting-edge' technology in steam engines.

Such pre-eminence was not to last. By the end of the nineteenth century, foreign competition was depressing the prices of both tin and copper and the mines rapidly ceased production – 100 years later there was only one working mine left at South Crofty. This finally closed in 2008 and what remained of the industry was parcelled up and turned into an 'industrial heritage site' appealing to tourists. Some miners went overseas to use their skills; most remained unemployed. Though there are still some industries related to mining in Cornwall (particularly china clay pits), it is clear that there will never be the levels of employment in this area seen when it was one of the most affluent parts of Britain.

Another industry that has seen rapid decline in the region is fishing. Cornwall had a huge pilchard industry in the nineteenth century. There was such an abundance of the fish that lookouts were paid to watch out for shoals of fish from the clifftops, but overfishing took its toll. Levels of fishing are now managed through an EU quota system, with levels heavily influenced by advice from the International Council for the Exploration of the Sea. Cornish fishers accuse the body of underestimating fish stocks, but relations have improved since they started taking the scientists out to sea on their boats and 'showing' them what fish there were. At the same time, Cornwall has diversified its fishing industry. There are far more species of fish in the waters around Cornwall than there are in the colder North Sea, and, being a narrow isthmus, the county has plenty of ports where the fish can be landed and handled quickly while fresh. Cornish fishers now bring in species such as monkfish, crab and lobster (the latter two often sold to France). Though there are barely 1,000 people left working full time on the boats, it must be remembered that, for every one at sea, there are about four jobs on land processing and marketing the catches.

Though this is clearly another industry that is not going to maintain the levels of employment it had 100 years ago, more can be done than simply limit catches and diversify the species that are caught. Measures can also be taken to increase supply through aquaculture (see Chapter 5). The ERDF supported a National Lobster Hatchery in Padstow in Cornwall (it is the only one in England; there is another in Scotland close to Orkney). Lobster is the most valuable sea creature caught in the UK (lobster catches are currently worth about 40 million euros annually), and unsurprisingly this means a threat to stocks (there is a similar threat elsewhere in the EU, for instance in the Mediterranean). However, a great deal can be done through hatcheries. A female lobster carries about 20,000 eggs in the abdomen, of which only one on average survives in the wild. In the hatchery, that survival rate can be increased a thousand-fold. In 2011, 32,000 juvenile lobsters (by which time they were stroppy adolescents with a much increased chance of making predators think twice) were released into the sea from the Cornwall hatchery, and the expectation is that this figure will be doubled in 2013. Whereas restricting catches reduces jobs, aquaculture creates them, both directly in the hatchery itself and indirectly through boosting supplies for the fishing industry. The hatchery also attracts visitors (40,000 in 2012) and has important links with marine conservation and scientific research, so it ticks boxes where education, research and tourism are concerned.

Cornwall has faced a problem of how to adjust to the 'post-industrial' era which bears some similarities to the problems experienced in parts of Wales, Scotland and the North of England (indeed it is always simplistic to talk of a 'north–south' divide in terms of wealth and poverty in the UK; a less simplistic – though still limited – description would talk of a large wealthy bloc in London and the South-East and increasing poverty the further away you move from that part of the UK). Up until 1999, the county had been part of a shared regional programme with the neighbouring county of Devon, but during the mid-1990s a team led by the former Chief Executive John Mills made the push for separate 'Objective One' designation. Cornwall's GDP of 72 per cent of the EU-15 average was averaged up by Devon's more affluent economy of around 86 per cent. The resulting average would be too high for 'Objective One' funding (the main criterion for which is that GDP per head should be less than 75 per cent of the EU average). After 15 months of lobbying, the Cornish arguments were finally accepted. In 2000, the area covering Cornwall and the Scilly Isles (a small group of islands with a population of around 2,000 located about 30 miles from the south-western tip of Cornwall) was classified by the EU as an Objective One region. As a result, Cornwall's 2000–6 allocation rose to a countywide 700 million euros, larger in size than the previous shared programme for Devon, Cornwall and west Somerset!

In 2007, when the next round of EU funding allocations was made, the area was awarded 'convergence status', the main criterion for which was again GDP per head less than 75 per cent of the EU average (Cornwall and the Scilly Isles were judged to be at 70 per cent). This made available about 600 million euros for the 2007–13 budgetary period. Hence something over 1 billion euros had been allocated during the first decade and more of the twenty-first century. Attention is now being paid to the next budgetary period, that of 2014–20.

What has been done during this period as a result of (or at least with the assistance of) European funding? Fortunately the funding has not all been funnelled into the service industries (as so often is the case with 'post-industrial' parts of the world). Cornwall has always been a popular tourist destination, particularly for those wanting to go as far from London as they can without going 'abroad' (it has a population of about half a million, but over 5 million visitors per annum). That could have been made the basis of a possible 'regeneration' strategy: support the tourist industry, reopen a mine or two as an industrial heritage site, brand a rundown area of east Cornwall the 'gateway to the Cornish Riviera' and do up a few picturesque villages with moth-balled fishing industries as ideal holiday destinations for jaded Londoners with an undiscovered longing for the sea. However, there would be shortcomings in such a policy, certainly if it were the only approach taken. Tourism would have generated more seasonal than full-time jobs, the jobs would have been more unskilled than skilled and they would have been in a notoriously badly paid sector of the economy. It is always a mistake to think that employment is an automatic way out of poverty. Moreover, Cornwall would have been vulnerable to economic developments outside its control. Holidaymakers who poured into Cornwall during a recession might return to the continent after it was over, making the county paradoxically a victim of economic recovery and reopening the gaps in income between this region and the rest of the UK.

The emphasis of the EU is more upon what its Europe 2020 Strategy calls 'smart, sustainable and inclusive' growth. Indeed, the Commission's intention, as it made clear when presenting its proposals for the budgetary framework of 2014–20, was to make the funding for this seven-year period contribute to achieving the quantified targets set out in the Europe 2020 Strategy (I have already mentioned why this approach has become even stronger since the budgetary framework was finally decided in 2013). 'Smart' growth means that the focus is upon investment in education, research and innovation. 'Sustainable' refers to the agenda discussed in Chapter 8, the targets being the '20:20:20 by 2020' ones related to reduced energy consumption and greenhouse gas emissions and the promotion of renewable energy. 'Inclusive' means boosting employment (to 75 per cent of the workforce) and reducing poverty (by 20 million). As pointed out in the previous paragraph, these targets are not necessarily the same – people may be in work and in poverty at the same time, particularly in unskilled and part-time jobs associated with much of the tourism business.

In many of these areas, the UK as a whole is lacking. To remind ourselves of the figures that needed to be worked on in the second decade of the twenty-first century: R&D in the UK stood at 1.77 per cent in 2010 (the target by 2020: 3 per cent). The UK's national target under the EU's climate and energy package – a 34 per cent reduction in greenhouse gas emissions from 1990 levels by 2020 – stood in 2010 at a reduction of 19.1 per cent. The amount of energy the UK as a whole obtained from renewables was much lower than its target for 2020:

the target for 2020 is 15 per cent, whereas the level reached in 2010 was 2.9 per cent, up from 1.3 per cent in 2005. Investment in these areas can therefore help not only Cornwall but the country itself in areas where it is lagging behind its targets. Moreover, whereas the R&D target is not binding, the other two are.

Since this is the emphasis of European funding, how has it affected Cornwall? The EU's emphasis upon job creation in innovative and highly skilled areas of the economy has been particularly useful for this region, as has the stress upon environmental impact. Cornwall is an ideal location in which to combine these two. Its long coastline is ideal for wind and wave energy, its granite backbone is perfect for geothermal energy, its (relatively) sunny climate makes it suitable for solar energy and its position at the south-west tip of England has enabled it to develop a distinctive ecosystem. Moreover (again partly because of its location), it is an area with a distinctive character that has contributed to a high level of cooperation between business, research and academic groups. This should not be exaggerated. It may have its own flag and its own language, but it is still very much a part of the UK. Even so, a strong sense of community identity helps 'connectivity'.

The hope, where Cornwall is concerned, is that this part of the UK might once again be placed in the industrial forefront by encouraging investment in the areas just described, such as renewable energy. As said, this is an area where the UK as a whole is far behind in meeting its targets for 2020 and at the same time it is where Cornwall's natural strengths lie.

Wave energy is a good example, because Cornwall juts out into the Atlantic and therefore (as every surfer knows) faces the prevailing western oceanic swell. European funding has supported the development of Wave Hub, a site of 8 square kilometres located on the sea bed about 55 metres below the surface of the Atlantic some 20 kilometres off the north coast of Cornwall (north-east of St Ives). On the seabed are some electrical hubs (in lay terms, sockets into which wave generation devices can be plugged); 25 kilometres of undersea cable then provide a link to the UK grid. Developments at Wave Hub are supported by a research institute (Peninsula Research Institute for Marine Renewable Energy) made up of about 60 academics from the

Figure 10. Hot Rocks.

universities of Exeter and Plymouth, which both have courses in renewable energy, in the neighbouring county of Devon. There is also an important wave energy test site in Cornwall's Falmouth Bay, developed for industry to test scale models of wave energy devices. Not only is this important for bearing in mind the close partnership between the scientific community and industry, and for recognising how many jobs, real and potential, are involved in the renewable energy sector, but it serves as a reminder that the technology is constantly developing and that figures for what is or is not obtainable from renewable energy sources (as well as for the costs of doing so) are under constant revision. A renewable energy source that is not cost effective today may well become so tomorrow.

Another important source of energy in which Cornwall has a pioneering role is deep geothermal. At the Rosemanowes project near Penryn in Cornwall (see Figure 10), scientists and engineers began work in the 1970s, funded by the UK Department of Energy and the European Economic Community, on extracting heat from deep within the rocks. Heat is caused by the radioactive decay of minerals within the granite, and Cornwall's 'granite spine' means that the heat is brought relatively close to the surface, cutting the cost of drilling.

In the early 1990s the Rosemanowes team worked on a European-funded geothermal (or 'hot dry rocks') project in Soultz-sous-Forêts in France which produced the first commercial deep geothermal plant in Europe. Some of the same team are now working with Cornwall's Eden Project to finish what was started at Rosemanowes some 20 years ago. The partnership between the Eden Project and a Penzance-based company called EGS (engineered geothermal system) Energy is of course on a small scale. Drilling is located in one of the Eden Project's car parks. Cornwall's first geothermal energy plant will provide enough energy for about 3,000 households. But, once again, it is important to be clear that pioneering work with new technologies is bound to be on a small scale. Though it is always best not to anticipate too much where renewable energy is concerned, geothermal energy has the potential to achieve much more. In April 2013, Balfour Beatty and Parsons Brinckerhoff, two global companies, joined the Eden Deep Geothermal Plant project. On the other hand, the same month saw the UK government withdraw its support from another deep geothermal project in west Cornwall on the grounds that it had failed to attract sufficient private investment.

Nevertheless, such projects respond to an inescapable need for new energy sources that the UK government cannot escape. As said, the UK must have 15 per cent of its energy from renewable sources by 2020; it must reduce its CO_2 emissions by 34 per cent by 2020. At the same time, the technology of the seabed and of 'hot dry rocks' provides a twenty-first-century equivalent to what was once the leading underground technology of those working to bring tin and copper out of the earth. This would enable Cornwall to be 'cutting edge' again (though the phrase is so overused that it deserves a ban), at the forefront of a new industrial revolution.

Jargon phrases such as 'skills base' and 'innovation agenda' describe this belief that new forms of energy will require pioneering research by the Davys and Trevithicks of the twenty-first century and will generate work in sufficient numbers to offset some of the losses from traditional industry (there were about 9,000 jobs in deep geothermal in Germany alone by 2013). To do that there must be linkage between scientific research and industrial applications, and this is another emphasis of EU regional funding. Much of it has been built around the Combined

Universities project, which brings together five further and higher education institutions: two that have already been mentioned, the universities of Plymouth and Exeter in the neighbouring country of Devon, and three in Cornwall itself. Cooperation between these five institutions made it possible for projects to be developed that would have been beyond the capacity of any one of them.

Linked to the universities are various centres that have been specifically created to promote businesses. The Environment and Sustainability Institute, for instance, is an offshoot of the University of Exeter located in its Cornwall campus near Falmouth. The institute cost £30 million to get off the ground, £23 million coming from the ERDF and £7 million from the South-West Regional Development Authority (unfortunately, Regional Development Authorities have since ceased to exist). A group of about 100 academics and researchers study the impact of environmental change and at the same time maintain close contacts with local enterprises. Though the jargon used to describe this can be overwhelming (the institute has a team of 'knowledge exchange managers' who busy themselves with 'knowledge transfer projects'), the practical benefits are clear. Local enterprises look to such institutes for suggestions, and the focus of researchers has to be upon the needs of the businesses around them. The sustainability agenda is the key to much of its work. For instance, Cornwall's 600 dairy farmers are interested in new techniques for the disposal of slurry or the use of biogas (Sir Humphrey Davy comes in again here – he was the first to discover in 1808 that methane was present in gases produced by cattle manure, and the University of Exeter devised a system for using a septic tank in order to produce gas lighting in 1895). The National Lobster Hatchery is seeking advice on its restocking programme. The Kraft Maus project has developed portable renewable power systems using both wind and solar energy that are not connected to any grid, which interests the military because military forces often have to operate in remote locations.

Similar partnerships can be found at other centres that have received support from European funding, such as the Academy for Innovation & Research (AIR), home of business and research collaboration at Falmouth University, and Cornwall's three 'innovation centres', described as 'business acceleration facilities'.

One of the biggest projects being developed in Cornwall is that of an 'eco-town', based on six sites that were formerly used for china clay mining. The plan is to build over 5,000 homes (using clay waste materials in the construction process), with at least 40 per cent being low cost and making use of renewable energy. One of the advantages of 'sustainable living' is that energy costs tend to be low so that there is a benefit in terms of reducing poverty levels; and, as pointed out in Chapter 8, energy prices started to rise worryingly during 2013, and there is every sign that they will be an important issue in UK politics in the years to come.

There is often talk of the need for infrastructure improvements in the context of regional regeneration, and there has been some support in terms of improving roads and part of the main railway line that is still single-track, but Cornwall will always be several hours away from London by car or train (it takes about as long to get to London from Penzance as it does from Edinburgh). Therefore the focus in terms of infrastructure is on the roll-out of superfast broadband rather than on physical infrastructure. As for its distance from London, this has had some positive spin-off in terms of encouraging the region to connect with similar regions in other countries and form a kind of 'coalition of the peripheries' in order to assert its identity. Such connections enable Cornwall to link up with other parts of the EU and help to compensate for some of its difficulties in connecting with the rest of the UK. For instance, there is close cooperation (through a grand-sounding Protocol of Cooperation – *Protocole de coopération*) with Finistère in Brittany, based on the cultural links between the two areas (Celtic roots, the Cornish and Breton languages) and their similar status both as peripheral maritime regions and as areas that are heavily reliant on the tourism industry.

Such linkages should be borne in mind by visitors from elsewhere in the UK as they cross the Tamar and point in wry amusement at a few fishing vessels bobbing up and down on the Saltash side of the river, sporting the Cornish flag of a black cross on a white background. What may surprise them, as they wait to be further amused by the signs in the occasional supermarket that are in Cornish as well as English, is not the amount of Cornish they hear (in reality still very little) but the amount of French. Cornwall may be becoming more 'Cornish', but it is also becoming more European.

Conclusion

The regions introduced a new dynamic into European policy making and the complexities of multi-level governance. They did so partly by accident, as an indirect result of the growing use of regionally targeted funding in order to appease national discontent. Nevertheless, the results are fascinating as the Community and regional levels find themselves allied against the national, although in reality the different levels form various alliances with and against one another. Of course, the implications vary according to the strength of the sub-national actor involved. This chapter has deliberately avoided looking at sub-national regions in which the prospect of independent statehood is being seriously discussed, such as Scotland and Catalonia. Instead it has looked at a part of the UK where (with due respect to Mebyon Kernow, the Party for Cornwall) independence is not an option but where a European identity has some significance.

The particular ways in which the European Union, the UK and Cornwall itself have chosen to support the development of this, the poorest region of England, have focused on providing skilled rather than unskilled work. They emphasise developments in the energy and environmental areas that play to Cornwall's strengths and also enable it to help the country as a whole meet important environmental targets. They provide work that can be seen as representing a form of continuity with Cornwall's industrial past. And they play on its sense of identity as a way of getting business, research and academic institutes and civic organisations to work in partnership.

It would be wrong to say that EU funding has 'pulled Cornwall out of poverty'. It has not. GDP per head is still below 75 per cent of the EU average (it has not yet officially reached the 'transition' status of 75–90 per cent). Of course it could be argued that, without such funding, Cornwall's position would be even worse, but what is clear is that EU funding alone cannot provide the answer to a region's problems. Intelligent assistance has to come at every level. Whether Cornwall's continuing difficulties come from the inadequacies of support at the EU level or inadequacies at the national level (or both) is a matter of debate. This chapter has merely tried to describe some of the projects that have been supported in the region and the way in which they form part of an overall EU strategy to help it recover some of the assets that it once enjoyed as an industrial pioneer.

7

External relations

This chapter is entitled 'External relations' rather than, for instance, 'Is there an EU foreign policy?' or 'Will there ever be an EU army?' because the European Union tries to link many aspects of external relations together, both those that involve so-called hard power and those that involve 'soft power'. The preferred EU strategy is to be comprehensive in its approach to external relations. This will be made clear in terms of a particular example. First, however, it is essential to highlight some of the context and historical background.

The dangers of overreach in the defence field

There has been an understandable wariness about anything that might appear too ambitious in terms of advancing integration in the area of foreign and defence policy. Member states are aware of the fact that it was the attempt to create a European Defence Community in the 1950s, the so-called Pleven Plan of 1954 (see Chapter 2), that nearly scuppered the whole sovereignty-sharing enterprise that had begun with the Coal and Steel Community. A year later, at Messina in Sicily, the member states were seen to have scuttled back to the economic arena when their ambitions turned to the creation of the European Economic Community and the European Atomic Energy Community, which came to fruition in the Treaties of Rome. A common Defence Community was out; a Common Market was in.

It is true that there were particular circumstances that gave rise to the Pleven Plan. The Six needed a solution to the problem of how to rearm Germany as part of a credible defence strategy against what was increasingly being perceived as the Soviet threat without letting a rearmed Germany become – as it had become in the past – a danger to European security. Allowing Germany to rearm under the auspices of a supranational institution appeared to be one possible solution. There were also particular circumstances leading to the rejection of the plan, most notably growing confidence in an enduring US commitment to the defence of Western Europe through NATO. Nevertheless, these circumstances did not alter the feeling that a breakthrough in managing the relations between nation-states had nearly been lost through vaulting ambition o'erleaping itself. The message seemed to be that there were areas where sovereignty-sharing was acceptable and areas where it was not. Defence was one area where it was not.

However, there were (and are) strong reasons for developing an effective EU programme in the sphere of external relations. The Union was (and is) often embarrassed by criticism of its perceived inadequacies in the foreign policy arena. The idea of the EU being 'an economic giant, a political dwarf and a military worm' (attributed to Mark Eyskens, the Belgian foreign minister at the time of the Gulf War, and possibly a way of saying that the EU was like Belgium itself) is often bandied about. So is the famous remark by Henry Kissinger, 'Who do I call if I want to call Europe?', which he never actually made but which is associated with the lack of a common foreign policy. Kissinger was national security adviser and secretary of state with a key role in US foreign policy from 1969 to 1977 (serving under both Presidents Nixon and Ford). The apocryphal phone story (which is often taken out of the 1970s and applied 40 years later) is a way of saying not only that there is no one person who can be contacted for information on EU foreign policy positions but that a different reply might be forthcoming from the phones picked up in London, Paris, Berlin and so on.

As in other areas we have discussed, it is important to approach such criticisms without presuming that problems can simply be solved by turning the EU into a single state (with one number to ring, one army to make it a military giant and one government to determine a clear foreign policy position) or into nothing more than several states that have to be telephoned in turn, with a clear understanding that their separate armies may be deployed in different ways or not at all. As a unique entity, the EU will have a unique way of dealing with external relations.

From World War II to the years of détente

Many West European countries recognised from the moment that World War II ended that they needed to work together in foreign policy. The Treaty of Dunkirk between the UK and France in 1947 was seen as representing a vital commitment by the UK to the defence of the mainland (at that time Germany was considered the most dangerous potential aggressor). The following year, the Treaty of Brussels extended this agreement to include the Benelux countries (Belgium, the Netherlands and Luxembourg). But, as Chapter 2 pointed out, the 'big prize' so far as West European security was concerned was a commitment by the USA to its defence. This was the whale that Ernest Bevin's sprats were set to catch. Hence the formation of NATO in 1949 tended to dwarf these earlier agreements, as it did the agreement to form their successor, the Western European Union (WEU).

The WEU added Germany and Italy, the 'axis' powers during World War II, to the countries that had signed the Treaty of Brussels, and might have been seen as a remarkable coming together of former opponents in order to form a united response to a common threat from the East. But it arose out of the crisis surrounding the rejection of the European Defence Community mentioned in the previous section. This almost destroyed the sovereignty-sharing initiative that was the very heart of the 'European project', and so the WEU was inevitably seen as a hasty reaction to an emergency.

Ironically, the WEU (which came into force in 1955) brought about precisely what France wished to avoid through the Pleven Plan for a European Defence Community, namely a rearmed Germany as a full and equal member of NATO. French problems then intensified under de Gaulle. As has been argued in Chapter 2, de Gaulle was one of the two great nationalist leaders of major European powers in the late twentieth century (the other was Margaret Thatcher), both of whom faced an impossible dilemma. On the one hand, they were both fervent intergovernmentalists, always suspicious that a European 'superstate' was around the corner. On the other hand, they were both incapable of achieving anything unless they worked with the others.

While de Gaulle was president of France (1958–69), some of the ambiguities thrown up by this dilemma were laid bare. He disliked NATO, withdrew France from the military wing of it and sought to develop a common foreign and defence policy for the six member states of the EEC through the Fouchet Plan (see Chapter 2). The Fouchet Plan called for a 'Union of European Peoples' on purely intergovernmental lines, reflecting de Gaulle's own belief that all important decisions should be made at national level or at least be open to the possibility of national vetoes. But if it was to be truly intergovernmental, then there was no way in which the views of the other five (themselves, after all, independent nation-states) could be ignored. And they did not (for instance) share de Gaulle's hostile view of NATO. They treated the Fouchet Plan with scepticism, believing that it was a way of trying to mould the foreign policy position of the other five according to that of France. Even when a second version of the plan was drawn up, introducing a foreign affairs committee meeting four times a year, they were unclear what it would be able to achieve in terms of forging a common foreign and defence policy. The plan was finally rejected in 1962.

De Gaulle then tried to replace it with an exclusive Franco-German arrangement, leading to a Treaty of Friendship and Reconciliation signed at the Elysée Palace in January 1963. This followed traditional intergovernmental lines in simply promising that the two states would consult each other on all questions of foreign policy before taking a decision and 'with a view to' (but by implication without an assurance of) reaching 'an analogous position'. Just in case the point was not clear enough, the German parliament added a codicil during the process of ratification making clear the country's overriding commit-ment to NATO. Thus Germany was consenting to find a position that agreed with France so long as France adopted the policy on NATO advocated by Germany (even more so when Adenauer was replaced as leader by Erhard three months later). De Gaulle was finding out that he could not create a common foreign policy position among the Six based on the acceptance by the other five of what France wanted.

Unsurprisingly, the discovery made progress on the external action front very difficult while de Gaulle remained in office.

It was 1970 (and a year after the resignation of de Gaulle) before further moves on foreign policy coordination were made through the creation of European Political Cooperation. It was proposed as no more than a way of coordinating meetings between foreign ministers, but at first it aroused suspicions among the other five of a revival of the Fouchet Plan. However, it soon became clear that European Political Cooperation was not attempting to harness the foreign policy wishes of the other states to those of France. Its weakness lay in the opposite direction: by no longer being an instrument for bending the foreign policy positions of the other five to those of France, it ended up as something of a rudderless ship. It was managed by the country holding the six-monthly Council presidency (aided by the previous and future president in a kind of ever-shifting troika). As member states were later to argue when, in the Treaty of Lisbon, they agreed to top-slice the functions of the rolling six-monthly presidency and create a Council president and a high representative (Herman van Rompuy and Catherine Ashton at the time of writing), playing musical chairs with potentially powerful political positions may be 'democratic' but endangers policy coherence.

Weak in structural terms European Political Cooperation may have been, but it still represented a very important step. After the failure of the European Defence Community, there had been a tendency to think that, because member states had finally rejected supranationalism in the defence and foreign policy field, there was no point in trying to coordinate their activities. The same reluctance to coordinate was produced by the debacle over the Fouchet Plan – in this case the fear was that 'coordination' would mean subordination to French policy. Although it was a relatively minor step in institutional terms, the establishment of the European Political Cooperation framework at least demonstrated that trying to coordinate foreign policy positions was worthwhile, even though different positions would often be taken by individual member states. Its modest administrative machinery involved regular meetings of foreign ministers and of various working groups to follow up on their deliberations. It was loose and optional in its arrangements and technically not even part of the institutional life of the Community, but it was nevertheless significant. Like much else in the history of the EU, it provided a toe in the water and was attended by grandiose statements that, if they were not to appear ridiculous, would require more effective organisational arrangements in the future. Moreover, this was the time when the Community began to enlarge (the UK, Ireland and Denmark became members of the Community in 1973) and enlargement was likely to generate more disagreements on foreign policy issues (Ireland, for instance, was not a member of NATO).

Cold War tensions and the collapse of communism – the 1980s

Grandiose statements multiplied during the tense period between détente and Gorbachev that marked the years of the first Reagan presidency in the USA. The German and Italian Foreign Ministers produced a Draft European Act calling for more Community competence in the external relations field, and a summit at Stuttgart in 1983 produced a Solemn Declaration on European Union, couched in very general terms but with the interesting observation that a united Europe was 'more than ever necessary in order to meet the dangers of the world situation'. In the following year, French President Mitterrand called for a permanent secretariat for the conduct of defence policy and a common defence effort. For the first time an increasingly isolated Washington wondered whether its allies in Western Europe (this was a period of mass demonstrations against the deployment of cruise missiles on the continent) might really be developing a common foreign policy against it. Such fears proved groundless, but they did reflect an increasing European concern about the international situation and with it the conviction that this was an area of policy that could not simply be ignored. The result of this conviction was the formal recognition of European Political Cooperation in the Single European Act. It was now part of the team. The act said that member states would 'endeavour jointly to formulate and implement a European foreign policy'. That was certainly one of those statements referred to earlier that would need to be fleshed out in institutional terms if they were not later going to appear ridiculous. A European foreign policy was not going to be achieved by informal chats between foreign ministers.

A very important point was made in the Stuttgart Declaration mentioned above, one that was to play a significant role in the way in which the Union developed its activities in the field of external relations. When it spoke of a united Europe meeting the dangers of the world situation, it went on to say that such a Europe would be 'capable of assuming the responsibilities incumbent on it by virtue of its political role, its economic potential and its manifold links with other peoples'. That reference to 'economic potential' is crucial. External relations were becoming important precisely because the EEC was a large trading group whose common positions had to be taken seriously on the world stage and indeed often led to controversy (for instance over agriculture). And the more it became a global trading and economic power, the more the EEC became a global power in the *political* sense, because those with considerable economic clout can wield it to considerable effect, even if they have very little in the way of military power. This is the mistake that the simple 'economic giant, military worm' juxtaposition often makes, even accepting the fact that military forces have to be developed too. The EEC felt that it was able to develop effective foreign policy positions partly because it was making progress towards becoming a (growing) single market.

Certainly no 'European foreign policy' emerged in the 1980s with the fall of communism in Central and Eastern Europe (which no one had predicted) or with the Iraqi invasion of Kuwait at the beginning of the following decade (it was the response to the Gulf War that led to the Belgian Foreign Minister's remark about the Community as 'an economic giant, a political dwarf and a military worm'). But the combination of growing economic strength and the need for the Community to live up to its own rhetoric about a European foreign policy, however disappointing the initial results, was likely in time to bring administrative machinery in its wake, and this began to arrive with the Maastricht Treaty in the early 1990s.

War in Europe: the lessons of the 1990s

The three-pillar structure of Maastricht recognised that a Common Foreign and Security Policy would be intergovernmental, and therefore separate from the first pillar, the supranational European

Community pillar. But, by giving it a clearly identified role as part of the whole 'building', it made clear that even acting on an intergovernmental basis was compatible with providing vital work in holding up the whole EU 'edifice'. There was no need to think that those who were calling for a more coherent foreign policy were somehow trying to smuggle in supranational elements to an area that was traditionally intergovernmental. They were not. They accepted the hybrid character of the EU, accepted that it was built on separate pillars, but at the same time were seeking to make each pillar work effectively. In practical terms this meant not closing off the Parliament and the Commission from the foreign and security policy arena but allowing them a (limited but in time growing) part to play.

There are, indeed, many spheres of EU activity where the fact that the area concerned is primarily a 'national competence' does not mean that there is not considerable demand for joint actions. Education has already been mentioned. Member states pay for the building and running of schools and decide on matters such as the national curriculum. But the Directorate-General (DG) for Education and Culture still has a key role to play in coordinating the various programmes – Comenius, Erasmus, Leonardo da Vinci, Grundtvig – that allow students and teaching staff from one member state (and from other parts of Europe, through the European Higher Education Area) to attend courses in other countries.

Put together degrees, put together armies. The French general chairing the EU's Military Committee in 2013, Patrick de Rousier, spoke of the need for a 'military Erasmus initiative', with military personnel spending time acquainting themselves with the forces of other member states. Such a development would speed up the process of achieving interoperability. At the very least, forces could be assembled that were capable of supporting very specific moves ('joint actions') – in effect small groups acting in a peacekeeping role taken to support commonly held objectives. Examples from the first decade of the twenty-first century would be the EU Police Mission in Bosnia and Herzegovina agreed in 2002 or the joint action of 2008 to promote the rule of law in Kosovo.

These interventions followed a decade (the 1990s) in which the EU's limitations in the foreign and security policy sphere were exposed as they had never been before. This was because the problems that affected the EU in that decade were problems in Europe. It was all very well to be teased by the Belgian Foreign Minister about the failure to have an effective European position on the Gulf War; it was quite another to see wars erupting in Europe itself and the EU unable to do anything effective in response. This was an attack on the whole European 'narrative' of postwar reconciliation between France and Germany laying the foundation for a peaceful continent of the future, sweeping away right-wing dictatorships in the South and then communist dictatorships in the East as it grew to embrace a whole continent. As post-communist Yugoslavia imploded, the EU's attempt at a peace conference was replaced by the Dayton peace accords, effectively organised by the USA. When the Kosovo crisis erupted in 1998, the military response that finally came a year later was again led by the USA and was a NATO intervention.

The implication of this was – and is – twofold. On the one hand, the nations of South-East Europe have to be brought into the EU and absorbed into the partial sovereignty-sharing framework, which really does increase the chances of (but can never guarantee) peaceful cooperation. Surrounded as they are by existing members of the EU, most or all of these countries – Slovenia (a member since 2004), Croatia (a member since July 2013), Serbia, Kosovo, Bosnia Herzegovina, Montenegro, Albania and the Former Yugoslav Republic of Macedonia – will probably (in some form or other) join the EU over the next decade. The sense of unfinished business, of the need to restore a narrative of bringing peace to a traditionally war-torn continent, will demand it.

However, the second implication is this. If these states are really to become members of the EU, then any future conflict that arises – even though there are genuine reasons to expect that it will not – must be dealt with by the EU itself. NATO intervention on the fringes of the EU was bad enough; NATO intervention within the EU would be unthinkable. Thus the Union has to have the capacity to use force effectively, if not in order to keep the peace in far-off corners of the world, at least in order to be able to keep its own peace.

Consciousness of failure in the Balkans added a sense of urgency to the EU's attempts to develop more effective structures in the foreign and security policy field. Some changes came with the Treaty of Amsterdam in 1997. One was the creation of the post of high representative, though attended by rather weak language about what the holder of the post might do – 'contribute to' the formulation and implementation of policy and 'assist' the work of the Council, as if this were a person who did not give direction but merely carried out Council decisions. However, there was going to be a Policy Planning and Early Warning Unit working under the new high representative, and in 2001 the Nice Treaty expanded this unit to include the newly formed European Union Military Staff. An effective administrative structure was developing in Brussels, including not only civilian but military staff.

Increased cooperation between Amsterdam and Lisbon

Though the decade between the Amsterdam and Lisbon treaties is often portrayed as a time of further disarray in the foreign policy field, as European countries took diametrically opposing positions on US military intervention in Iraq (there were also some differences over its involvement in Afghanistan), important changes began to take place that presaged more coordinated action in the foreign policy field in future. Three factors are crucial.

The first was a sense in all EU countries (if not on the part of all their governments) that in the post-Cold War era Europe would fall down the list of US priorities. If one recalls Bevin's 'sprat to catch a whale' in the later 1940s, seeking to woo US forces onto the European mainland through the creation of NATO, then one can see how after the end of the Cold War the whale might seek to move elsewhere, to some extent taking NATO with it. Where President George W. Bush upset a lot of Europeans (it needs to be remembered that some 75 per cent of EU citizens opposed US military intervention in Iraq, even if their governments acted otherwise) by the nature of his policies, President Obama has upset them through the nature of his priorities, when they see him focusing more attention on Asia than on Europe. Arguably this is an inevitable consequence of economic and political changes that have taken place over the last two decades. It means that Europe will not be able to assure itself that differences over foreign policy issues can all take place within a comfort zone of overarching US protection. A European foreign policy, which de Gaulle sought in order to deny the USA too much influence, will to some extent be necessary in order to live with the USA's new priorities.

The second crucial factor has already been mentioned: the need to develop a capacity to use force at the very least within the borders of the (expanding) EU itself. In 1999, a European Council meeting in Cologne launched the European Security and Defence Policy (ESDP), which was formally introduced by the Nice Treaty two years later, and which sought to give the EU what an Anglo-French Summit in St Malo in 1998 between President Chirac and Prime Minister Blair had demanded, 'the capacity for autonomous action backed up by credible military forces and the means to decide to use them'. This was necessary in order to be able to carry out the so-called Petersberg (a town near Bonn) tasks associated with peacekeeping and rescue missions. These tasks had been identified some seven years earlier, but it took the conflicts in South-East Europe during the intervening period to force the EU to make progress.

Six months later the EU set a headline goal of 60,000 troops, deployable within 60 days and sustainable for up to a year, to be achieved by 2003. This goal was not reached (and in the meantime divisions over Iraq started to dominate government thinking), but arguably that did not matter as much as it might have done. The ESDP was going to have a military committee and military staff as well as a political committee. Once there was a sizeable group of military as well as civilian officials working on EU defence and security issues, they would start to make things happen – as indeed they did. By 2003 the EU had not managed its 60,000 troops, but it had made progress on the civilian aspects of crisis management, being able to deploy a police force of 5,000 within 30 days, backed up by civilian administrators and legal experts. This was a case not of turning from 'hard' to 'soft' power but of developing the ability to use influence in several different ways. The military aspect did not disappear, and by the end of 2004 defence ministers had pledged up to 165,000 troops to make up a series of EU 'battlegroups', each deployable within ten days and with two kept in a state of constant readiness.

By the end of the decade it was clear that the EU was capable of putting 'battlegroups' into troublespots worldwide – one is examined later in this chapter. Over 20 civilian and military missions had been launched, many of them in the former Yugoslavia. That concentrated the mind of EU leaders in a way that was not overshadowed by their divisions over Iraq. No one has made this point better than former Conservative minister and EU External Relations Commissioner Chris Patten, speaking in 2004:

> The people of the Western Balkans are our fellow Europeans. We cannot wash our hands of them. Let us remember the consequences of our refusal to get involved. The shattered ruins of Vukovar. The ghastly siege of Sarajevo. The charnel house of Srebrenica. The smoking villages of Kosovo. The European Union did not commit these crimes. But 200,000 fellow Europeans died in Bosnia and Herzegovina alone. As Europeans we cannot avoid a heavy share of responsibility for what happened.[1]

The third crucial factor encouraging more cooperation between member states in the defence sphere is financial. Military technology pushes up defence expenditure. Costly weapons systems rapidly become obsolescent and have to be replaced. It makes sense to do things together when it is unaffordable to continue doing them alone. It also makes sense to minimise duplication and incompatibility. The USA is often portrayed as advising the EU to increase its military spending, but the real EU problem is the *way* it spends money on defence. EU spending amounts to something like 70 per cent of the military expenditure of the USA, but it can put into the field nowhere near 70 per cent of the forces that the USA can deploy. It is interesting to note that the two most powerful member states (militarily), the UK and France, have achieved an unprecedented level of cooperation simply by dint of neither being able to operate effectively on its own. A Franco-British summit in St Malo between Labour Prime Minister Tony Blair and President Jacques Chirac, in December 1998, discussed defence cooperation between their two countries as well as the development of an EU military capability, though this was very much in the shadow of the need to intervene in the Kosovo crisis and the EU's clear inability to do so. Twelve years later, a Conservative prime minister arguably went even further: David Cameron agreed with

President Nicolas Sarkozy of France that the two countries would work together on nuclear testing technology (a key issue for France because it no longer conducts tests on the Mururoa atoll). Between them they would ensure that there was at least one aircraft carrier at sea at any one time, ready for use by planes from both countries. There would be common programmes of training and maintenance on the transport aircraft that they were both buying. There would be joint research work on drones, satellite communications and dealing with mines. Interestingly, they agreed to form a 'joint expeditionary force', which could provide the means for joint military intervention. All this was more *entente frugale* than *entente cordiale*, but arguably none the less significant for being a product of practical necessity rather than emotional warmth. The implication, of course, is that wider European defence cooperation will also be driven forward by ballooning costs and that other countries too will be drawn into further coordination. What is surprising about this? The retiring chairman of the European Union Military Committee, Swedish General Håkan Syrén, declared at the end of 2012:

> There are several (over 12) manufacturers of armoured vehicles in the EU. Do we need that? We are buying four types of combat aircraft right now. Do we need that? Do we have the money for that?

As countries find their defence budgets under increasing strain because of economic recession at the same time as they strain to maintain or even extend their commitments, there can be only one answer. Do things together or you will not be able to do them at all.

The creation of the European External Action Service

The most recent changes in the external relations field, made under the Lisbon Treaty, are complicated but interesting. The treaty provided for the setting up of a new body, the European External Action Service (EEAS), which was founded in January 2011 and is still to some extent finding its way within the European institutional labyrinth. Its purpose was to bring more coherence in an area where, as we have seen, coherence often seemed to be lacking. Partly this coherence came from having the same person chairing meetings of foreign affairs ministers in the Council, rather than whoever was the foreign minister of the country holding the rolling six-monthly presidency. It also came from making the high representative (a post already in existence for more than a decade) at the same time a vice-president of the Commission. The value of this is that two institutions that are easily portrayed as antitheses – the Council of Ministers as 'intergovernmental', the Commission as 'supranational' – are represented by the same person (Catherine Ashton until the end of 2014), who brings coherence by having a foot in both camps. Before Lisbon there was a high representative working for the Council and a separate commissioner for external relations heading a particular Directorate-General of the Commission (DG RELEX). Now one person has assumed both roles and the 1,400 staff of the EEAS are drawn from both the Council Secretariat and the former DG RELEX, together with members of the diplomatic services of member states. This last group has arguably been a very useful catalyst for cooperation between the other two, which formally worked apart from and sometimes against each other.

A dry couple of paragraphs on the structure of the EEAS runs the risk of turning readers off, but in defence of doing so it is worth reiterating the point made at the start of this chapter, namely that unless the whole issue of external relations is seen in the round, then the significance of the EU approach is lost. Though Catherine Ashton is the external relations commissioner as well as high representative, there are other commissioners who are clearly involved in the work of external relations – Commissioner for Development Andris Piebalgs, Commissioner for International Cooperation, Humanitarian Aid and Crisis Response Kristalina Georgieva, and Commissioner for Enlargement and European Neighbourhood Policy Štefan Füle (these names will probably change at the end of 2014). Catherine Ashton is a 'coherence maker' not only between institutions but between different departments of the same institution, ensuring that all those involved have regular meetings.

The point is not just one of making sure that different institutions work with rather than against each other. It is that the favoured EU 'comprehensive' approach to international problems seeks to engage both 'soft' and, where necessary, 'hard' power in order to find solutions. A development commissioner and a commissioner for

Figure 11. Operation Atalanta: An EU naval force off the coast of Somalia.

humanitarian aid are as important to dealing with a problem as an
admiral or a general. Since they are all vital, they have to be brought
together in order to turn a 'comprehensive' approach from theoretical
strategy to practical outcome. The following section looks at a
particular example of this 'comprehensive' approach.

Example: the Horn of Africa

As this chapter has tried to show, the famous comment about the EU as
'an economic giant, a political dwarf and a military worm' was in one
respect very naïve. These are not separate blocs so far as the EU's
influence in external relations is concerned. Precisely because it
remains an economic giant, the EU is able to exercise considerable
influence around the world. Of course there is a limit to economic
influence, but economic clout means that when the EU becomes
involved in a troublespot such as the Horn of Africa, it can combine
aid programmes and trade negotiations on the one hand with the use
(or threat) of force on the other. The EEAS emphasises an approach
that breaks down into what might be called 'hard' and 'soft' elements

but involves both. Addressing the problem of Somali piracy, for instance, means using helicopters to destroy arms dumps on beaches, but it also means projects to educate judges and police forces in law enforcement, together with development aid to Somalis in need.

These may seem like very different things, but they are in fact closely linked. There is limited benefit from capturing pirates if they cannot then be prosecuted. Similarly, there is limited benefit in arresting and prosecuting pirates if the economic conditions make piracy seem an attractive (or the least unattractive) option for making a living. Problems have to be addressed on all fronts, especially when dealing with a poor country (Somalia) of 9 million people riddled with inter-clan rivalry that has at times devastated its capital Mogadishu, and which has produced an estimated 1 to 1.5 million people who have been forced out of their homes ('internally displaced'). Added to this are spillover problems from neighbouring conflicts (such as that between Ethiopia and Eritrea), the ability of terrorist and other armed groups such as the Lord's Resistance Army to take root in remote parts of the country and the exacerbation of tensions caused by scarce resources such as water (which climate change has arguably made worse). These problems are themselves only further aggravating factors to add to the complex geography of this part of Africa, where traditional nomadism across borders has often produced conflict with the strict lines of demarcation produced by (and originally for) different European nation-states as a result of a century of colonial occupation.

The 'comprehensive' approach 1: military force

To improve security at sea, the EU launched Operation Atalanta in December 2008, a naval operation including at various times between four and seven surface combat vessels, together with auxiliary ships and reconnaissance aircraft. Vessels were provided from a number of countries, including some not automatically seen as maritime nations – in December 2012 a Romanian frigate completed Romania's first counter-piracy operation as part of Operation Atalanta. At that time the surface vessels on deployment came from Belgium, Spain, France and Germany, assisted by reconnaissance aircraft from the Netherlands, Germany, Luxembourg and Sweden. The make-up of countries participating changes regularly, but this snapshot shows that several are involved at any one moment. The Council of the EU later decided to extend the operation until December 2014, by which time it will have been running for six years, with an option to extend it further.

The headquarters of the operation is in the UK, at Northwood, and the operation commander as of January 2013, who has to coordinate actions with the political and military authorities of the EU, was Rear Admiral Robert Tarrant of the UK Royal Navy, in which he has served for over 30 years, beginning his career with a stint on the destroyer HMS *Antrim* during the Falklands conflict. UK vessels have, of course, been part of the EU task force. The UK's frigate HMS *Northumberland* was involved from the beginning, escorting a World Food Programme ship (which had been ambushed by pirates in the past). One thinks of those charity requests that talk about a gift of £10 'feeding five people for a week'. In this case one frigate can feed 50,000 Somalis for a month. Once again, the point is the interlinkage: successful aid does not depend upon generous donor countries and individuals alone; it has to overcome problems of logistics in order for that aid to be successfully delivered. In this instance, that could only be done with a frigate. In fact the main task of the EU naval force is to escort merchant vessels carrying humanitarian aid for the World Food Programme (80 per cent of the food aid to Somalia arrives by sea). And it is clearly 'hard' power. Within two weeks of the launch of Operation Atalanta it had its first military engagement, involving a German frigate that used helicopter fire to deter a pirate attack in the Gulf of Aden. The pirate ship was later boarded and all the arms and equipment thrown overboard. As explained already, helicopters have been used to destroy arms dumps on beaches. Over 100 pirates have been captured and handed over for prosecution.

Piracy levels fell by 95 per cent between the end of 2011 and the end of 2012, and 'hard' power had a lot to do with that success. But these achievements would have been impossible unless, for instance, the Director-General of the EU Military Staff had been in close contact with the European Commission's Humanitarian Aid and Civil Protection department (ECHO), which was supporting the World Food Programme and knew that security escorts were needed for its food aid ships. There is doubtless a wonderful diagram of EU institutions liaising with one another that could be drawn up to show how all this interlinkage is arranged. It would end up looking like the alimentary canal of a large mammal and is largely unnecessary. The EEAS is successful because it bangs heads together and coordinates activities at several levels.

Moreover, operations such as Atalanta have a bearing upon the sort of military cooperation between member states that was discussed earlier in this chapter in terms of the Blair/Chirac St Malo summit and David Cameron's later discussions with President Sarkozy. An EU naval force working together inevitably raises questions concerning how to develop and buy equipment together. Patrolling the Gulf of Aden (an area larger than the EU itself) requires airplanes for air-to-air refuelling (this was one of the areas for cooperation between the UK and France agreed by Cameron and Sarkozy), and expensive military capabilities such as this can be maintained only through a pooling of resources – particularly at a time when EU member states are making cuts in their defence budgets amounting to some 30 billion euros. The European Defence Agency, an EU agency created to foster defence cooperation, has been pushing cooperation in the defence sphere forward since 2004.

It might be said that this naval force is doing NATO's job, but NATO cannot be everywhere and do everything (as it is frequently at pains to point out to its European members). Besides, Operation Atalanta is being carried out in full cooperation with NATO, which has its own Operation Ocean Shield. There is no difference of opinion over the issue of piracy in the Somali Basin and the Gulf of Aden, just a need to use the forces of both organisations in order to deal with it. NATO's reach is much wider and its forces are much bigger, but it would be wrong to say that there is no use of 'hard power' at the EU level and wrong to suppose that it is impossible to assemble a military force from a large number of member states. Interestingly, there was also increasing cooperation between the EU and the Chinese navy in the summer of 2013, when an Italian warship handed over escort duties to a Chinese vessel, CNS *Mianyang*, to ensure safe passage of a ship carrying aid under the World Food Programme to Djibouti. More cooperation was planned for later in 2013.

At the same time, efforts are being made to develop the 'hard power' capacity of the countries in the regions themselves. EUCAP Nestor – a capacity-building effort in the Horn of Africa and the Western Indian Ocean under the Common Security and Defence Policy – is designed to do this, building up the maritime capacity of Somalia, Djibouti, Kenya, Tanzania and the Seychelles, while placing particular emphasis on a land-based coastal police force in Somalia. As with any form of military engagement, there has to be an exit strategy, and it usually involves both reducing the problem that gave rise to conflict in the first place and handing over the management of whatever conflict remains to local and regionally based forces after a period of capacity-building. The same applies to the EU's strategy of working with the African Union, a regional union of over 50 African countries that has just celebrated its half centenary and that is building up the size of its forces in the region through the African Union Mission in Somalia. The EU has committed over 400 million euros to this mission through its African Peace Facility.

The comprehensive approach 2: creating effective forms of governance

The second part of the comprehensive approach involves the legal, political and administrative capacities of Somalia itself. Handing over 100 pirates for prosecution is useless if they are not going to be tried and tried fairly. To some extent this problem can be bypassed through arranging the transfer of suspected pirates out of Somalia (the EU has arrangements to do this with Kenya, Mauritius and the Seychelles). But a more lasting solution is to support the justice systems of countries *inside* the area. The EU does this in a joint partnership with the United Nations Office on Drugs and Crime. The aim must be to support police and justice institutions so that eventually all the piracy trials take place in Somalia itself. At the same time, there is an EU Training Mission (EUTM Somalia) involving about 100 troops from a dozen different countries under an Irish commander which has given military and legal training to about 3,000 Somali soldiers in the hope that such action will both help to embed the rule of law and provide support to the Transitional Federal Government and thereby prevent the country falling back into civil war. Hopes rose in August 2012 when the National Constituent Assembly adopted a Provisional Constitution and a new Federal Parliament came into being, electing a president and giving a vote of confidence to his ten ministers (two of them women, including the Minister for Foreign Affairs).

No one knows whether any of this progress will last, and there were plenty of reminders of the precarious situation of the country in 2013 (for instance, the murder of the journalist Mohamed Ibrahim Rage in April and a car bomb killing seven people in the capital Mogadishu in May). Indeed, the fact that the headquarters of the training mission is in Uganda (Ugandan Defence Force officers assist with the military training) and that it is only gradually transferring its training capacities to Somalia is itself an illustration of the continuing problems of security in a country that has had many years of civil war. But without progress in the area of security, the provision of aid can have no real effect.

The comprehensive approach 3: economic development

The third part of the comprehensive approach concerns what some might consider the 'root causes' of the piracy, namely the lack of economic development. The EU is the largest development donor to Somalia: over 200 million euros was spent through the EU Somalia Special Support Programme between 2008 and 2013. Here also the EU does not work alone. Links with the United Nations Development Programme and with Save the Children have been established, and EU Flight Services are offered to and from (as well as within) Somalia for organisations implementing aid programmes in the country.

Such help is doubly needed at a time of economic recession because, like many other developing nations, Somalia (which has a wide diaspora) receives a great deal of help from remittances (about US$1 billion annually, of which one-third goes directly to individual households and the rest into private investment). The aid programmes of individual countries and the EU have broadly been maintained through the recession, but the level of remittances has fallen as Somalis living abroad have felt the impact of recession. Remittances fell by 25 per cent in the first quarter of 2009, for instance, as the economic crisis began to bite – a loss of some US$250 million and of perhaps US$100 million delivered directly to individuals, without any of the indirect funnelling of funds that often leads aid programmes into corruption and waste. This money would have been spent on basic essentials such as food, clothes and education, thereby supporting local producers.

ECHO has been supporting projects in Somalia since 1998, but as its tortuous name makes clear, it is not just necessary to have something to give; there also has to be the means to hand it over. As the use of naval forces to deliver humanitarian aid has shown, there is no point in providing aid that is not deliverable, and this requires an adequate security context. In 2008, some 37 aid workers were killed in Somalia, two-thirds of the total number of deaths of aid workers worldwide. Aid workers were declared legitimate 'targets' by various armed groups. This made it necessary, until the security situation could be addressed, to deliver aid (if at all) by a kind of remote control, directing delivery through Somali intermediaries in the south of the country from various centres in the north or from Kenya.

Lack of security and a breakdown in social order can very easily undo the work of any aid agency. This is a very important constraint and one that justifies the EU in adopting a comprehensive approach and avoiding a list of its 'achievements' without any consideration of whether these can be made lasting. The problems of an approach that is not comprehensive is well illustrated by considering statistics given by DG EuropeAid, as the department of the European Commission that has the task of devising development policies and delivering aid is now called. It provides a statistical overview of its success in implementing the Millennium Development Goals (eradicate extreme poverty and hunger, achieve universal primary education, promote gender equality and empower women, reduce child mortality and promote maternal health, ensure environmental sustainability) formulated by the United Nations in 2000. It goes through 'key results' on a goal-by-goal basis, using them as benchmarks against which it claims 'successes' for the period 2004–9.[2] Where Somalia is concerned (see 'Further reading' for this chapter), we are told that 150,000 Somalis have benefited from social transfers (cash, seed, agricultural equipment), primary school teachers have been trained (23,000), schools have been built or repaired (more than 100), new female students have been enrolled in secondary education (13,000), health facilities have been improved (148), births have been attended by skilled health personnel (over 6,000), Somalis' drinking water has been improved (for nearly 1 million) and many have been connected to sanitation facilities (120,000). Great stuff. Then we discover from BBC News (2 May 2013) that between 2010 and 2012 (just after all these 'achievements' had been run up) over a quarter of a million people died from famine in Somalia, half of them children under five. By October 2013, Somalis had become one of the largest groups of asylum seekers willing to risk their lives and those of their families to cross the Mediterranean and find or be denied sanctuary in the EU.

No one doubts that 'key results' are a useful illustration of the sort of priorities that the EU has adopted in cooperation with the United Nations. Development is rightly seen as inseparable from providing basic health facilities and education; education must particularly focus on female students; the need for safe water is often greater than the need for food; and the best way of providing food aid is to provide the means of cultivating the food locally (seeds and equipment – and, in the context of factors that are unavoidably making the situation worse, such as climate change, the emphasis needs to be on developing drought-resistant crops and cattle as well as effective irrigation schemes). But none of this gets us very far (or even anywhere at all) if the approach is not comprehensive in the sense outlined above: for instance if there is not a stable security situation or if there is a collapsed infrastructure. Farmers need roads, market centres and slaughterhouses as well as animal feed and seeds. There is no point in repairing 100 schools one year if 200 are destroyed in a civil war the next year. If 100 schools were built or repaired between 2004 and 2009, we need to know how many were destroyed or damaged during that period, or how many are still standing five years later.

Moreover, a comprehensive approach demands a stable and viable economic environment. There is no point in delivering seeds and equipment if a farmer cannot make a living out of cultivating them. Nothing makes the work of increasing food production and preventing famine more difficult than the presumption that farmers simply need the technological know-how to produce more, when what they in fact require is the ability to be confident of an enduring return on their investment in agriculture. The huge (and eventually excessive) boost in agricultural production in the EEC (see Chapter 5) stemmed from guaranteed floor prices and a common external tariff. In just the same way, boosting food production in Africa has to be seen in the wider context of the economy taken as a whole. The situation is not helped by the fact that Somalia is one of the countries onto which the EU dumped its excess food production (see Chapter 5) in the past, though this has now stopped.

The comprehensive approach to this and other regional conflicts is the only one that is practical through mixing 'hard' and 'soft' power, but this principle applies to the provision of development aid itself. Security without aid fails to address the root causes; aid without security – including a secure economic environment – goes to waste.

The EU's alternative employment strategy is another aspect of its policy in the region, one that requires a broad approach in order to have any chance of being successful. Mindful of the effects of piracy, the EU has tried to support programmes specifically designed to encourage 'alternative livelihoods' to crime. Agriculture dominates the economy, mostly in terms of livestock (the biggest source of employment in the country), followed by crops and fruit. However, a proposal that former pirates might be lured into livestock production seemed unlikely to be successful. New funds were therefore earmarked in 2011–13 specifically to support the fishing industry as a practical alternative to piracy in coastal communities.

It is true that the fisheries sector has great potential, with only about 3 per cent of the country's possible sustainable catch being exploited domestically. The problem is that the difficulties in doing so relate only in part to the state of its fishing fleets. Once caught, the fish have to be stored, processed and distributed, making it necessary to improve the overall infrastructure even beyond the coastal area (most of Somalia's 22,000 kilometres of roads are in very poor condition). Moreover, drawing boundaries at sea is notoriously difficult (even for the EU itself) and other states have been predators in the area, making it necessary to reach agreements over fishing with neighbouring countries. And if you ask the Somali fishermen who has been most effective in keeping these 'foreign predators' at bay, then the answer is: 'The pirates!'

One might have begun by thinking that the need is to provide a few seaworthy vessels and some training in the use of nets. One ends up recognising that creating a viable Somali fishing industry requires international agreements, infrastructural renewal and investment in warehousing with refrigeration facilities. Only then is it worth thinking about ships and courses for 'upskilling' pirates as fishers.

It has to be borne in mind that government collapse has meant that in recent years many of the basic services in Somalia, such as education and health, have been delivered – where they have been delivered at all – by the private sector, usually in urban centres and usually to those who are able to pay for them. It is true that the involvement of a variety of non-state actors in service provision is a positive thing, and through DG EuropeAid the EU has given support to non-state actors such as women's groups and community associations. Often it is local and community networks that are the most resilient and effective forms of governance when there is administrative breakdown at national level. They can help to promote democracy at grassroots levels as well as solving conflicts that might otherwise renew outbreaks of civil war. Nevertheless, such positives come in the context of an overarching negative – the absence of a functional central government. A long-term objective, while supporting these grassroots developments, has to be that of reinvigorating the public sector through restoring political stability to the country as a whole, where popular elections are planned for 2016.

Whether the comprehensive approach will work in Somalia has yet to be determined. There is no doubt that there are still regular reports of terrorist attacks and of groups linked to al-Qaeda working in parts of Somalia where there is little or no security. But what is clear is that only a comprehensive approach has any chance of success. Building a school is useless if there is no way of guaranteeing that it will not be destroyed by further conflict or used for some completely different purpose. Arresting pirates is no good if there are no legal systems under which they can be effectively tried, and, even if there are, success is unlikely in the long term if there are no other forms of employment for them to move into. And those other forms of employment require, in turn, more than a dollop of aid to build a fishing boat or provide a tractor. They require work on the whole infrastructure of the country. Such is the complexity of this that coordinated work with other agencies becomes imperative. The danger of being sucked in so that you cannot easily get out is such that this policy also requires capacity-building on the part of local and regional authorities, from community groups to the African Union, in order to take over in the longer term.

Inevitably, this comprehensive approach entails a complex relationship between the EU institutions that are part of putting it together. Effective help to developing countries is lacking precisely because approaches are not coordinated. Either there is bombing by people who 'don't do peacemaking' or there is peacemaking by people who cannot produce a peace that lasts. The 'hard' and 'soft' elements have to be put together. This is where the EEAS can play a vital coordinating role.

Conclusion

Given the remarks in this chapter, it comes as no surprise that the European Council of December 2013, which included an important discussion of defence issues, had the pooling and sharing of military capabilities on its agenda from the previous spring, when it was decided under the Irish presidency that Theme 1 for the forthcoming Defence Summit (as it was already called) would be: 'That resources available to EU Member States will remain in short supply necessitating pooling and sharing'. There is no other way for member states to maintain (let alone extend) a broad military commitment without significant increases in their defence budgets (and these are generally being cut in the context of economic recession). Proud and independent nations such as the UK and France, for instance, are forced to come together and share an aircraft carrier if they want to be able to land their planes at sea at any time.

Such sharing is likely to be the beginning of much more cooperation in the defence field. It will require coordination at the European level, not as a way of impinging upon national sovereignty but as a sensible way of managing things that can best be done at that level. The principle of subsidiarity does not mean doing everything at the national level; it means doing everything at the *appropriate* level – regional, national or European.

The EEAS has such a coordinating role, but not just in bringing together the military capacities of the different member states in order to promote operations such as Atalanta. Such coordination also requires a comprehensive working together of 'hard' and 'soft' power. It requires work on the economic and domestic security front as well as the military front. It requires liaising with other bodies – such as the United Nations and regional groupings such as the African Union – and pursuing joint ventures. And it means bringing together the different departments of the EU (or simply of the Commission), which themselves need to recognise the necessity of a comprehensive approach.

A wordless two-minute display of EU missions around the world (see 'Further research' for this chapter) was produced by the EEAS in 2012. It was clear that most of the missions were very small contributions to very large problems (Iraq, Afghanistan, etc.), but in the case of Somalia the EU had really become involved at several levels and could claim to be playing a major role. Will it prove successful in the medium term? Nobody knows, but, by seeking to be comprehensive, it at least has a chance. If it does succeed, then it will be because it has not just handed out dollops of cash but has tried to address the problems of governance without which cash aid is useless. This in turn has to recognise that the only long-term solution is for Somalis to govern themselves, so any actions by the EU have to involve helping them to do so. A comprehensive approach has to be enabling rather than simply represent a new form of European takeover in Africa. This hardly makes it easy and in the end it may not work (things do not look very hopeful at the end of 2013), but it is hard to deny that it is the right approach in principle.

Academics will be able to enjoy themselves discussing whether and in what sense the EEAS is an 'EU institution', but the fact is that it is one of the most cheerful and open EU bodies, happy to be finding its way through the institutional labyrinth and scoring some notable successes in terms of member state cooperation. The demand for such cooperation has practical necessity on its side, whether in terms of member states trying to maintain their individual commitments in the context of rising costs and falling budgets, or in terms of the requirement that development aid is lasting and effective. For that reason alone the workload and importance of the EEAS can only increase in the future. It has the confidence of an organisation that friends and foes alike know is here to stay.

8

The greening of Europe?

The beginnings of environmental policy

The interesting thing about environmental policy is that, in the early days of sovereignty-sharing, no one thought of having one (there was no mention of the environment in the Treaties of Rome). They were struggling with the creation of a Common Market and a Common Agricultural Policy (CAP). They were deeply aware of the recent rejection of a European Defence Community and had high hopes of being able to reduce disparities at the regional level. But the environment was nowhere on their radar (or anyone else's). Perhaps in the context of a continent that had been torn apart by war and half-destroyed by catastrophic bombing, people saw peace as the best way of ensuring a better environment. It took another generation to realise that the process of recovery from war had itself created a new threat to that environment.

Hence the dates at which key developments took place in the emergence of an environmental policy look relatively late: 1973 for the Commission's first Environmental Action Programme, 1979 for a committee of the Parliament dedicated to environmental matters, 1981 for a department (Directorate-General) of the Commission specifically concerned with the issue, 1989 for the first commissioner tasked with environmental policy, 1993 for the introduction of Qualified Majority Voting (QMV) into most areas of environmental policy (meaning that environmental laggards could no longer wield a veto), the end of the century before the language of 'sustainable development' started to enter the vocabulary of EU-speak as a central objective and 2010 before there was a Directorate-General for Climate Action (DG CLIMA) and a climate action commissioner, Connie Hedegaard. She is the Danish commissioner, an unsurprising choice in the context of Denmark's place at the forefront of renewable energy use.

It might be said that, though relatively late, this represents real progress, and certainly compares well with what has been happening (or not happening) elsewhere in the world (for instance in the USA, Russia or China). It is certainly true that on environmental issues Europe has come a long way, and the fact that pollution knows no borders has helped to encourage cooperation between member states.

Environmental policy illustrates how the tangle of institutions that make up the European Union may nevertheless allow radical policies to seep through the interstices and be adopted. On the one hand, it has never been a major concern where the European Council is concerned. National leaders may try to advertise their green credentials, but their priorities lie elsewhere. Nor has the environment been championed by any president of the Commission. But precisely because it has not received a major push from the top, it has been better able to slip under the radar through pressure from below. Moreover, it needs to be borne in mind that the environment receives significant support from a powerful element of 'multilevel governance' that is often missed as people tour the institutions from local up to international and back, namely the pressure group (or 'interest group'). Before almost all of the milestones in the emergence of an environmental policy within the EU recorded above, the European Environmental Bureau was created (in 1974) by environmental pressure groups that recognised the inadequacy of operating at the national level alone. Of course there are also business groups in Brussels and elsewhere lobbying hard (in most but not all cases) on behalf of a different point of view, but this only reinforces the point that the important 'actors' are not just the institutional ones.

Environmental policy as a networking phenomenon

This is the fascination of environmental policy, which more than the other policies under consideration here has been developed from below, in terms of both pressure groups outside the web of institutions and (sometimes in connection or even collusion with them) influential (but below the top layer) representatives inside the web.

As a result, it is a policy with the capacity to network. It has developed from the province of one department of the Commission into a policy area to be considered elsewhere. Of course, like any other department it has never been able to work in isolation. It is not difficult to see how in many areas of policy DG Environment has to contact other Directorates-General, not only those with an obvious relationship to the environment such as DG CLIMA but also departments concerned with economic matters such as trade and employment. However, environmental policy has moved beyond that to setting certain standards to be followed by *all* departments in the Commission.

Once the Treaty of Amsterdam had made environmental policy a central objective of the EU, every part of the Commission had to explain its 'sustainable development strategy'. Those working in DG Agriculture had to explain how farmers would operate as 'custodians of the countryside'; those in DG Energy had to explain how they planned to obtain more energy from renewables; those in DG Move (Mobility and Transport, though they did not become a separate DG until 2010) had to explain how they intended to reduce pollution from vehicles; and so on. It is true that there is a detailed academic debate about whether leaving the 'policy ghetto' actually weakens you by making your department susceptible to counter-attacks from others who try, for instance, to make environmental policy more transport conscious rather than transport more environmentally conscious, but this book will steer through rather than into the muddy waters of so-called reverse integration.[1]

Environmental policy is adept at befriending other policies and making them its own. For example, the first Barroso Commission (2005–9) pointedly identified the delivery through the Lisbon Agenda of more 'jobs and growth' as its overriding priority. But what is pointedly meant (if it was) does not have to be pointedly taken. Renewable energy creates jobs in abundance, and being a world leader in green technology provides numerous opportunities for exports and growth. Those who wanted to push environmental policy knew that there was no need (and no point in trying) to make the Barroso Commission change its mind on its priorities. What they did was to applaud the priorities and seek to demonstrate that the greening of Europe was one of the best means of achieving them. Hence the Commission's Climate and Energy Package, proposed in 2007 and passed with some changes by the Council and Parliament in the following year, spoke of over 400,000 new jobs being created by the target of a 20 per cent contribution of renewables to the EU's energy supply by 2020, and another 400,000 jobs from a 20 per cent increase in energy efficiency by the same date. This presumed job-creating potential was what enabled the Climate and Energy Package to form part of the Europe 2020 Growth Strategy, which was the centrepiece of the Barroso Commission's overall plan.

Energy and the environment

Though environmental concerns date from the 1970s, energy has been a concern from the beginning. Sovereignty-sharing was launched through the Coal and Steel Community and then, after the setback of the failed European Defence Community, it was partly relaunched through the European Atomic Energy Community (EURATOM). The interest in renewables could therefore be seen as the latest step in a long history of Community action in the energy field, the environmental concerns being integrated with those connected to employment and job creation.

A report from the Directorate-General for Energy, *Renewables Make the Difference*, was published in 2011 and provided an overview of the different sources of renewable energy: solar, wind, wave, geothermal and bioenergy. But the emphasis in the introduction was upon 'boosting the economy':

> 'Hi-tech', green, industrial development brings new value added green jobs and builds on Europe's industrial strengths. European companies

currently dominate the global renewable energy manufacturing sector, employing over 1.5 million people with a turnover of over EUR 50 billion. With continued strong growth the sector could provide another million jobs by 2020 and double or even triple its turnover.[2]

This quotation could have been a plea for boosting the car and aviation industries. The plea for renewables was decked out with the best 'jobs and growth' jargon to make Barroso's priorities look as if a few more wind turbines could save the European economy.

Environmental policy has been able to adopt other areas of concern besides the drive for economic growth, even some that might at first sight appear to be largely irrelevant to it, such as national security. This is made clear in the same introduction to *Renewables Make the Difference* under the heading 'Making our energy supply more secure':

EU countries are highly and increasingly dependent on imports of fossil fuels (particularly oil and gas) for their transport and electricity generation. [...] Europe benefits from increasing the range of fuels available to produce energy [...] Such diversity reduces the risk of cuts in supply and price volatility and encourages efficiency by increasing competition in the energy sector.[3]

It was a powerful argument to a European Union that had recently learned the risks of dependence upon imports from Russia. (Supplies were temporarily interrupted when a row blew up between Russia and Ukraine over 'transit fees' for transporting natural gas across Ukraine; some EU member states had several unpleasant weeks in midwinter as a consequence.) The introduction of the Common Agricultural Policy (CAP) was partly defended on the basis of claiming that dependence upon imports for something as basic as food imperils the security of the Community (see Chapter 5). Now the same arguments were starting to appear in the energy sector.

Moreover, these arguments would only grow stronger with time. World demand for energy supplies is growing, a trend liable to increase both costs and political tensions as countries compete for access (unless supply can keep pace with demand, though there are environmental implications concerning various methods being proposed in order to boost supply, such as fracking). In addition, the EU has become increasingly dependent upon energy imports. Imports supplied about 40 per cent of its energy needs in the 1980s and well over 50 per cent in the 2010s. In certain sectors it is very dependent indeed, importing over 60 per cent of its natural gas and 85 per cent of its crude oil from outside the EU. Furthermore, the EU is increasingly dependent upon just a few suppliers, and, as the previous paragraph pointed out, they are not always reliable.

Where oil is concerned (2011 figures), about 36 per cent of EU imports are from countries in OPEC (Organization of the Petroleum Exporting Countries) and 32 per cent is from Russia; where gas is concerned, about 40 per cent is from Russia. The second-largest source of gas, Norway, can be considered reliable (it is a member of the European Economic Area even though it had twice voted – narrowly – to reject membership of the EU), but the third-largest supplier, Algeria (15 per cent), is less so. Dependence on a few suppliers that are not entirely reliable can produce difficulties. Moreover, it is not easy to find new suppliers, for instance by creating a new pipeline bypassing Russia through the Southern Gas Corridor. This is a project that the EU decided to push ahead with in 2011 but is one that has its own difficulties, not least its reliance upon Azerbaijan, Georgia and Turkey as the new suppliers, countries that are not necessarily models of reliability themselves.

In such a situation there is a considerable incentive to drive through changes that might otherwise encounter resistance from member states keen to protect their own energy sectors. Unlike in the case of food (except perhaps where obesity is concerned, though this rarely results from items supported through the CAP), lowering consumption is a viable way of reducing energy dependence, and this fact undoubtedly boosts the attractiveness of energy conservation measures. Moreover, 'homegrown' sources of energy in the form of renewables also help to reduce the level of dependence upon others in the energy sector (as well as introducing more 'efficiency' and 'competition', another careful ticking of a Barroso 'growth and jobs' box, not to mention that favourite word 'diversity', usually reserved for a more socio-cultural context). Such considerations provided part of the impetus behind the EU's acceptance of the '20:20:20 by 2020' target in its 2008 Climate and Energy Package (a 20 per cent reduction in greenhouse gas emissions, a 20 per cent increase in energy efficiency and a 20 per cent contribution of renewables to the EU's overall energy supply). As already mentioned, its potential to create jobs was another factor behind the incorporation of a 'green agenda' into the Europe 2020 Strategy.

However, the energy sector also illustrates how other policy considerations can inhibit progress in the environmental field rather than encourage it. Key energy infrastructure projects designed to reduce grid deficiencies in European gas and electricity networks were cut substantially in the budget framework for 2014–20 agreed by member states during acrimonious meetings in 2013, despite the fact that this would help the EU both politically (by reducing dependence on outside suppliers) and environmentally (by reducing consumption). As has already been pointed out in Chapters 5 and 6, the big-spending areas within the EU budget tend to be ones where member states can easily read off 'what's in it for them': a list of landowners receiving direct payments under the CAP, a list of regions benefiting from support as 'less developed' or 'transition' regions. When it comes to pan-European projects such as the Connecting Europe Facility, such 'national' benefits are harder to calculate. As a result, key improvements in the energy and transport sector have remained underfunded, making it much more difficult to make environmental improvements through reducing energy consumption and boosting public transport.

A further reason not to do enough in this area (see Chapter 4) is that there are plenty of 'national champions' in the energy sector for whom a more connected Europe provides unwelcome competition, whatever the savings involved. The result is high prices both for consumers and for companies, holding back industrial recovery (a point made frequently as energy prices rose during 2013), while companies complain that 'we are ignoring the benefits of European cooperation' (Fulvio Conti, CEO of ENEL, the Italian utility) in the energy sector.

The Emissions Trading System

Despite the setbacks they face, environmental policy makers have the flexibility to make their own interests part of satisfying the 'mainstream priorities' of the EU and allaying some of its main concerns. They understand that some tactics work and some do not, though even the ones that work often do not work very well. One example is the Emissions Trading System (ETS), a key part of the Climate and Energy Package. This is a system with an international pedigree, having been supported by the USA in UN negotiations over the Kyoto Protocol to the United Nations Framework Convention on Climate Change in 1997 (which the USA did not sign up to in the end), and having been explored already by some of the member states themselves at national level. Adopting it was a good example of 'policy entrepreneurship'. At the time of the Kyoto negotiations, the preferred approach of the EU to cutting emissions was through a carbon tax, but taxation is a national competence and any new tax system would require a unanimous vote from member states. Moreover, if there is one thing that any state dislikes doing, it is introducing a new tax.

The ETS was developed as a way of reducing emissions without taking the taxation route. It was launched in 2005 on the 'cap and trade' principle. There is a 'cap' or limit on the total amount of certain greenhouse gases that can be emitted, with companies receiving allowances. At first these were provided free, but starting from 2013 companies were required to buy an increasing number of their credits in national auctions. Should they emit more than their allowances cover, they are forced to buy allowances from other companies; should they emit less than their allowances cover, they can sell the rest to companies whose allowances cannot cover their emissions. Control is therefore kept over the level of total emissions, and economic incentives to reduce emissions are provided.

The idea is to make the system tougher as it goes along. Thus the total number of allowances is being reduced over time, so that in 2020 it will be more than one-fifth lower than it was at the start of emissions trading in 2005. At the same time, the system will be extended to industries that are not currently covered by it, such as petrochemicals, ammonia and aluminium. In 2013, about 45 per cent of emissions were covered by the scheme.

It has to be admitted that there have been considerable problems with the system. The trouble was that some companies and some member states (especially those such as Poland that still have a huge reliance upon coal) were won over by an agreement to hand out an excessive number of credits. On top of this political pressure came an economic slowdown that led to a sharp cutback in industrial activity. A huge surplus of permits was the result of these two factors, meaning that in 2013 the price of carbon allowances nosedived. Carbon prices had been as high as 30 euros in 2008, leading companies to invest huge amounts in renewables. But by 2013 they were at one-tenth of the earlier level. To make matters worse, an attempt by the Commission to delay the scheduled auctioning of credits was narrowly overruled by the Parliament in a vote in April 2013, a decision that in effect threatened to turn carbon credits into the ecological equivalent of junk bonds. In July 2013, the Parliament partially reversed that decision, but the price remains too low.

The system operates at present for the 28 member states of the EU and for three states that are outside it – Liechtenstein, Iceland and Norway. Linkage with the Swiss ETS is also being pursued. In principle, however, it could be extended further. There could perfectly well be a global emissions trading system, or at least something trans-continental linking up willing participants from around the world that already have emissions trading schemes of their own (the USA, Japan, New Zealand, Australia). The European Commission has been exploring the possibility of linking the ETS with Australia's, starting from 2015 and achieving full implementation by 2018, though the 2013 election in Australia may have changed that. Companies would be able to use carbon units from either the EU or the Australian ETS for compliance under either system. But low prices have discouraged other ETS countries such as the USA both from further developing their own systems and from linking up with the EU. After all, California sold its carbon allowances in early 2013 at US$14 a ton. Why would it link up with an EU selling them at about US$4 a ton, thus bringing down its own 'pollution price' to unacceptable levels? Analysts who at the end of the last decade expected a world carbon market worth US$2 trillion (about 1.5 trillion euros) hardly found the next decade providing the figures that they were expecting.

In 2012, the UK increased coal-burning for power generation more than 30 per cent, while cutting back gas use by a similar amount. Had the cost of carbon been higher, it might well have decided otherwise. In the EU as a whole, several new coal-burning plants are being planned. Worse still, industrial companies in Europe and elsewhere have less incentive to invest in greenhouse gas abatement projects – for example, wind farms in developing countries such as China – because these projects generated credits that such companies could use to offset their emissions elsewhere. So many credits have been produced by such projects and have been added to the existing oversupply that, by the middle of 2013, they were trading at about 0.30 euros each. The result was not only fewer 'green' investments in Europe but also fewer in the developing world.

Bad though this is, it shows how effective the system would be if only such an oversupply were avoided. In a perverse way, the problems of the ETS scheme only underline how important it could still be if it were ever to be managed effectively. A properly run EU system would have positive knock-on effects elsewhere in the world. However, given the current problems of the EU scheme, it is possible that it will be the rest of the world that manages to develop a viable scheme first. South Korea plans to introduce one in 2015, and China launched a pilot programme in 2013 which is to be extended nationwide in 2015. By then a new European Commission and Parliament may be waking up to the fact that they have fallen behind those for whom they previously saw themselves as setting an example.

The current economic recession makes environmental concerns less of a priority, but paradoxically it also makes them seem more effective than they are. A fall in greenhouse gas emissions may simply be the result of falling production levels stemming from the recession, and have nothing to do with greener policies. The obverse of this paradox is that economic recovery may produce an increase in harmful emissions at precisely the time that people are more prepared to give priority to environmental concerns. Statistical 'trends' therefore have to be treated with great care, and where the inevitable 'targets' are concerned it has to be remembered that countries may be doing well in reaching them for reasons that have nothing to do with their implementing environment-friendly measures.

The importance of binding legislation

As stated at the very beginning of this book, there is every reason to beware of 'targets', a system that often ends up as one of promise without delivery. Are the goals of the EU's Climate and Energy Package (20:20:20 by 2020) a serious target or a figure plucked from nowhere because of its catchiness? Achieving any target depends to some extent upon unpredictable developments in the political and economic spheres. But the likelihood of hitting a target also depends on the powers available to those entrusted with reaching them.

Within the '20:20:20' goal itself, the 20 per cent cut in carbon dioxide emissions and the 20 per cent reliance upon renewables are binding targets; the 20 per cent reduction in consumption, in contrast, is voluntary (one reason, according to the President of the Commission, why this is the least likely target of the three to be met). It is the binding nature of many of the targets in the environmental field that makes for a higher degree of confidence that they will be achieved in this area than in others.

This becomes clear when the environmental field is compared with, for example, education and employment. The 20:20:20 goal by 2020 is only one part of the Europe 2020 Strategy for Growth. There are plenty of targets in other policy areas too: the strategy talks of having 20 million fewer in poverty, a 40 per cent take-up of tertiary education, 75 per cent of 20–64 year olds in employment by 2020, an overall investment of 3 per cent of GDP in research and development, and so on. But areas such as education and employment are national competences. The Commission cannot do much beyond offer what it coyly calls 'the benefits of its overview position'.

It is true that various measures have been taken to try to narrow the difference between the areas in which binding directives can be applied and the areas in which the Commission can only recommend. After all, the Europe 2020 Strategy is the successor to the Lisbon Strategy (which had lots of growth targets for the first decade of the twenty-first century), one of whose failings has been identified as the 'need for stronger governance'. But such measures have to confront the fact that many member states are flatly opposed to anything suggestive of binding directives in areas such as education and employment.

The search has been on to devise a form of 'stronger governance' that does not involve a further extension of sovereignty-sharing. Much has been made of the 'open method of coordination' (OMC), but OMC does not mean that targets become binding. It means that overall targets are translated into national targets for particular member states, that the member states have to report on their progress towards meeting them (in the spring of each year), and that the Commission reads these reports, coordinates the various responses through something called the European Semester and reaches country-specific recommendations in the early summer, which may include 'policy warnings'. These are then passed on to the European Council for its endorsement. It reads like one long Examiners' Meeting, and, though the requirement to report and be assessed might seem like a good way of 'shaming states into action', it could also provide the worst of both worlds, with none of the resentment against EU meddling at national level going away, and gaining by way of compensation none of the effectiveness that such 'meddling' can bring when it comes in the form of binding directives.

The limitations of these other parts of the Europe 2020 Strategy only highlight the importance of the fact that the environmental area is one in which member states *have* been prepared to accept binding directives. Indeed it is awash with them: Drinking Water Directive; Biocides Directive (particularly concerned with the use of pesticides in parks and sports grounds); Habitats and Wild Birds Directive (protecting the habitats of endangered species, including many inside cities); Urban Wastewater Treatment Directive (sewerage systems must be in place and minimum standards must apply for wastewater); CAFE (Clean Air for Europe) Directive (designating limits for air pollutants and defining 'air quality zones'); Large Combustion Plants and Waste Incineration Directives; Fuel Quality Directive; Carbon Capture Storage Directive; directives on packaging, on batteries, on the disposal of electrical equipment and end-of-life vehicles; and so on, often with new directives replacing one or more older ones. But this means that many policies in the environmental area are legally binding and therefore enforceable, making the targets associated with them much more likely to be achievable.

Of course, being subject to an EU directive is not a guarantee of targets being met, but it increases the chances considerably. The 20 per cent cut in carbon dioxide emissions and the 20 per cent reliance upon renewables are, as said, binding targets. Member states are legally obliged to reach a certain target but are free to choose their own method of doing so. The figure is not 20 per cent for each country but varies according to their circumstances. Targets range from 10 per cent in the case of Malta (whose use of renewable energy in 2005 was zero) to nearly 50 per cent in the case of Sweden, which in 2005 already sourced nearly 40 per cent of its energy from renewables. The target for the UK (which in 2005 sourced 1.3 per cent of its energy from renewables) is 15 per cent, a figure that it will find it hard to meet (see the discussion of Cornwall and the Scilly Isles in Chapter 6). Nevertheless, the binding character of these targets ensures that member states will make every effort to reach them.

Even in the area of reducing energy consumption, where the 20 per cent reduction by 2020 is not binding, there are important directives that *are* binding and that will help to produce economies. There is also the pressure of consumer interests, which seek to avoid high energy bills. For instance, 40 per cent of the EU's energy consumption is attributable to buildings (buildings also account for 36 per cent of its carbon dioxide emissions), and the Energy Performance of Buildings Directive requires action to be taken to reduce these. The range of measures to be taken is often of a highly specific nature – for instance making cement using vertical rather than horizontal kilns which require less energy, or using computer technology to create 'smarter' buildings through daylight sensors that control lighting. Such specific requirements show that this is an area that promotes new jobs and skills and is not simply a question of 'energy refits' through further insulation.

One way of making clear how binding legislation can drive forward environmental improvements is to consider a specific policy area. The rest of this chapter will therefore focus on a matter of particular environmental concern, vehicle emissions. Through this example it should be possible to highlight precisely how (and how far) EU directives in the environmental field can be effective.

Figure 12. Reducing carbon dioxide emissions.

Example: vehicle emissions

Addressing the issue of vehicle emissions is only a part of dealing with traffic congestion and the pollution it causes. It may well be the case, as the executive director of the European Environment Agency, Jacqueline McGlade, reported in 2012, that the necessary reduction in greenhouse gas emissions produced in the transport sector cannot be met by technical improvements alone but will also require a significant reduction in transport demand. There may, for instance, be an overall growth in vehicle use, meaning that even if each vehicle is cleaner, overall emissions levels will rise. The approach outlined here, which has nothing to do with exhorting people to walk or get on trains (or making it easier for them to do so), certainly has its limitations. It reinforces a point made earlier, that no part of the European Commission can do its work in isolation. There are certainly wider questions of overall transport policy. But, by being able to take on some of the most powerful industries in Europe, both in terms of employment and in terms of their flag-waving capacity as 'national champions', and bring them into line with perhaps modest but still very effective requirements for limiting emissions, the EU managed to make an important contribution to reducing pollution when it tackled vehicle emissions.

Taming the car industry

The car industry is both a fundamental source of employment for member states (especially if ancillary services are taken into account) and a source of environmental damage. Therefore the issue of vehicle emissions provides both a good illustration of what happens when there is an apparent clash between securing jobs and avoiding pollution and a nicely controversial subject in terms of which to consider what can actually be done.

The focus here is upon light vehicles (cars and vans) and particularly upon cars. Cars alone are responsible for about 12 per cent of total EU emissions of carbon dioxide, and attempts to reduce them can be dated back to the 1990s. However, in the 1990s the approach was one of asking companies to reduce their emissions through a voluntary agreement. This got nowhere. The new century therefore saw the first proposals for something binding as opposed to voluntary – and unsurprisingly this led to conflict. The European Parliament passed a resolution in 2005 in support of mandatory CO_2 emission standards to replace voluntary commitments. In the following year the Commission began to draft a proposal to do so, even though it was clear that the Commission itself was divided on the issue. Anand Menon quotes a letter written by Industry Commissioner Günther Verheugen to the President of the Commission (this was during Barroso's first term as president) and revealed by the *Financial Times* on 23 November 2006:

> Our environmental leadership could significantly undermine the international competitiveness of part of Europe's energy-intensive industries and worsen global environmental performance by redirecting production to parts of the world with lower environmental standards.[4]

By such curious argumentation, the Industry Commissioner managed to suggest that trying to reduce car emissions would end up having a harmful effect on the environment! But the opposite point of view was also plausible, namely that because the EU's single market was now the biggest trading bloc in the world, outstripping even the USA in terms of total GDP, it was likely that producers from outside the EU with lower environmental standards would make an effort to raise their standards, precisely in order to have access to the lucrative EU market. It should never be forgotten that the EU can have environmental clout (not to mention clout in the external relations arena generally) partly because it has economic clout.

It is possible to read the debates at the time in terms of different national perspectives. Unlike (on the whole) the French and the Italians, Germans tend to make big cars. Fiat did not feel affected when the Commission first proposed to reduce car emissions to 120 grams of CO_2 per kilometre, but BMW and Mercedes were not amused. Verheugen was the German commissioner and Germany was about to assume the presidency for the first half of 2007. Though Verheugen's nationality was meant to be irrelevant to his role as commissioner, and Germany's presidency was not meant to be an opportunity for it to advance 'German interests', there is no doubt that they did have such an effect. Was there really likely to be progress on the Commission's proposals during 2007?

The fact that there *was* progress owes much to political pressures pushing in the other direction, including international opinion (the EU was aware of the need to have something for the 'second commitment' period agreed under the Kyoto Protocol) and a powerful environmental lobby within the EU itself. Moreover, other considerations were involved besides the environmental; it was also a question of energy security. This chapter has already mentioned the EU's concern about its dependence upon a small number of (in some cases unreliable) suppliers in order to meet its energy needs, and anything that reduces consumption by increasing fuel efficiency is seen as a contribution to that security. Hence the drive towards reducing energy consumption had both environmental and political components by the end of 2007. Interestingly, the conclusion to the key Commission document putting the case for reducing CO_2 emissions to the Parliament and Council in 2007 began: 'the EU must reduce its dependence on imported oil', a consideration that, though it was not discussed in the text itself, was obviously on everyone's mind at the time.

Hence the initial proposals of the Commission were watered down but not so as to become totally ineffective. What *had* been ineffective was the voluntary system used in the 1990s when the car companies were 'asked' to reduce emissions and failed to do so. What German pressure managed to do was to lower the emission reduction targets for new cars but not to abolish them, and it also led to a later target date for implementation. Under EU legislation that was finally adopted by the European Council and Parliament in 2009, the fleet average to be achieved by all new cars was 130 grams of CO_2 per kilometre instead of the 120 grams originally planned by the Commission. Where the Commission originally planned 120 grams per kilometre for 2012, the eventually adopted target of 130 was for 2015 (by which time all newly registered cars must comply with the ruling), with further reductions to follow by 2020. 'Fleet average' means that firms will still be allowed to make heavier cars with higher emission levels, provided that by way of compensation they also make lighter cars with emission levels that are lower than the target. Manufacturers can pool their fleets in order to receive a collective target, and special derogations (exemptions) are granted to smaller manufacturers (those that produce fewer than 10,000 cars a year and are not connected to another manufacturer).

The Commission did not get what it wanted in terms of binding legislation, but it did get binding legislation. Companies were and are required to comply. Instead of the voluntary policy that failed in the 1990s, this is a much stronger approach that combines carrot and stick. If the average level of CO_2 emissions of a manufacturer's fleet exceeds its limit value in any year, the manufacturer has to pay an excess emissions premium for each car registered (5 euros for the first gram over the target, 15 for the second, 25 for the third and 95 for the fourth and subsequent grams, thus introducing more severe penalties for a larger overshoot). On the other hand, manufacturers are incentivised to support innovative technologies by receiving 'emission credits' if they equip their vehicles with such technologies. They are also incentivised to produce vehicles with extremely low emission levels (below 50 grams per kilometre), being able to count each low-emitting car as three cars in 2013, 2.5 in 2014 and so on down to one car from 2016 onwards. There has been some debate about whether this system is a way of promoting electric and hybrid cars or a way of maintaining gas guzzlers at the other end of the spectrum. It is arguably both, but so long as the average falls it does not matter.

Harnessing the consumer

A further very practical reason why the pressure for lower emissions is difficult to resist is the interests of the consumer. People have a natural concern about fuel costs, particularly at a time when petrol is expensive, and this means that fuel-efficient cars will easily find a market. EU legislation requires member states to provide relevant information to consumers, including a label showing a new car's fuel efficiency and CO_2 emissions. In 2013, the EU published a report from two consultancies, Cambridge Econometrics and Ricardo-AEA, showing that, although the average car will cost about 1,000 euros more in 2020 as a result of alterations made in order to meet the reduced vehicle emissions target of 95 grams per kilometre (for 2020 – though after more German objections in 2013 it may now be 2024), that extra cost will be offset (for the average car owner) through fuel savings within three years. As in so much that has propelled market liberalisation forward (see Chapter 4), the interests of consumers will eventually prevail over those of producers (who, of course, are also themselves consumers). A further knock-on effect of the proposals is that more fuel-efficient vehicles tend to be quieter, producing a benefit in terms of reduced levels of noise pollution.

In July 2012, the Commission proposed a similar approach for the 2015–20 period, driving the target down further, as mentioned in the previous paragraph, to 95 grams per kilometre by 2020. This proposal was accepted by the Parliament and the Council in June 2013 and, subject to their formal confirmation, will become binding legislation. They may not provide this. In September 2013, Germany, backed by the UK, once again stood in the way of progress, insisting that the target for CO_2 emissions be pushed back to 2024. Since the Commission had been asked to produce by 2015 even more stringent targets for 2025, so that the decline in carbon dioxide emissions could continue, there will presumably also be a delay in these targets too. Nevertheless, as with the original proposals, member states with powerful car lobbies can delay but not stop the process of curbing vehicle emissions.

In line with the environmental approach highlighted earlier in this chapter, the Commission is careful to stress the job-creating potential of such targets, with the consultancy report mentioned earlier claiming hundreds of thousands of new jobs. This figure has been contested, but there is no doubt that the technology needed to reach such targets – making lighter cars from aluminium, using stop-start technology that turns the engine off and on at lights and so on – does require the application of new methods. Hence the smelting industry has been enthusiastic about the proposals, whereas the oil refiners have obviously not been.

Early evidence showed that the policy was working. Companies' behaviour could be monitored fairly easily. From 2010 member states were obliged to collect data on the number of new passenger cars registered, their average size and their emissions, all broken down according to the model of car and sent to the Commission as from 2011. Doubtless some states might have been inclined to resent a further example of 'bureaucratic interference' from Brussels, but the data were essential to making the policy work. And they did. As pointed out above, there was very little else that the companies could do apart from comply. If they did not, they either incurred huge fines or forwent entry to a massive market – neither outcome would be acceptable. The only way of avoiding the necessity of adapting their vehicles was for carmakers to manipulate the tests measuring fuel consumption and harmful emissions. There is some evidence that this has taken place,[5] but the introduction of a new test, the World Light-Duty Test Cycle, expected from 2016, should close that loophole. It is significant that the agreement reached between the Council, the Commission and the Parliament in June 2013 called for more realistic test procedures.

Despite the danger that figures achieved in tests do not match the figures taken from real-life performance on the road (where fuel efficiency is concerned, consumers have been careful to measure this for themselves and have often found the official figures over-optimistic), progress in reducing emissions has been made. In December 2012, the European Commission adopted a decision confirming provisional findings that average CO_2 emissions from new cars in the EU fell by 3.3 per cent in 2011: 12.8 million new cars were registered in the EU in 2011, with average CO_2 emissions of 135.7 grams per kilometre, a fall of 4.6 grams as compared with 2010. This would suggest that car manufacturers are on track to reach their target of 130 grams per kilometre by 2015. Since these targets are backed up by measures to enforce compliance, they seem to be achievable so long as the tests are reliable.

Cars are not the only source of vehicle pollution. Mandatory targets have also been agreed for vans or 'light commercial vehicles' (175 grams per kilometre by 2017, falling to 147 grams by 2020). Then there is the question of heavy-duty vehicles (buses and lorries), where emissions limits are assessed differently – by measuring engine energy output (grams per kilowatt hour) rather than by measuring driving distance (grams per kilometre). Progress has been made here too, with stricter limits on pollutant emissions having come into force in early 2013. 'Heavy motor vehicles' (lorries or trucks) have had to reduce their nitrogen oxide emissions by 80 per cent and their emissions of particulate matter by 66 per cent as compared with a 2008 baseline. This is particularly important in view of the fact that road freight traffic is increasing (raising some of the general questions about transport policy mentioned earlier).

Proposals in April 2013 for more aerodynamic lorries offered another approach to reducing emissions from heavy goods vehicles. Rounded cabins and flaps at the back of the trailer would improve safety (granting drivers an increased field of vision), reduce fuel costs (through a more aerodynamic structure) and are a further example of the way in which 'greening' Europe can be good for employment.

The Italian industry and entrepreneurship commissioner for 2009–14, Antonio Tajani, had a completely different approach, where stronger measures to control emissions are concerned, from that taken by his predecessor as industry commissioner for 2004–9, the German commissioner Günther Verheugen. Whereas Verheugen had argued that such measures would *threaten* exports, Tajani argued that they would *boost* exports. The Commission had deliberately introduced procedures and standards for testing heavy vehicle emissions that would give EU lorries the same emission limit values as those (stricter ones) that apply in the USA. He was therefore able to declare in early 2013:

> Today's emission reduction will help clean up the air we breathe and improve the competitiveness of Europe's automobile industry [...] we will have cleaner trucks and buses, which will be trendsetters and exportable worldwide.

This enabled Tajani to talk of a 'win–win' situation for both economic and environmental interest groups. Whereas Verheugen had warned of higher standards causing environmental damage by redirecting production to parts of the world with lower standards, Tajani's response shows the opposite view, namely that higher standards encourage the rest of the world to improve in order to be able to export to the EU (in this case, of course, it was the EU that improved in order to be able to export to the USA). As stated earlier, a huge market such as the EU can have high environmental standards for itself that in turn induce others to have higher standards themselves in order to be able to penetrate the EU market. There does not always have to be a 'race to the bottom' where competitive markets are concerned – there can also be a race to the top.

For this reason, Transport Commissioner Siim Kallas was able to describe his aerodynamic lorries in terms of 'a greener truck for the global market', supporting the 'race to the top' position that a more environmental approach can in fact boost exports. In the same way, vehicles with lower emissions will be an attractive export to countries with serious pollution problems, particularly in major cities such as Beijing. The Air Quality Index in the Chinese capital went off the charts in January 2013, producing numerous 'airpocalypse' tales, and northern China was again affected in October 2013. The problem is clearly not going to go away.

It is worth emphasising what has *not* been done in order to reduce vehicle emissions. The Commission has steered clear of fiscal measures. As stated earlier in the discussion of the ETS, taxation is jealously guarded as a national competence. The EU recognised the failure of its attempt to have a 'carbon tax' introduced in the 1990s, and turning to the ETS was a way round that problem. Similarly, though several member states have adopted fiscal measures to promote the purchase of cars that emit less CO_2, the Commission has not been tempted to try to turn this into a Council Directive requiring compliance. Instead its focus has been upon reducing vehicle emissions in the manner described above, the emphasis where the consumer is concerned being on extra savings (in fuel efficiency), even if there is some initial outlay (a higher purchase price). Studies have shown that this appeal to cost-saving is very successful in the environmental field, with people prepared to pay to insulate their houses, for instance, so long as they can see that they will save more in terms of heating bills in the medium term.[6] In the case of both cars and homes, people accept a greater initial outlay if what they own is then cheaper to run. In addition, of course, there are the benefits to the environment as a whole.

Conclusion

The environmental field is one in which the EU likes to claim to be a world leader. Whether or not that is the case, it has no cause for complacency, as the problems with the ETS outlined earlier in this chapter make clear. In this area, it may well be other parts of the world that adopt a successful scheme first.

The achievements of the EU have come only partly because of the natural interest in environmental matters that follows from increasing concern about climate change. They also owe much to the sort of 'policy entrepreneurship' that adopts priorities such as 'jobs and growth' or 'energy security', and show that progress in these areas can be an indirect result of investment in 'green' policies. Policy entrepreneurship is valuable but runs the risk of underplaying the environmental benefits of a sound environmental policy. Moreover, there are other considerations outside the environmental field that may militate *against* certain environmental measures, such as the implications of more integration in the energy field for the support of 'national champions' or the fact that it is difficult to read off specific national benefits from measures to improve overall infrastructure rather than help 'this particular region'.

Policies in the environmental area manage to attract popular support when it is clear that green alternatives are (at least in the medium term) cheaper, avoiding a system of 'green taxes' (which member states would not accept anyway). Such taxes would have the opposite effect of making green policies something everyone has to pay for rather than something that means they end up paying less.

Two other factors have been essential to the success the EU has enjoyed in the environmental area. One is the power of the single market, which is big and attractive enough to persuade manufacturers that they should conform to its requirements. The other is the acceptance of binding legislation, as opposed to voluntary agreements, which rarely if ever work. Where reducing vehicle emissions is concerned, this is clearly the case. Not only must laws concerning such emissions be passed (following the usual amendments to Commission proposals that can be expected from both the Council and the Parliament); they must be enforceable. In the case of vehicle emissions, this means that manufacturers must collect data in a fair and transparent manner, that national governments must receive these data from the companies and pass them on to the Commission and that the Commission in turn must assess the data and, if necessary, fine companies that have exceeded permitted limits. There have been some problems along this 'chain of command', but overall the policy shows signs of working. There can be little doubt that, in the environmental area, the power of enforceable secondary legislation, backed up by the attractions of the single market, can make 'green' behaviour not only morally desirable but commercially compelling. It needs to be both.

9

Conclusion

This book set out to explain what the European Union is in terms of a general outline of its history and structures. Its fundamental argument was that the EU is unlike any other organisation of states. It tried to develop this by looking at the history of the EU from the beginnings of the European Coal and Steel Community in 1951 (but with a brief consideration of earlier attempts to manage relations between European states). It also examined its overall structure and the institutions that make it up.

In doing so it had a central narrative. The EU is neither 28 states desperate to escape from each other and find their own separate space, nor a single state in the making. These apparently opposite views of the EU are in fact very similar. They can think of nation-states relating to one another only in the traditional manner – at a distance. The 'eurosceptic' would return Europe to being a continent of separate nations that will be more likely to return to the traditional animosities of the past. The 'eurofederalist' (if that is the right word to use for this position) would create a superstate that will knock against the other 'superstates' bestriding the world: the USA, Russia, China and perhaps others to come. Both scenarios are based on the view that nation-states cannot be brought into the sort of close-knit relationship that has enabled them not only to retain their separate identities but also to cooperate and integrate to an extent that makes conflict effectively unthinkable.

Against those who advocate that the EU should 'finish off' the process of becoming a single state or of breaking up into 28 'properly independent' states, this book argues that the EU has developed a uniquely close relationship between states that has been of benefit to all of them. Unfortunately, the advocates of these 'eurosceptic' and 'eurofederal' positions tend to feed off each other as they turn the EU into a candle burning at both ends. Since both agree that the EU in its present form is unworkable, the victories of one side are immediately seen by the other as a justification of its own position. The more one side cries for 'more Europe', the more the other side calls for 'less Europe'. In the resultant cacophony, what is needed above all is a calm assessment of how far the EU has gone in building up the postwar European order. However, in deference to the eurosceptics, it is equally necessary to have a calm assessment of areas where the EU should not try to go in developing that order further. It is not state-building.

Later in the book, five areas were examined within which such a close relationship between member states has proved useful. It is not the intention of this final chapter to present nation-states as in difficulty and then the EU riding in like a knight in shining armour to put everything right. For instance, labour mobility facilitated by various EU exchange projects will not end unemployment in member states (Chapter 4). More than a decade of European funding has not taken Cornwall's GDP per head above 75 per cent (Chapter 6). A naval task force in the Horn of Africa, and even a 'comprehensive' approach that joins this to development and retraining projects in Somalia itself, will not end the country's problems (Chapter 7), or why would so many Somalis be so desperate to leave their country for the EU that they are prepared to risk (and in some cases suffer) drowning? It would be ridiculous to suggest that, when the 'Wonderpets of the EU' come flying in, the nation in danger is set free. The concrete examples given are simply an attempt to suggest that the jargon of 'multilevel governance' has some resonance. The presence of a Community level in addressing problems can help in their resolution – as can that of a powerful sub-national and regional level. Nation-states are not the only game in town.

Moreover, the recognition of a Community level can help to change the perception of problems at the national level. When people in the

UK, for instance, say that a large number of migrants from Eastern Europe arriving in the UK creates problems, they are right. It does. But those problems are the other side of an opportunity that not only allows Romanians to work in the UK but allows the British to be jobseekers throughout Europe. Cornwall's problems are not 'solved' by the EU, but projects that link it to the far-flung coastal areas of neighbouring countries help to strengthen its own identity.

There is no doubt that the binding nature of European Law enables important decisions to be made at the Community level that can succeed in having an effect when voluntary agreements fall short. Chapter 8 sought to illustrate this in the case of vehicle emissions. The environmental area is one where increasing numbers of people recognise that binding legislation is the only way forward. But even in areas such as the environment, where the EU is widely given some credit, the book has been careful to point out that it falls short in a number of respects, as the current state of the Emissions Trading System shows. It has also been quick to point out the failings of the Common Agricultural Policy; indeed, the EU's success in the field of organic farming, though important, is to some extent a product of its failure to deal with the central problem of how to cure the problem of overproduction without alienating farmers (Chapter 5).

To end as this book began, 2014 is a good point at which to present an introduction to the EU. Elections are producing a new Parliament and a new Commission is being formed. A new multi-annual financial framework (let us call it 'budget') is in place until 2021 and the EU has its Europe 2020 Strategy with its various 'targets'. In that sense, 2014 should give a good idea of where the EU thinks it is going for the rest of the decade.

But that is not all that is happening. There is a severe recession in the world and a crisis in the eurozone, both of which have sent shock-waves through the system. There may be a member state (the UK) voting (for the second time) on whether to leave the EU altogether. (If the UK does have a vote and the vote is 'Yes', then by the end of the decade the UK will have left – if there is a UK, given that 2014 sees a referendum on Scotland's future within the UK.) Thus 2014 is not just a year when the EU will 'settle in' a new Commission and Parliament and start to make a serious attempt to realise its 'targets' for 2020. It is bound to be the start of a politically unsettling and even traumatising period, during which many member states (not just the UK) are likely to go through the sort of painful reconsideration of the whole 'European project' that is further exacerbated by a dire economic situation and in particular a huge rise in joblessness.

One thing is clear. Either it is recognised, in a practical and down-to-earth manner, that there is an EU dimension to solving the economic and environmental crisis that we are in, or the Community itself is unlikely to survive. It all began with the perception on the part of France that it could use Germany's desire for national survival as an instrument of its own national recovery. It will continue if the nation-states that are in the EU now continue to find it as useful to them as it was to the six founders in the 1950s. Practical considerations (at the national level) began the process, and it is practical considerations (again, largely at the national level) that will sustain it.

The most important practical consideration is that a system of managing the relations between nation-states has been built up that minimises the chance of their going to war again. For that alone the EU deserved its Nobel Peace Prize in 2012. A European dimension provides a wider perspective that can help to make bitterly felt regional and national tensions less all-consuming. Macedonia is an official candidate country to join the EU, but its accession has been held up by a dispute with Greece over its name (there is also a region of Greece called Macedonia). When I spoke to a group of Macedonian students visiting the Commission, it was perhaps trite of me to mention that there is a region of Belgium called Luxembourg, which did not seem to have provoked conflict with the Grand Duchy next door, and to quote Shakespeare's *Romeo and Juliet* to the effect that 'a rose by any other name would smell as sweet'. I am sure that they rightly saw through my lack of knowledge of the complexities of Balkan history. But I still think that there is as much value for them in having a broader European perspective as there doubtless is for me in knowing more about the history of South-East Europe.

Where the UK and Ireland are concerned, it is clear (to Ireland definitely, to the UK less so) that a broader European perspective has helped to foster the peace process in Northern Ireland. Of course that broader perspective may paradoxically encourage separatism, in that it reminds Scotland and Catalonia that they would hardly be exceptional in terms of size if they were to become separate members of the EU. But that is the whole point. A European dimension is supposed to provide support for the national and sub-national levels of governance, making them more confident about their own identity. Perhaps also (and this, I suspect, is the underlying source of the visceral dislike of the EU among many in the UK) it provides a better context within which nations can flourish than the UK's own peculiar 'Union', in which (ignoring the complexities of Northern Ireland for the moment) three nations awkwardly co-inhere, with a parliament or assembly for the two smaller ones, Scotland and Wales, but not for the larger one, England, and no attempt to enable them all to come together (as in Germany) in a regionally based second chamber, which instead is set apart for unelected appointees.

It is not the facile slogans on the huge banners suspended from the Berlaymont building in the Brussels rain that will change anyone's mind about the EU, any more than the omnipresent faces of Lenin and Marx in the former communist countries of Central and Eastern Europe persuaded anyone in Czechoslovakia or Poland that their societies were part of a stateless utopia. It is a range of practical and useful arrangements that show the next generation how much is to be gained by living among states who agree to a partial sharing of sovereignty. When the cry goes up 'What has the EU ever done for us?' the reply needs to be eminently practical if it is to persuade. This book has tried to suggest an equivalent to the aqueducts, the central heating, the villas and the wine which, as mentioned in the Preface, reminded John Cleese of the benefits of the Roman Empire in Monty Python's classic *Life of Brian*. If it has fallen short in its presentation of every stripe on the quagga, the book may at least have provided some idea of what the creature tries to do. Of course, in the case of the quagga its usefulness made no difference to the fact that the hunters wiped it out. It remains to be seen whether in this less hopeful respect the quagga and the institution to which I have compared it are alike.

Notes

Preface

1. Hewitt, Gavin, *The Lost Continent* (London: Hodder & Stoughton, 2013).

Chapter 1

1. Benedetto Croce quoted in Wilson, Kevin and van der Dussen, Jan, eds, *The History of the Idea of Europe* (Milton Keynes: Open University, 1995), p. 144.
2. See Michelle Cini's chapter on 'Intergovernmentalism' in Cini, Michelle and Pérez-Solórzano Borragán, Nieves, eds, *European Union Politics* (3rd edition, Oxford: Oxford University Press, 2010), p. 91.
3. Those wanting to explore the theories further could try Dimitris N. Chryssochoou's *Theorizing European Integration* (London: Routledge, 2009). The author plumps for 'organised synarchy'.
4. Rosamond, Ben, 'New theories of European integration', in Cini and Perez-Solórzano Borragán, *European Union Politics*, p. 107.
5. Ibid., p. 120.
6. McCormick, John, *Understanding the European Union: A Concise Introduction* (5th edition, London: Palgrave Macmillan, 2011).
7. Menon, Anand, *Europe: The State of the Union* (London: Atlantic Books, 2008), p. 71.
8. Ibid., p. xiii.
9. Laffan, Brigid, O'Donnell, Rory and Smith, Michael, *Europe's Experimental Union: Rethinking Integration* (London: Routledge, 2000).
10. Corner, Mark, *The Binding of Nations: From European Union to World Union* (London: Palgrave, 2010).

Chapter 2

1. For more detail see Corner, Mark, *The Binding of Nations: From European Union to World Union* (London: Palgrave, 2010), chapter 2.
2. Cooper, Robert, *The Breaking of Nations* (New York: Atlantic Monthly Press, 2003), p. 58.
3. Davies, Norman, *Europe: A History* (London: Pimlico, 1997), p. 568.
4. A year after the Papal States had been forcibly turned into a republic and the Pope put into prison (1798), the German romantic poet Novalis was lamenting the good old times when 'Europa ein christliches Land war' (when Europe was a Christian land), and three years later the French writer Chateaubriand was emphasising the political cohesion brought by Christianity in his *Génie du christianisme* (1802).
5. See Fimister, Alan Paul, *Robert Schuman: Neo Scholastic Humanism and the Reunification of Europe* (Oxford: Peter Lang, 2008).
6. Quoted in Phillips, Walter Alison, *The Confederation of Europe* (New York: Fertig, 1966), p. 183.
7. Thomson, David, *England in the Nineteenth Century* (London: Penguin, 1991), p. 27.
8. As the title of one of the most well-known works on the years leading up to World War I makes clear, lack of general conflict or all-out war between European states ran alongside a state of perpetual tension. See Taylor, A.J.P., *The Struggle for Mastery in Europe 1848–1918* (Oxford: Clarendon Press, 1971).
9. Quoted in Wilson, Kevin and van der Dussen, Jan, *The History of the Idea of Europe* (London: Routledge, 1995), p. 96.
10. May, Alex, *Britain and Europe since 1945* (London: Longman, 1999), p. 5.
11. Judt, Tony, *Postwar: A History of Europe since 1945* (London: Penguin, 2005), p. 94.
12. May, *Britain and Europe since 1945*, p. 15.
13. Judt, *Postwar*, p. 150.
14. See May, *Britain and Europe since 1945*, pp. 99–100, for extracts from Churchill's speech and later 'clarification' by Churchill of what he meant to say.
15. This and the following quotation can be found in the useful selection of Schuman's speeches by David Heilbron Price and reproduced on his (massively untidy!) website, www.schuman.info, together with information about his Schuman Project and useful analysis of the difference between 'federalism' and 'supranationalism'. Price has a bone to pick with what he sees as people who underrate Schuman (particularly by allowing Monnet to eclipse him), but his material is nevertheless helpful – albeit much of it laid out like a collage in the making.

16. Duchêne, François, *Jean Monnet: The First Statesman of Independence* (New York: W.W. Norton & Co, 1994), p. 347.
17. Ibid., p. 347.
18. Milward, Alan, *The European Rescue of the Nation-State* (London: Routledge, 1999).
19. See Dinan, Desmond, *Europe Recast: A History of European Union* (London: Palgrave, 2004), p. 40.
20. Bálint Szele, '"The European lobby": The Action Committee for the United States of Europe', *European Integration Studies*, Vol. 4, No. 2 (2005), pp. 109–19.
21. This quotation from Alain Peyrefitte's *C'était de Gaulle* can be found in Alain Menon's *Europe: The State of the Union* (London: Atlantic Books, 2008), p. 214.
22. See May, *Britain and Europe since 1945*, p. 45. For more detail, see Bell, P.M.H., *France and Britain, 1940–1994: The Long Separation* (London: Longman, 1997).
23. From Roy Denman's *Missed Chances: Britain and Europe in the Twentieth Century* (London: Cassell, 1996), p. 249. As the title suggests, the book is a fairly critical account of Britain's failure to manage its relations with the rest of Europe, written just as the Major government was busy imploding over this very question.
24. Cecchini, Paolo, *The European Challenge, 1992* (Aldershot: Wildwood, 1988).
25. The European currency unit was calculated on the basis of a basket of currencies in order to try to stabilise exchange rates before the adoption of the euro, at the rate 1 ECU = 1 euro in 1999.
26. Thatcher, Margaret, *The Downing Street Years* (London: HarperCollins, 1993), p. 547.
27. Dinan, Desmond, *Ever Closer Union: An Introduction to European Integration* (London: Palgrave Macmillan, 2010), p. 84.
28. See the report in the *Guardian*, 27 August 2002.

Chapter 3

1. Dinan, Desmond, *Ever Closer Union: An Introduction to European Integration* (London: Palgrave Macmillan, 2010), p. 205.
2. Ibid., p. 310.
3. Quoted in Kapsis, Ilias, 'The courts of the European Union', in Cini, Michelle and Perez-Solórzano Borragán, Nieves, eds, *European Union Politics* (3rd edition, Oxford: Oxford University Press, 2010), p. 177. The chapter provides a useful overview of the main cases.
4. Quoted in Nugent, Neill, *The Government and Politics of the European Union* (7th edition, London: Palgrave Macmillan, 2010), p. 213.

5. See Kapsis, 'The courts of the European Union', p. 184. Case Study 11.4 looks at *Francovich and Bonifaci v. Italy* (1991).
6. Nugent, *The Government and Politics of the European Union*, p. 220.
7. Dinan, *Ever Closer Union*, p. 223.
8. See the report in the *Guardian*, 22 April 2010.
9. See the article 'Why do MEPs fear electoral reform?' by Liberal MEP Andrew Duff in the *EUobserver* of 14 March 2012, http://euobserver.com/opinion/115596 (accessed 31 January 2014).
10. Dinan, *Ever Closer Union*, pp. 319–20.
11. See the chapter 'Interest groups and the European Union' by Rainer Eising and Sonja Lehringer in Cini and Perez-Solórzano Borragán, eds, *European Union Politics*, especially the section on 'The Europeanisation of interests', pp. 202–4.

Chapter 4

1. Quoted in Ó Tuathail, Gearóid, Dalby, Simon and Routledge, Paul, eds, *The Geopolitics Reader* (2nd edition, London: Routledge, 2003), p. 115.
2. Fukuyama's article was originally published in *The National Interest* in 1989, and then expanded into a book, *The End of History and the Last Man* (New York: Free Press, 1992).
3. See the EUR-Lex website, which provides access to cases involving European Union Law. The specific case involving Belgium and margarine (Judgment of the Court of 10 November 1982) can be found at http://eur-lex.europa.eu/smartapi/cgi/sga_doc?smartapi!celexplus!prod!CELEXnumdoc&lg=en&numdoc=61981J0261 (accessed 3 February 2014).
4. McCormick, John, *Understanding the European Union: A Concise Introduction* (5th edition, London: Palgrave Macmillan, 2011), p. 155.
5. Thatcher, Margaret, *The Downing Street Years* (London: HarperCollins, 1993), p. 540.
6. There is a fascinating account of the Conservative government's attitudes to economic integration between 1979 and 1997 in Jim Buller's *National Statecraft and European Integration* (London: Continuum, 2000), pp. 70–1.
7. Menon, Amand, *Europe: The State of the Union* (London: Atlantic Books, 2008), p. 52.
8. *OECD Economic Surveys: European Union 2012* (OECD Publishing, 2012), http://dx.doi.org/10.1787/eco_surveys-eur-2012-en (accessed 3 February 2014).
9. The *Wall Street Journal* article ('EU aims to boost worker mobility throughout region') can be read online at http://online.wsj.com/article/SB10001424052748703518704576258501173219510.html (accessed 3 February 2014).

10. To read it online, go to http://ec.europa.eu/social/BlobServlet?doc
    Id=6324&langId=en (accessed 3 February 2014). Copies of the journal
    can also be ordered as a periodical – see the website of DG Employment,
    Social Affairs and Inclusion, http://ec.europa.eu/social/home.jsp?
    langId=en (accessed 7 February 2014).

Chapter 5

1. Dinan, Desmond, *Ever Closer Union: An Introduction to European
   Integration* (London: Palgrave Macmillan, 2010), pp. 346–7.
2. See Fouilleux, Eve, 'The Common Agricultural Policy', in Cini, Michelle
   and Perez-Solórzano Borragán, Nieves, eds, *European Union Politics*
   (3rd edition, Oxford: Oxford University Press, 2010), p. 352.
3. D'Oultremont, Clémentine, 'Introducing more equity in the CAP: A
   difficult challenge', Egmont Paper 55, June 2012, p. 22 (produced by the
   Royal Institute for International Relations in Brussels and published by
   Academia Press in Ghent, Belgium). It is available in PDF form at www.
   egmontinstitute.be/paperegm/ep55.pdf (accessed 4 February 2014).
4. See Rousseau, Sandra and Vranken, Liesbet, 'Green market expansion by
   reducing information asymmetries: Evidence for labeled organic food
   products', *Food Policy*, Vol. 40 (2013), pp. 33–4.
5. A brief overview of EU legislation on organic production and the labelling
   of organic products is to be found at http://ec.europa.eu/agriculture/
   organic/eu-policy/eu-legislation/brief-overview/index_en.htm   (accessed
   25 February 2014))

Chapter 6

1. Menon, Anand, *Europe: The State of the Union* (London: Atlantic Books,
   2008), p. 161.

Chapter 7

1. Quoted in Dinan, Desmond, *Ever Closer Union: An Introduction to
   European Integration* (London: Palgrave Macmillan, 2010), p. 565.
2. See 'The EU and the Millennium Development Goals' at http://ec.europa.
   eu/europeaid/what/millenium-development-goals/index_en.htm
   (accessed 5 February 2014).

Chapter 8

1. Fears of 'reverse' integration were discussed in an article by A. Liberaroe
   entitled 'Problems of transitional policy making: Environmental policy in

the EC', *European Journal of Political Research*, Vol. 19, Nos 2–3 (1993), pp. 281–305. They were taken up a decade later (after the environment had spread its wings, or tentacles, into other departments) in a book edited by Professor Andrew Jordan, *Environmental Policy in the European Union* (London: Earthscan, 2002). The revised second edition (Earthscan, 2005), subtitled 'Actors, Institutions, and Processes', considers how far 'reverse integration' has occurred.

2. European Commission, *Renewables Make the Difference* (Luxembourg: Publications Office of the European Union, 2011), p. 5.
3. Ibid.
4. The letter is quoted in Menon, Anand, *Europe: The State of the Union* (London: Atlantic Books, 2008), p. 144.
5. As reported by BBC News on 14 March 2013; see www.bbc.co.uk/news/business-21759258 (accessed 6 February 2014).
6. See Audenaert, Amaryllis, De Boeck, Liesje and Beliën, Jeroen, 'The governmental policy of subsidizing the investment in PV panels from the viewpoint of the average Flemish household: Evaluation and suggestions', in Lohani, Sunil Prasad, ed., *Renewable Energy for Sustainable Future* (iConcept Press, 2013); available at http://iconceptpress.com/books/renewable-energy-for-sustainable-future (accessed 6 February 2014).

General observations concerning sources

Introduction

One very important point to make is that, precisely because this book has set out to be specific, it is bound to suffer from the instant obsolescence of any attempt to be contemporary. Shortly after submitting the final version of this book, I went through the latest edition of the weekly *European Voice* and found that some details of what I had written about the Citizens' Initiative, the Common Agricultural Policy budget for 2014–20 and the Emissions Trading System were already behind the curve. This is inevitable, but it has implications for research and reading. Though books will always be (in my opinion) the most important teaching and learning resource, it is vital that anyone studying the EU reads the latest articles in newspapers and journals (some of them in shops and some available only online) and also the articles produced by some of the leading research institutes and think tanks, partly because these will provide the most up-to-date material. It is also advisable to consult EU websites, particularly those of the Commission. It is true that these will not provide material overtly critical of the EU, but astute readers of what the Directorate-General (DG) for Employment, Social Affairs and Inclusion has to say, for instance, will see plenty of implied criticism of 'Commission policy' and will easily recognise that in many policy areas there are in fact several Commission views.

There are useful websites that can be accessed as a complement to using books. For example, Oxford University Press has published an excellent multi-authored textbook, *European Union Politics*, edited by Michelle Cini and Nieves Pérez-Solórzano Borragán, and also provides complementary material through its online resource centre (see http:// global.oup.com/uk/orc/politics/eu/cini4e, accessed 21 February 2014). The complementary material includes PowerPoint presentations, maps, video updates, tables and figures, links to journal articles and an email alert to update you on new entries as they happen.

Online sources

EU websites are (on the whole) clear and informative (as well as being multilingual).

www.europarl.europa.eu is the homepage for the European Parliament, with up-to-date accounts of its activities and the different political groupings.

www.consilium.europa.eu is the homepage of the European Council.

www.curia.europa.eu is the official website of the Court of Justice and provides access to case-law, enabling you to read up on key rulings.

www.ec.europa.eu is the official website for the European Commission, and will contain obvious links to priorities such as the Europe 2020 Strategy. However, you will probably want to investigate the work of a particular department (or DG). Simply look at the list of departments on the homepage and click on whatever one you want. Top of the list, for instance, is Agriculture and Rural Development (DG AGRI). Click on that for the Commission's presentation of particular issues such as the Common Agricultural Policy or organic farming.

The EU bookshop (https://bookshop.europa.eu) is an online book-shop and an archive of publications from the European institutions. It is managed by the Publications Office of the European Union in Luxembourg, and hard copies of texts can be purchased online using a credit card. PDF versions of the texts, on the other hand, are available free online. A brief and simple overview is offered by *Europe in 12 Lessons*, and under the heading 'The EU explained' a series of illustrated pamphlets describe EU activity in various policy areas (competition, agriculture and so on). 'How the European Union works: Your guide to the EU institutions' can be downloaded free or ordered as a 39-page illustrated pamphlet from the EU bookshop (http://bookshop.europa.eu/en/how-the-european-union-works-pbNA3212336). Published in 2012, it is a very helpful introduction to the institutions.

Not all the publications of the EU bookshop are rudimentary. At a more sophisticated level, it also publishes Professor Klaus-Dieter Borchardt's *The ABC of European Union Law* (http://bookshop. europa.eu/en/the-abc-of-european-union-law-pbOA8107147), published in 2012. This is an excellent account – by an EU official who is also an honorary professor of law at Würzburg University in Germany – of the most important, distinctive and difficult element of the EU anatomy, European Law, and provides 140 free pages (in PDF format) of discussion.

BBC Parliament's *Politics Europe* provides the best online BBC material about the EU. Adam Fleming's 30-minute 'An insider's guide to the EU' is not a bad introduction to the institutions. BBC News Europe, on the other hand, is much less useful and is short of analysis. It produced a useful glossary of what it called 'European Union jargon' in 2010 – see www.bbc.co.uk/news/world-europe-11767037. Though it could do with updating, its definitions are helpful.

Newspapers and journals

The Economist has a section on Europe (including a weekly Charlemagne column) and publishes each quarter its *Economist Intelligence Unit Country Reports* and *European Policy Analyst*. These are packed with economic information and will necessarily provide a more up-to-date account of ongoing problems, such as the eurozone crisis, than any book can. The *Financial Times* is the daily with the best coverage of EU matters. Both *The Economist* and the *Financial Times* have useful websites, though access has to be paid for. The Financial Times Brussels Blog (http://blogs.ft.com/brusselsblog) provides useful up-to-date material on the eurozone crisis and other EU matters.

European Voice is an excellent and informative weekly specifically focused on EU issues. It is produced and (largely) sold in Brussels but can be consulted online (www.europeanvoice.com), though it requires a subscription for full access. *EUobserver* (www.euobserver.com) is balanced and informative and access is free.

Think tanks and research institutes

There are well over 20 think tanks based in Brussels alone, but many of them are essentially pressure groups and find it hard to absorb a view of the world beyond the sides of their own tanks. One of the best is the Centre for European Policy Studies (www.ceps.be). Also useful are the European Policy Centre (www.epc.eu), the Centre for European Reform (www.cer.org.uk), based in London rather than Brussels, and The Bruegel Institute (despite the hints of fine art, Bruegel is actually a ponderous acronym for Brussels European and Global Economic Laboratory, which is a think tank producing a lot of material on economic policy (www.bruegel.org).

Two research institutes should be mentioned. Chatham House in London (www.chathamhouse.org) provides an excellent resource for international affairs and is very useful for material concerning the EU (one of its current projects concerns assessing the future of the UK in the EU). The Egmont Institute in Brussels (www.egmontinstitute.be) has a similar focus on international affairs, but with a great deal of useful EU-related material.

Academic journals

The most useful is the *Journal of Common Market Studies* (published by John Wiley), which contains many good and readable articles. One of its editors, Michelle Cini, is also one of the editors of *European Union Politics*, the best multi-authored general introduction to the EU (published by Sage). Wiley also publishes *Political Studies*, which has some useful discussions of democracy and legitimacy in an EU context.

Books

Recommended reading, together with useful definitions and abbreviations, will be provided on a chapter-by-chapter basis in the next section.

Statistics

It is very important to have reliable statistics on matters such as unemployment rates, growth rates, poverty levels, migration rates, and so on. Often this means having an understanding not only of figures but of the definitions on the basis of which they are arrived at (for example, how do you define a person who is unemployed; what is your definition of poverty?). Statistical tables do not always make this clear. Material produced by DG Eurostat is an excellent source of information, both online (http://epp.eurostat.ec.europa.eu/portal/page/portal/statistics/themes) and in the form of the *Eurostat Regional Yearbook*, which contains graphs and explanations of how the statistics are arrived at. *The Eurostat Regional Yearbook 2013* (Luxembourg: Publications Office of the European Union, 2013) was available in the autumn of that year, based on statistics collected at the beginning of the year (in most cases – and it specifies which). The same will apply in subsequent years.

Abbreviations, definitions and further reading

This section will contain useful material for both background and further reading on a chapter-by-chapter basis. It does not provide an exhaustive list.

Many textbooks already provide extensive lists of terms and abbreviations. See, for instance, the glossary at the back of Cini, Michelle and Pérez-Solórzano Borragán, Nieves, eds, *European Union Politics* (3rd edition, Oxford: Oxford University Press, 2010), pp. 437–53, and the list of abbreviations on pp. xxvi–xxxi.

What is provided below is a limited glossary and list of abbreviations, namely those that are used in this book (which has tried as far as possible to steer clear of them), together with some useful definitions (sometimes amounting almost to short essays) and recommendations for futher research.

Chapters 1 & 2: Introduction and History

Abbreviations and definitions

Referring to the European Union and its predecessors

It is very important to understand the abbreviations that mark the (complex) development of what eventually became the European Union (EU). Essentially they are all stages in the development of partial sovereignty-sharing between nation-states. This began with the ECSC (European Coal and Steel Community). There was then (in

1954) a failed attempt to set up a European Defence Community (EDC) and bring it together with the ECSC under the single umbrella of a European Political Community. In 1957 the Treaties of Rome added to the ECSC two other communities, the EEC (European Economic Community) and EURATOM (European Atomic Energy Community). There were now three communities, and though in 1965 they agreed to share the same institutions they remained formally separate (the ECSC, set up for half a century, was finally dissolved in 2002). Naturally enough, attention was focused on the EEC, which was often called the Common Market in the English-speaking world (and this description was used when the UK had its referendum in 1975 on whether to remain part of the EEC). The 1992 Treaty of Maastricht dropped the 'economic' and referred to the Economic Community (EC) as one of the three pillars of what was now called the European Union (EU). The Treaty of Lisbon dropped the pillars and it is now usual simply to refer to the EU.

One source of confusion lies in the fact that these abbreviations are often confused with similar abbreviations used for institutions of the EU. Thus EC might refer to European Community, but it might also refer to European Commission. Since the love of abbreviations overcomes all fear of ambiguity, it is necessary to judge from the context. See the 'Abbreviations and definitions' section of Chapter 3 for a discussion of abbreviations used to describe institutions.

Referring to treaties

Treaties are referred to by their name (Paris, Rome, Maastricht, Amsterdam, Nice and Lisbon) with the exception of the Single European Act, which is sometimes given the abbreviation SEA (there is an abstruse discussion about the sense in which it was 'really' a treaty – in fact it was arguably one of the most important).

Referring to other organisations

The OEEC (Organisation for European Economic Co-operation) was the forerunner of the OECD (Organisation for Economic Co-operation and Development), formed in 1961 and with its head-quarters in Paris.

EFTA (the European Free Trade Area) was set up in 1960 as a counter to the EEC. The main difference between the two was the lack of a common external tariff in the case of EFTA. Some EFTA members went on to become members of the EEC, and others sought special economic ties with the EEC despite remaining outside it. The result of this was the creation in 1994 of the EEA (European Economic Area), which essentially allowed Liechtenstein, Norway and Iceland to have a degree of access to the internal market without being formally part of the EU. Some people think this could be a model for the UK if it leaves the EU.

NATO is the North Atlantic Treaty Organization.

There is also an alphabet soup of other regional groupings worldwide that bring countries together but do not involve sovereignty-sharing. Those referred to in the text (apart from the United Nations, or UN) are the African Union (AU) and the Association of Southeast Asian Nations (ASEAN).

Referring to EU policies

The text refers to the CAP (Common Agricultural Policy), to QMV (Qualified Majority Voting) and to abbreviations on the way to a single currency, notably EMU (Economic and Monetary Union), the EMS (European Monetary System) and the ecu or ECU (European currency unit). These will be defined in the 'Abbreviations and definitions' section of Chapter 4.

Further reading

Though a decade old, Desmond Dinan's *Europe Recast: A History of European Union* (London: Palgrave, 2004) is still an excellent introduction to the development of the EU. Anand Menon's *Europe: The State of the Union* (London: Atlantic Books, 2008) is a profound and passionate survey of the EU 50 years after the Treaty of Rome was signed. Clive Archer's *The European Union: Structure and Process* (3rd edition, London and New York: Continuum, 2000) is still a good introduction, and he has since published *The European Union* (Abingdon: Routledge, 2008) in Routledge's 'Global Institutions' series.

John McCormick's *Understanding the European Union: A Concise Introduction* (5th edition, London: Palgrave, 2011) is excellent, and more recently he has published *Why Europe Matters: The Case for the European Union* (London: Palgrave, 2013). The writings of Alasdair Blair are also simple and concise without being in any way simplistic. He published *The European Union since 1945* (2nd edition, Harlow: Pearson, 2010) as part of Pearson's 'Seminar Studies in History' series, and more recently *The European Union: A Beginner's Guide* (London: Oneworld, 2012) as part of Oneworld's 'Beginner's Guide' series.

Chapter 3: Anatomy

Abbreviations and definitions
Referring to EU institutions
The most dangerous confusion is between the Council of Europe (CoE), the body formed in 1949 whose structure the early pioneers of the European Coal and Steel Community specifically sought to avoid, and the European Council, a body that has existed since 1975 and that is one of the seven institutions of the EU, the one at which heads of state have their quarterly meetings. This is a confusion based not on abbreviations but on similarity of title; it is nonetheless a very important one. In similar vein, beware confusing the European Court of Justice (ECJ), another of the seven institutions of the EU, based in Luxembourg and responsible for the application of European Law, with the ECHR (the European Court of Human Rights), created by the CoE and with its headquarters in Strasbourg.

Other frequent abbreviations for EU institutions include CoA (Court of Auditors), CoR (Committee of the Regions), COREPER (Committee of Permanent Representatives, advisory body to the Council of Ministers), ECB (European Central Bank), EESC (European Economic and Social Committee), EIB (European Investment Bank), EP (European Parliament) and MEP (Member of the European Parliament). There are many others related to particular policy areas, which will be considered in the 'Abbreviations and definitions' for other chapters.

One very useful set of abbreviations to know concerns the different departments (or DGs – Directorates-General) of the Commission.

Sometimes they are obvious and sometimes not (it can depend on the language that is being used for the abbreviation). Sometimes the title of the department appears to be as mysterious as the abbreviation. Here is a full list with abbreviations:

Agriculture and Rural Development (AGRI) Hence something will be referred to as 'a matter for DG AGRI' and so on . . .

Budget (BUDG)

Climate Action (CLIMA)

Communication (COMM)

Communications Networks, Content and Technology (CNECT)

Competition (COMP)

Consumer Policy (in place since July 2013; abbreviation to come – could be DG CO but see the note below on DG SANCO)

Economic and Financial Affairs (ECFIN)

Education and Culture (EAC)

Employment, Social Affairs and Inclusion (EMPL)

Energy (ENER)

Enlargement (ELARG)

Enterprise and Industry (ENTR)

Environment (ENV)

EuropeAid Development & Cooperation (DEVCO)

Eurostat (ESTAT) This is the EU's statistical office and produces excellent and reliable statistics on a range of social and economic matters related to the EU – for example, fertility rates, growth rates, unemployment rates, migration rates. It is well worth consulting and often includes material for candidate countries, including Turkey.

Health (SANCO) The Consumer Affairs part of the old DG for Health and Consumers was hived off to create a 28th commissioner when Croatia joined the EU. SANCO – which comes from the French words *santé* (health) and *consommateurs* (consumers) – may have to become DG SAN, but don't expect anything so logical.

Home Affairs (HOME)

Humanitarian Aid and Civil Protection (ECHO)

Human Resources and Security (HR)

Informatics (DIGIT)
Internal Market and Services (MARKT)
Interpretation (SCIC)
Joint Research Centre (JRC)
Justice (JUST)
Maritime Affairs and Fisheries (MARE)
Mobility and Transport (MOVE)
Regional Policy (REGIO)
Research and Innovation (RTD)
Secretariat-General (SG) This department has a gatekeeper role. It sets the agenda and takes the minutes for meetings of the College of Commissioners. Based in the Berlaymont building, headquarters of the Commission, it is arguably the last hurdle any proposal from another DG has to clear – and can be the reason why some proposals from other DGs sink without trace.
Service for Foreign Policy Instruments (FPI) This body works alongside the EEAS (European External Action Service) in implementing foreign policy initiatives.
Taxation and Customs Union (TAXUD)
Trade (TRADE)
Translation (DGT)

Further reading

There are a number of textbooks that provide a competent trawl through the institutions. They are regularly updated so readers should make sure they get the latest edition. Neill Nugent's *Government and Politics of the European Union* (7th edition, London: Palgrave, 2010) and Desmond Dinan's *Ever Closer Union: An Introduction to European Integration* (4th edition, London: Palgrave, 2010) are very good, though new editions of both are needed. A more succinct and accessible introduction is provided by John McCormick in his *Understanding the European Union: A Concise Introduction* (5th edition, London: Palgrave, 2011). These also have the benefit of being by one author, which helps to maintain coherence in a complex subject area.

The Oxford University Press (OUP) has produced several weighty tomes for its 'New European Union' series, the covers all featuring a thick cable made up of several differently coloured wires. In line with this metaphor (and modern fashion), the volumes all have different contributors. John Peterson and Michael Shackleton provide a lot of sophisticated analysis in *The Institutions of the European Union* (3rd edition, Oxford: OUP, 2012), as does *The European Union: How Does it Work?*, edited by Elizabeth Blomberg, John Peterson and Richard Corbett (3rd edition, Oxford: OUP, 2012), but whether these books really manage, as they claim, to 'demystify' the complex systems their cable metaphor alludes to is a moot point.

Chapter 4: The single market

Abbreviations and definitions

The route to the euro is awash with abbreviations. It began with the Werner Report in 1970 and the plan for EMU (Economic and Monetary Union). As part of that process, attention had to be paid to the exchange-rate fluctuations that followed the USA's action in ending the Bretton Woods system in 1971 and in effect floating the dollar. At first (and with a welcome outburst of imagination), states attempted the 'snake in the tunnel' (no known abbreviation), which tried to bind currencies within certain narrow limits while allowing them a degree of wiggle room (the snake can wiggle but only inside the tunnel). The snake did not survive the oil crises of the 1970s and was replaced by the EMS (European Monetary System). This tried to provide similar wiggle room to currencies, but set up a European currency unit (ECU), essentially a weighted average of all the currencies inside the EMS which would be the new 'tunnel' against which to measure the wiggles. By the early 1990s this had failed to do its job and currency fluctuations were out of control again. Many people concluded that the only way of preventing fluctuations was a single currency (the euro) managed by the ECB (European Central Bank), whose forerunner was the EMI (European Monetary Institute), and by the ESCB (European System of Central Banks), which would have independent control of monetary policy.

Nowadays ERM II is the Exchange Rate Mechanism for managing the relation of the euro to other European currencies, and provides an important criterion for potential new eurozone members seeking to meet the convergence criteria (essentially ERM II enables them to peg their national currencies to the euro for two years prior to entry into the eurozone). After joining the eurozone, member states are required to meet certain other criteria after they become members (the Stability and Growth Pact), and, if they get into difficulty in the eurozone and require so-called 'bail-outs' (but remember, these are loans, not some kind of debt forgiveness), much tougher conditions are set. Whether or not the rigours of eurozone membership will eventually produce the Economic and Monetary Union spoken about in 1970 is unclear, as is the final achievement of the single market as a whole.

Further reading

Since so much of the EU concerns the single market, summaries in the major textbooks are not always very good. They end up getting bogged down in a repetition of 'everything you always wanted to know'. Chapter 4 ('Making the market') of Anand Menon's *Europe: The State of the Union* (London: Atlantic Books, 2008) stands out as an exception to this rule. Anand Menon is also one of the editors of *The Oxford Handbook of the European Union* (edited by Erik Jones, Anand Menon and Stephen Weatherill), which has a useful chapter on 'The Single Market' (Oxford: Oxford University Press, 2012).

At a more straightforward level, the EU itself has produced material in booklet form such as '20 years of the European Single Market', covering 1992–2012, though it has the limitations of a 'what we have achieved' approach. Readers might find the small booklet 'Your Europe: Your rights', looking at opportunities for citizens and businesses in the single market, more useful and revealing because it concentrates on practicalities such as how to continue to receive unemployment pay when looking for a job abroad. The situation changes all the time, so these booklets, produced in 2012, may have been updated or supplemented by 2014. For a more critical account, Tinne Heremans, a research fellow at the Egmont Institute in Brussels, produced a working paper in 2011 entitled 'The Single Market in need of a strategic relaunch'. It is available in pdf format at www.egmontinstitute.be/paperegm/ep43.pdf.

The best way to stay up to date is to use web links. For instance, it is helpful to consult the department of the Commission responsible for the internal market and services, DG MARKT. See http://ec.europa.eu/ internal_market/index_en.htm. Two examples of useful material on this website are:

(i) A 'scorecard' of how well member states have applied EU Law in the area of the single market. See http://ec.europa.eu/ internal_market/score/index_en.htm. The UK improved the rapidity of its national transposition measures considerably between 2012 and 2014.

(ii) Details of the latest developments related to the Single Market Act anticipated in the Tinne Heremans article mentioned above (passed in two stages in 2011 and 2012 and designed to support the market as an 'engine for growth'). See http://ec.europa.eu/internal_market/smact/ index_en.htm.

Material from DG Employment, Social Affairs and Inclusion (http:// ec.europa.eu/social/home.jsp) is useful less for analysing what the single market has achieved than for how to mitigate the effects of what has *not* been achieved (after all, with unemployment reaching record levels in 2013 and growth stalling near zero, a list of achievements is arguably not quite enough). It is here that material can be found on promoting young worker mobility through the pan-EU job search network EURES (http://ec.europa.eu/eures/home.jsp?lang=en) and various other initiatives.

For a tough but useful read, Chapters 6 and 7 of *Europe's Experimental Union* by Brigid Laffan, Rory O'Donnell and Michael Smith (London: Routledge, 2000), entitled 'Market' and 'Money', are still useful, as are Chapters 3 and 4 of Clive Archer's *The European Union: Structure and Process* (3rd edition, London: Continuum, 2000), entitled 'Completing the Single Market' and 'Economic and Monetary Union'. Of course a lot has happened since 2000, and a more up-to-date view (2010) is provided by Chapters 5, 6 and 7 of *Policy-Making in the European Union*, edited by Helen Wallace,

Mark A. Pollack and Alasdair R. Young as part of OUP's New European Union series. The chapters cover the single market, competition policy and Economic and Monetary Union. A book edited by George Anderson, *Internal Markets and Multi-level Governance: The Experience of the European Union, Australia, Canada, Switzerland and the United States* (Oxford: Oxford University Press, 2012) provides an interesting comparison between the EU's single market and attempts at similar economic arrangements under different political systems.

As Chapter 4 tried to point out, the single market involves social as well as economic matters – for instance those regarding mobility, training and employment. The useful articles in the quarterly *Journal of European Social Policy* (edited by Jochen Calsen and Traute Meyer) – in which ESM usually stands for European Social Model – show the obvious overlap between progress towards economic and monetary union and progress towards (or failure to achieve) full employment and an end to poverty.

Chapter 5: Agriculture and aquaculture

Definitions, abbreviations and further reading

There is a careful analysis of the economic principles underlying the CAP (Common Agricultural Policy) in the text. For further research, Eve Fouilleux's chapter in *European Union Politics*, edited by Michelle Cini and Nieves Pérez-Solórzano Borragán (Oxford: Oxford University Press, 2010), is a useful introduction to the general arguments and lists helpful blogs and websites concerning the CAP. For a critique of the CAP (and regional policy) as being too focused upon redistribution, see Chapter 5 ('The broader economy') in Anand Menon's *Europe: The State of the Union* (London: Atlantic Books, 2008). Commission websites on agriculture and aquaculture are easily accessible via www.ec.europa.eu/agriculture and www.ec.europa.eu/fisheries, respectively. Alan Matthews, Emeritus Professor of European Agricultural Policy at Trinity College, Dublin, has produced excellent and readable work on reforming the CAP (see http://capreform.eu). A useful article written in December 2012 by Clémentine D'Oultremont on 'Introducing more equity in the CAP: A difficult challenge' produced by the Egmont Institute in Brussels (see Egmont Paper No. 55, available at www.egmontinstitute.be/paperegm/ep55.pdf) has not lost its relevance as the dust settles on agreements over the place of agriculture within the 2014–20 multi-annual financial framework. Those seeking to know who gets what from the CAP (always a contentious political issue) can consult http://farmsubsidy.org, although this useful online database cannot provide a complete list of beneficiaries.

Where aquaculture is concerned, DG MARE (Maritime Affairs and Fisheries) produces a useful brochure called 'Fisheries and aquaculture in Europe' (the figures I quoted were from Edition No. 59 produced in December 2012), and for an interesting perspective on the dangers of antibiotics in agriculture see the website of APUA (Alliance for the Prudent Use of Antibiotics) at www.tufts.edu/med/apua.

A comprehensive analysis of the attempts to reform the CAP between 1992 and 2003 (it was written shortly before the 2008 'Health Check', which arguably amounted to very little) is provided by I. Garzon in *Reforming the Common Agricultural Policy: History of a Paradigm Change* (London: Palgrave, 2007), though readers may wonder whether paradigm change (at least in the sense of the term to describe revolutionary change, as originally used by Thomas Kuhn in *The Structure of Scientific Revolutions*) is precisely what has *not* occurred with the CAP. Berkeley Hill provides a more up-to-date analysis in *Understanding the Common Agricultural Policy* (Earthscan Food and Agriculture series, London: Routledge, 2011).

Chapter 6: A Europe of regions

Definitions and abbreviations
There is an alphabet soup of programmes where regional linkages and the various pots of funding attached to them are concerned and they are forever changing. This is a selection of ingredients from the present state of the soup:

General terms to refer to regional spending
Funding for 2014–20 is to be applied with the Europe 2020 Strategy in mind and within a 'Common Strategic Framework' (CSF) bringing together five programmes. The five programmes are:

ERDF – European Regional Development Fund. Within this block of funding, ETC (European Territorial Cooperation) is important for linking border regions of neighbouring states or regions of several states with a significant common link (for instance the Baltic states, or those bordering the Mediterranean or Alpine states), or regions without such connections that want to exchange experiences. It succeeds the INTERREG (short for interregional) programme that began in 1989.

ESF – European Social Fund.

CF – Cohesion Fund. Has a particular focus on transport and environmental and energy projects.

EAFRD – European Agricultural Fund for Rural Development.

EMFF – European Maritime and Fisheries Fund.

The first three are within the remit of DG REGIO, the last two are within the remit of DG AGRIC and DG MARE respectively, but all five funds will be brought within the Common Strategic Framework for the 2014–20 period in order to promote coherence (or 'synergies', as the EU likes to call it). Like other bodies, the EU goes through phases of dividing programmes up (for 'specificity' and 'targeting') and then putting them back together again (for 'synergy'). At present it is going through a synergy phase. The five programmes overlap: the European Social Fund, for instance, focuses on the need to promote employment and combat poverty, but that is the intention of all the other programmes too, so the difference is one of 'emphasis' and 'targeting'.

Regions may also benefit from two other funds that are not specifically linked to regional development:

EUSF – European Union Solidarity Fund. This is used to deal with natural disasters such as floods wherever they occur (23 member states have so far benefited).

IPA – Instrument for Pre-Accession. This is used to help candidate and potential candidate countries prepare for accession (for instance by developing the necessary administrative institutions for transposing European Law into their national legal frameworks).

Cross-border cooperation programmes

These are of great interest to peripheral and maritime regions such as Cornwall:

> CAMIS – Channel Arc Manche Integrated Strategy. Seeks an integrated maritime project in the Channel Area. Provides for Anglo-French cooperation on matters such as offshore renewable energy, marine tourism, transport and safety matters related to Channel crossings.
>
> FLIP – Fostering Long-Term Initiatives in Ports.
>
> MERIFIC – Marine Energy in Far Peripheral and Coastal Communities. This is for developing marine renewable energy.
>
> NEA II – Nautisme Espace Atlantique. This is for developing the leisure sector in several Atlantic coastal regions.
>
> PATCH – Ports Adapting to Change. Two departments of the Commission (DG REGIO and DG MARE – Maritime Affairs and Fisheries) are involved, together with the European Investment Bank, in order to fund a 'Blue Growth' strategy involving, among other things, cross-border cooperation in tidal and wave energy. The whole of the UK south coast is included, as well as ports in the north of France and West Flanders (a region of Belgium).
>
> RESGEN – Project RESgen (as it tends to be written) stands for Renewable Energy Sources generation.
>
> RFC – Regions for Sustainable Change.
>
> UNICREDS – University Collaborations in Regional Development Spaces.

Using the European Investment Bank (EIB)

Access to money at EU level is a question not just of receiving grants but also of being able to access cheap loans. The EIB (see Chapter 3) does not use money from the EU budget but finances itself by issuing bonds on world financial markets. It is prepared to commit itself to the sort of long-term lending that is appropriate to a number of projects in the environmental area, where returns cannot be expected in the short term.

Hence the ELENA (European Local Energy Assistance) facility, launched by the European Commission and the EIB in December 2009 to support more than 1 billion euros of energy efficiency and renewable energy projects in 2010. The high figure of 1 billion euros shows how useful the EIB, with its AAA rating, can be in leveraging loans. The system is essentially a sprat to catch a mackerel. The sprat is a degree of assistance (Project Development Assistance – PDA) from a relatively small budget under the Intelligent Energy Europe (IEE) programme, in order to put together a viable proposal – for instance, it might be a project for retrofitting buildings to make them more energy efficient. The mackerel is then a large loan from a private bank or from the EIB, which is where access to a slice of the 1 billion euros comes in.

Regional representation in Brussels
The complicated and ever-changing nature of EU funding means that it is imperative that regions have a strong base in Brussels and that they can effectively make their case for support. In the case of the UK and its South-West region, problems have arisen with the demise of the South-West UK Brussels Office (SWUBKO), formerly part-funded by the Regional Development Authority until the RDAs were closed down (they eventually disappeared in March 2012 and were replaced by 'local enterprise partnerships' (LEPs), which lacked their own budgets to administer. SWUBKO now became unviable, even though it had played a vital part in making links and gathering intelligence on European policies and funding opportunities (few member states would be without such representations). In the end, it metamorphosed into the South-West European Partnership, a charitable organisation, in order to try to continue its former work by drawing on support from private and civic organisations.

Further reading
Marco Brunazzo's chapter in Michelle Cini and Nieves Pérez-Solórzano Borragán, eds, *European Union Politics* (3rd edition, Oxford: Oxford University Press, 2010), interestingly entitled 'Regional Europe', highlights some of the complex issues raised at the regional level concerning who has the power to do what (unfortunately, the chapter was expunged from the 4th edition

published in 2013, which seems to have nothing to say on regional Europe at all, despite the clear importance of regional issues in the EU). Such issues are best seen in terms of how things work in practice, taking particular regions as examples. As mentioned at the end of 'Agriculture and Aquaculture', for a critique of regional policy (and the CAP) as being too focused upon redistribution, see Anand Menon's *Europe: The State of the Union*, Chapter 5 ('The broader economy'). DG REGIO's website http://ec.europa.eu/regional_policy/index_en. cfm will provide updated information on programmes for 2014–20 and country-by-country examples of what is being done. See also the website of the Committee of the Regions at www.cor.europa.eu.

Where up-to-date information about Cornwall is concerned, go to the Cornwall Council website at www.cornwall.gov.uk. Here you will find a number of interesting documents and references, including a pdf file (written at the end of 2011) entitled 'Post 2013 European funding: building on success'. This contains a certain amount of entirely hypothetical (and optimistic) material concerning the expected impact of European funding on the Council by 2020, but it is very useful for understanding and appreciating the region's approach and priorities.

As the chapter suggested, the regional issue raises interesting questions of multilevel governance. Editors Ian Bache and Matthew Flinders offer a collection of articles on this in *Multi-level Governance* (Oxford: Oxford University Press, 2005). On an equally detailed but more practical level, Robert Leonardi's *Cohesion Policy in the European Union: the Building of Europe* (London: Palgrave Macmillan, 2005) looks at the way the EU's cohesion policy was implemented in Central and Eastern Europe before the countries joined the EU in 2004. Leonardi, the Jean Monnet Professor at the European Institute in the London School of Economics, gives an account of what cohesion policy can do for new and future members of the EU. See also in this regard a work published by the European Movement in Serbia, *The Regional Policy of the European Union as an Engine of Economic Development* (Belgrade, 2010), in which Ognjen Mirić discusses ways in which the European Union is currently helping Serbia through the Instrument for Pre-Accession Assistance and how the country might benefit further after EU accession (something that is crucially significant given the history of regional and national conflict in parts of South-East Europe). Originally written in 2009, the work is available in pdf format at www.emins.org/uploads/useruploads/knjige/10-regional-policy-eu.pdf.

Chapter 7: External relations

Definitions and abbreviations
These are best given in the form of a brief historical summary.

Following the failure of the proposed EDC (European Defence Community) in 1954, Italy and Germany were admitted to the Western European Union (WEU) and became members of NATO (the North Atlantic Treaty Organization). Thus the WEU and NATO became the forums for discussion of foreign and defence matters. There was no forum within the confines of the EEC itself.

De Gaulle tried to impose a common foreign policy on French lines through the Fouchet Plan. When this failed, and with some trepidation, member states agreed to European Political Cooperation (EPC) in 1970, but this was a discussion forum outside the institutional format of the EEC. It did not attain official status within the EEC until the Single European Act was passed in 1986.

Though various statements were made at European Council meetings on the need for more foreign policy coordination (for example by the Stuttgart Declaration of 1983), progress only took off in the 1990s when the Common Foreign and Security Policy (CFSP) became one of the three 'pillars' of the European Union at the Treaty of Maastricht. The CFSP is still the mainstay of EU foreign policy, but within that there is what was at first called the European Security and Defence Policy (ESDP) and is now called the Common Security and Defence Policy (CSDP), which amounts essentially to all the components of the CFSP that give flesh to the EU's defence and military commitments.

The post of high representative (HR), in effect a 'foreign secretary lite', was created by the Treaty of Amsterdam. Lisbon joined the HR to the former commissioner for external relations (whose department was known as DG RELEX) to create a single post with a foot in both camps, the Commission and the Council. It also created a new body, the European External Action Service (EEAS), to service the holder of this new post (Baroness Ashton until 2014).

Since the Treaty of Nice, and in the wake of the five wars in the former Yugoslavia in the 1990s, permanent political and military structures have been set up in the EU. There is now a Political and Security Committee (PSC) staffed by ambassadors or their deputies which helps to define the approach of the CFSP. The PSC in turn seeks advice from the European Union Military Committee (EUMC), which is composed of the defence chiefs of member states, and from a civilian equivalent, CICOM (Committee for Civilian Aspects of Crisis Management). The EUMS(European Union Military Staff) works under the direction of the EUMC and ensures that there is a body to coordinate military actions under the auspices of the EEAS. The EEAS also has a body coordinating civilian crisis management operations, the Civilian Planning and Conduct Capability (CPCC).

It is all very convoluted, largely because the five wars in the former Yugoslavia in the 1990s forced the EU to take its defence responsibilities seriously, while at the same time this was the sort of sensitive area in which member states sought to keep control over anything that might be agreed. The result was a set of institutions to ensure that the EU could act in this field and another set of institutions to ensure that it could not (or at least that the member states could control any actions it might wish to adopt).

Nevertheless, the convoluted arrangements should not hide the real progress that has been made for reasons outlined in the text. The first formulation of European responsibility for peacekeeeping on its own continent as South-East Europe descended into bloody conflict in the early 1990s came from the WEU, outside the structures of the European Union (the so-called Petersberg tasks, focusing on peace-keeping capabilities, were first formulated by the WEU's Ministerial Council in June 1992). Yet they were later adopted as part of the Maastricht Treaty when the CFSP was created as one of the pillars of the EU, and became the core of the EU's European Security and Defence Policy. The WEU has since been wound up (in 2011), showing that there is at least acceptance within the EU itself of the need to have the resources and commitment for peacekeeping operations. Of course it has yet to be seen whether it can use them to play the role in any future European conflict that in the 1990s had to be left to NATO.

Further reading

Rather against the spirit of this chapter, Michelle Cini and Nieves Pérez-Solórzano Borragán's *European Union Politics* (3rd edition, Oxford: Oxford University Press, 2010) breaks up external relations into a chapter on the economic aspects (by Michael Smith) and a chapter on foreign, security and defence policy (by Robert Dover). For the same reason, I have difficulty with Anand Menon's entitling his chapter in *Europe: The State of the Union* looking at this area 'Beyond economics'. A glance at the ESDP newsletter for the winter of 2012/13 (No. 12) makes it clear that the EEAS is dedicated to a comprehensive approach that is not beyond economics but incorporates it. The website of the EEAS, www.eeas.europa.eu, is a mine of information about operations such as Atalanta, including a series of press releases going back several years. For the list of achievements in Somalia mentioned in the text, see 'EU contribution to the Millennium Development Goals' (European Union, 2010) listed at http://ec.europa.eu/europeaid/infopoint/publications/europeaid/documents/188a_mdg_en.pdf and produced by DG Development & Cooperation (EuropeAid). To be fair, most aid agencies behave in exactly the same way, encouraging the same misperception that aid can be dumped on a population with no consideration of the security and governance context.

There is an excellent website for 'Exploring EU foreign policy', at www.eufp.eu, managed by academics from the University of Leuven and the College of Europe based in Bruges, which provides useful links for further reading. One of the managers of the website, Professor Stephan Keukeleire, has published *The Foreign Policy of the European Union* with Tom Delreux (2nd edition, London: Palgrave Macmillan, 2014). This is as good a guide as any to ways in which the EU has developed towards having a foreign policy.

See also Michael E. Smith's *Europe's Foreign and Security Policy: The Institutionalisation of Cooperation* (Cambridge: Cambridge University Press, 2008). A number of think tanks and research institutes have useful papers on defence issues, especially Chatham

House, the European Policy Centre and the Centre for European Reform.

Chapter 8: The greening of Europe?

Definitions and abbreviations

The Institute for European Environmental Policy (IEEP) is an independent body seeking to promote an environmentally sustainable Europe. In a useful section headed 'Understanding the EU', its website (www.ieep.eu) provides an EU Glossary and what it calls 'Euro-Acronyms'. The Euro-Acronyms section contains abbreviations used in the environmental sector and others in general use that those working in the environmental field should know.

Further reading

The report mentioned in the text, *Renewables Make the Difference*, can be found at http://ec.europa.eu/energy/publications/doc/ 2011_renewable_difference_en.pdf. Commissioner Tajani's statements can be found at http://europa.eu/rapid/press-release_IP-13-4_en.htm. The earlier and different approach of his predecessor as industry commissioner, Günther Verheugen, was reported in the *Financial Times* (23 November 2006).

As for information within the EU itself, the constantly changing framework of EU environmental policy can be followed through the homepage of the relevant Directorates – http://ec.europa.eu/dgs/ environment (DG Environment), http://ec.europa.eu/dgs/clima/mis sion/index_en.htm (DG Climate Action) http://ec.europa.eu/energy/ index_en.htm (DG Energy) and http://ec.europa.eu/transport/ index_en.htm (DG Transport). However, many other DGs also have environmental concerns, such as DG Agriculture and Rural Development and DG Regional Policy (see Chapters 5 and 6). The very fact that there is increasingly a 'green component' to the strategies of most departments means that environmental issues can be found on the websites of most DGs.

Useful and up-to-date material and analysis can be found on the websites of the European Environment Agency (www.eea.europa.eu) and the IEEP (www.ieep.eu).

Professor Andrew Jordan (Professor of Environmental Sciences at the University of East Anglia) is a leading authority on environmental policy at the EU (as well as the UK) level. The third edition (edited with Camilla Adelle) of his *Environmental Policy in the EU: Actors, Institutions and Processes* (London: Routledge) was published in 2013. He also edited *Climate Change Policy in the European Union* (Cambridge: Cambridge University Press, 2010). Together with David Benson, Andrew Jordan also wrote the chapter on environmental policy in Michelle Cini and Nieves Pérez-Solórzano Borragán, eds, *European Union Politics* (3rd edition, Oxford: Oxford University Press, 2010).

Index